About The Author

Ian Wishart is an award-winning journalist and author, with a 30 year career in radio, television and magazines, a #1 talk radio show and five #1 bestselling books to his credit. Together with his wife Heidi, they edit and publish the news magazine *Investigate* and the news website www.investigatedaily.com.

In memory of Heidi Paakkonen & Urban Hoglin

Missing Pieces

Ian Wishart

HOWLING AT THE MOON PUBLISHING LTD

First edition published 2012
Howling At The Moon Publishing Ltd
PO Box 188, Kaukapakapa
Auckland 0843, NEW ZEALAND

www.howlingatthemoon.com
email: editorial@investigatemagazine.com
Copyright © Ian Wishart, 2012
Copyright © Howling At The Moon Publishing Ltd, 2012

The moral rights of the author have been asserted.
Missing Pieces is copyright. Except for the purpose of fair reviewing, no part of the publication may be copied, reproduced or transmitted in any form, or by any means, including via technology either already in existence or developed subsequent to publication, without the express written permission of the publisher and copyright holders. All Rights Reserved.
ISBN 978-0-9876573-7-4

Typeset in Adobe Garamond Pro and Facit
Cover concept: Ian Wishart, Heidi Wishart, Bozidar Jokanovic
Book Design: Bozidar Jokanovic

To get another copy of this book airmailed to you anywhere in the world, or to purchase a fully text-searchable digital edition, visit our website:
WWW.HOWLINGATTHEMOON.COM

LEGAL NOTICE: Criticisms of individuals in this book reflect the author's honest opinion, for reasons outlined in the text or generally known at the time of writing

Contents

Introduction	6
I Know You're Out There Somewhere	11
The Vanishing	20
Forever Autumn	36
The Breakthrough	49
Eyewitness Evidence	69
Seven Habits Of Successful Witnesses	83
To Hell In A Handcart	97
The Secret Witnesses	123
Don't Pay The Ferryman	137
Tamihere Cross-Examined	153
Urban's Body Is Found	178
A Frenzied Attack	184
A New Scenario	196
Back In The Gun	205
New Suspects	212
Where Is Heidi?	221
Your Verdict	230
Other books by Ian Wishart	240

Introduction

The book you are about to read has taken nearly 24 years to write. The story begins with the disappearance in April 1989 of two photogenic Swedish tourists – Sven Urban Hoglin and Heidi Birgitta Paakkonen. As the news director of a major Auckland radio station at the time, I had my 'troops' covering it.

When I joined TV3 in August 1989, I found myself quickly thrown into the case directly, covering the May 1990 court depositions hearing and the October – December 1990 trial of David Wayne Tamihere for the network. When Urban Hoglin's body was found by hunters in October 1991, my TV3 cameraman Pete Stones and I were the first TV journalists to reach the shallow gravesite in the Coromandel bush – helicoptered in to a place so remote that police had not even posted an overnight scene guard. Just a strip of tape, "Crime Scene – Do Not Cross", marked off Hoglin's final resting place.

In the mid 1990s after establishing a publishing company, I was given a manuscript written by convicted double-murderer David Tamihere from his prison cell, entitled "Operation Stockholm". Like many publishers around that time, we turned it down. Too hard, too guttural, and what if the cops had indeed convicted the right man?

Still, the issue nagged.

In 2010, one of the subscribers to our magazine, *Investigate*, passed away. His widow handed on some of his private papers to the magazine, including a lengthy report on the mystery of Swedish tourist

Introduction

murders. That information, which you will read in this book, proved to be a bombshell discovery.

In *Missing Pieces*, you will meet the protagonists – Heidi Paakkonen, Urban Hoglin and David Tamihere – and follow the accepted "narrative" of what happened: that the young couple met and were killed by Tamihere on Saturday 8 April 1989, in the vicinity of a distant Coromandel bush track known as "Crosbie's Clearing" – about three hours' walk from the nearest carpark at Tararu Creek Road, a few clicks north of Thames.

When you've seen how good the Crown case is against Tamihere, then we'll examine the evidence the jury never heard. After that you can make your own mind up on whether this conviction was safe, or whether the real killer/s may still be at large.

Justice, in the New Zealand context, works at two levels: punishment for the crime itself, and protection for the wider community by taking a dangerous offender off the streets. There is no question in this case that the price for the crime – as set by the courts – has not been paid. Tamihere served 21 years behind bars before finally being paroled in 2010. There is arguably no question that the second part of the justice equation has not been served – Tamihere had a string of serious crimes behind him, and was off the streets for a long time.

The real question, however, is "Did David Wayne Tamihere murder the Swedish tourists?" Because if he did not, if he just filled a "case closed" quota on the basis of "he'll do", then the New Zealand public as a whole were cheated of their public safety while the person/s who slaughtered Heidi and Urban remained at large, free to strike again.

The significance of this may not be immediately apparent to some of you, so a celebrated American case might help get the point across:

> "The cost to society of inaccurate eyewitness identifications is twofold," notes psychologist Rod Lindsay of Queens University in Kingston, Ontario. "It's a double error. Not only are you

7

convicting the innocent – or at least putting them through the process of having to get out of the situation – but the guilty are still out there doing the crimes."

A pointed reminder of the costs of misidentification is the case of Clarence Harrison. Wrongfully convicted of a brutal rape in Decatur, Georgia, Clarence Harrison spent nearly 18 years in prison before DNA testing proved his innocence – and showed the eyewitness evidence in his case to be false. After the exoneration, the District Attorney relayed that while the victim was upset by the DNA results, "she is more upset that this means the person who raped her is yet to be identified."[1]

It is often said that the public have no right to criticise a jury's verdict, because the public don't get to hear all the evidence, only the jury do. You'll hear that criticism often, but it is actually untrue. The evidence placed before a court, and therefore before the jury, is only the information that the prosecution or defence *choose* to let the jury hear, and it is usually a fraction of the total information. Ninety percent of the legal work in a court case has usually been done before the actual trial even starts, as both sides lobby the judge to block the introduction of certain evidence. The jury certainly hear more than the public, but they hear less than they think.

The Tamihere case was no different. There had been several hearings behind closed doors for precisely those reasons, hearings the jury was not allowed to know about.

One of the advantages of doing a book like this, particularly long after the events in question, is that fresh eyes re-examining *all* the evidence (and I do mean all), can introduce facts and information that the jurors never had a chance to consider; facts the police or the defence were sitting on and chose not to reveal.

In writing this, I have re-interviewed some witnesses (on rare occasions, as memories noted down closest to the events in question are

---

[1] From Eyewitness Evidence: A Policy Review, The Justice Project, page 9

Introduction

more likely to be accurate), I have perused hundreds of newspaper articles about the disappearance, the search and the eventual court cases. I have read through hundreds of pages of evidence given at Depositions, and a further 906 pages of the evidence transcript from the murder trial. I have read hundreds of pages of witness statements given to police at various stages of the investigation, and countless police job sheets recording investigations undertaken. I have read the submissions of the Crown and Defence, and the judge's summing up. I have read the Court of Appeal documents and the Privy Council application.

In short, I had access to all the information the jury were given, and much more information either withheld from the jury or simply not available when they handed down their guilty verdict. Additionally, I covered the court case at the time.

I am grateful to David Tamihere for providing the legal files dating from the moment of the Swedes' disappearance through to his failed Privy Council bid. All of the evidence in this book that readers may regard as incriminating Tamihere has come from the court and police files he handed me. This has allowed a thorough warts and all overview of the case. At no point did Tamihere request or have any editorial control over this book.

This is not a book that sets out to prove "Poor David". In fact, readers can approach this work knowing Tamihere has served and completed a life sentence for the double murder, and in fact served nearly double the time he could have served. He was eligible for parole more than a decade ago but refused to acknowledge his guilt. He accordingly stayed behind bars for more than 20 years. He effectively served around twice the jail time he was actually required to.

This is not a book that sets out to prove David Tamihere is innocent. Absent a watertight alibi, it is virtually impossible to prove anyone innocent. There are three possibilities as I see it. One, the jury convicted the right man for the right reasons (in other words the evidence was perfect and garnered a deserved conviction; Two, the jury convicted the right man for the wrong reasons (the evidence did not support a guilty verdict but it doesn't matter because we got the killer); Three, the jury convicted the wrong man for the wrong reasons (the Crown's evidence was flawed, leading to an innocent man's conviction).

What I, and indeed many in the news media, now realise is that it's time to take a more critical look at the Crown's case than we journalists gave it the first time around – and I include myself as one of those crime reporters who gave the police an easy ride.

There are calls for a retrial, and hopefully this book will help give the public some context to judge that against.

If he is guilty, Tamihere has done his time under the laws as they stand. If it turns out he is not guilty, then that's a story for another time. A retrial could be held to set the record straight, if required. The important thing about this book is that it's the first in-depth look at this case.

So *Missing Pieces* is a book for the victims – both the families of Heidi and Urban and the wider community – who deserve genuine closure, not a feel-good result akin to throwing a dog a bone to make it shut up. This is a book that takes a behind the scenes look at one of our most controversial murder mysteries and – having asked some very serious questions – discovers very sobering answers.

Answers that go to the heart of our policing and justice systems. Answers that could affect you…

CHAPTER 1
———

I Know You're Out There Somewhere

"We've now come to New Zealand...we haven't decided on a route yet, but we are staying here in Auckland some 5-6 days and then we'll try to get further north. Everybody we've been talking to in Australia has said that everything is a lot more expensive here in New Zealand. We got very surprised when we went out shopping today and found that the prices were about the same as in Australia; some things were even cheaper.

"Among other things, we bought some mince that cost some 15 krona ($3) a kilogram. We bought potatoes that are a lot nicer and tastier than at home. Soon, we are taking the bus to the city and we are going to a market, we may go to the zoo. They borrowed two pandas all the way from China, maybe because we are here! After that we are visiting the world's biggest underwater aquarium. We'll see how much we've got time for..."

– *letter from Heidi Paakkonen, Auckland, 7 December 1988*

In the right circumstances, it could have been a fairy tale. Young, blonde, blue-eyed and beautiful, the archetypal Swedish girl, 21 year old Heidi Paakkonen turned heads wherever she went: "I was going to phone you from Queenstown," she wrote home at one point, "but I had to go to the Post Office and exchange some money. In there, I met three Swedish guys who looked at me as if

11

I was a strange animal. They probably believed that I was a Swede, but they didn't dare to ask."

Whatever else they may say in the voluminous police files, Heidi Paakkonen is writ large in comment after comment from eyewitnesses: "striking", "very attractive", "a movie star look". At 176 cm tall (5 ft 9), the Swede stood head and shoulders above many other women.

Born 14 October, 1967, Heidi was the only girl of five children and, at 21, second youngest. Like all Swedish kids in the seventies, she began school at the age of seven, graduating from high school at 19. She dreamed of becoming a kindergarten teacher and planned tertiary studies to achieve that, but in her gap year had chosen to work at the cosmetics counter of a local supermarket, hoping to get some money in the bank.

With her on this trip of a lifetime to Australia and New Zealand, fiancé Urban Hoglin, a 23 year old from the same Swedish village both had grown up in – Storfors, 225km west of capital city Stockholm. Hoglin shared the same rugged good looks and athletic frame as his well-known older brother Johnny, a gold medallist at the 1968 Winter Olympics in France in the 10,000 metre speedskating final. There was a big age difference between the brothers. Johnny was born in 1943, the first of four children – Urban, born 2 December, 1965, was the youngest.

At 183 cm tall (6 ft) and around 75 kg, Urban had the trademark Scandinavian blue eyes and medium brown hair. He'd attended the same high school as Heidi, but with a two year age gap their paths didn't really cross till they worked together in the Storfors village supermarket, Domus, after Urban had completed his ten month military training at the age of 19.

Striking up a relationship, the couple became engaged on the Spanish island of Mallorca in September 1986, a month shy of Heidi's 19th birthday, and began living together back in Sweden that December. Their engagement rings were special, each wore a gold band engraved with the other's name on the inside.

On top of his army experience, Urban Hoglin was an outdoorsman by nature, accompanying one of his older brothers – Stefan – on frequent wilderness trips in Sweden:

"He was mainly interested in tramping and particularly fishing," Stefan Hoglin said in a briefing for the police inquiry team in 1989.[2] "I often used to go with Urban on fishing trips…We would go out overnight and sometimes up to ten days at a time. On these longer trips we would have backpacks and sometimes canoes, and would be up to 60 kilometres from any civilisation."

Urban, explained his brother, liked to be prepared, ensuring they carried more food and clothing than they needed, in case of emergencies. "He would have been even more careful on his own or when he was with Heidi."

On occasion, Urban would go camping in the Swedish summer without a tent, and "sometimes just sleep under a tree overnight, but never taking any risks."

The latter point is debatable, given Stefan Hoglin's next revelation:

"The forest in Sweden is quite open and you can walk through it quite freely, however there are the dangers of bear, snakes and sometimes wolves that you have to be aware of."

Coming to New Zealand, the bush here posed no such threat. Or so Urban Hoglin thought.

It was Urban's idea to come down under. He and Heidi signed up to a Swedish magazine published by the Scandinavian-Australian-New

---

2 Statement of Stefan Hoglin dated 22 September 1989

Zealand Friendship Union. The journal regaled readers with tales of fabulous fishing, hunting and sightseeing in the Antipodes. Urban and Heidi thrashed out an itinerary taking them from Stockholm to nearby Copenhagen and then onto Los Angeles for the famed Air New Zealand "Raro route" flight that stopped off in Tahiti and sometimes Rarotonga before arriving in Auckland.

Auckland was initially just a transfer point for a flight to Brisbane – the couple's adventure would start in the land made famous by the recent *Crocodile Dundee* movie. On their second arrival into New Zealand in December 1988, they planned to buy a car and drive around.

"Heidi and Urban left Sweden on Friday the 16th of September 1988," Heidi's 32 year old brother Johni told New Zealand Police.[3] "Their departure was very early in the morning and my parents drove them both to the airport in Stockholm to see them off. They had with them their two large green backpacks full of their property, and a small blue carry bag which had the name 'Salomon' on it."

Also stashed away were their sleeping bags, a tent and Urban's fishing and camping equipment. To all intents and purposes it was an ordinary airport departure, of the kind repeated at transit lounges across the globe every day. But unlike most, and unbeknown to anyone there that dark September morning, it was the last time any of them would see each other.

When they arrived in Australia 48 hours later, it wasn't all prawns on the barbie; or perhaps it was one too many prawns: a few weeks after arriving in Brisbane, Urban Hoglin was struck with a vicious infection. Doctors never got to the bottom of it, but he was hospitalised for two weeks in Alice Springs while the medics fought fevers peaking at 41 degrees. "I lost 6kg," a recovering Urban wrote to family in mid November 1988.

Then there was the Australian wildlife to deal with:

"I was looking mostly up in the trees because I was looking for

---
3   Statement of Johni Paakkonen, 22 September 1989

some tree kangaroos up there," Heidi wrote of the couple's experiences at Cape Tribulation in the far north. Since there were so many people on the path in front of her, she wasn't paying overly close attention to the ground.

"Just as I was putting my foot down I saw that something moved and it was a snake…The snake was not supposed to be deadly poisonous, but if I'd got bitten I would have believed it was poisonous and probably died of the shock!"

The tour guide later explained the snake was venomous to the point of making a victim sick "for some days".

Then, there was the Australian "wildlife" to deal with:

"We stayed in a backpacker's hostel in Darwin with a lot of odd people…the place only had two toilets and one shower, and one of the toilets was in the same room where the shower was. When Urban went to take a shower, a drugged girl came in and knocked with a wooden stick, she was going to the loo and couldn't wait. He hadn't started yet so he went out and let her start instead. When he came back in there was another drugged girl coming in but then he just closed the door. When I took a shower later she came again and if you could murder anyone with your eyes."

Heidi later discovered the second druggie had thrown a fully-clothed Swedish girl into the swimming pool apparently after failing to get access to the toilet.

"Before we fell asleep," she wrote, "there were some guys fighting out in the kitchen. It was rather unpleasant to stay there but we survived."

Hoglin's brush with death and hospital stay forced a two week extension to their Aussie adventure, and the couple didn't arrive back in Auckland until December 5, 1988. One of the first items on their NZ agenda was transport.

"We've bought a car, a Japanese wreck of a Subaru," Heidi told her family in a letter. The seller was another Swedish tourist – a BMW salesman back home – who turned out to be a neighbour. "He has a summer house just close to yours! Talk about a small world."

Heidi and Urban had been stunned at the prices of cars in Auckland at the Newmarket car fair. "We went around and checked them out and saw just a lot of bad expensive cars. Some of them were damaged and rusty and still they asked for some 8,500 krona ($2,100). At home you can find nicer ones in a garbage tin."

After turning down a 1970 VW Beetle for $4,000, the Swedish couple found their compatriot with the 1976 Subaru wagon. He wanted $2,200 but sold it to them for $1,750. Packs and camping gear loaded in the back, Heidi and Urban were off, albeit hesitantly at first.

"The people here in NZ are nice and very helpful," Heidi's letter continues. "We stayed in a private home in Auckland and the woman who owned the place…when she heard that we were a bit worried about how to get out of Auckland (big motorways, and it's important to get on the right road, in the right direction and on the right side of the road) she took her car and showed us all the way to the motorway."

One of the first tasks was to tune the car radio to one of Auckland's two FM stations – either the top rated 89FM or the less popular Magic 91. Evidently our playlists were a novelty to the young Swedes:

"I've heard another great song with a girl called Melissa Etheridge, have you heard anything from her at home? Is she popular?" Heidi wrote to a friend in December 1988. There was, she noted, "one song that is rather funny with a dark guy and that one is called *Don't Worry Be Happy*. We heard that a lot when Urban went to the hospital.

"I've heard another good song from the Moody Blues. The song is named, or at least they sing like this, 'I know you're out there somewhere', and that song is so beautiful."

Given what would transpire, the lyrics to the 1988 Moody Blues hit are more than poignant and bittersweet – they are downright eerie:[4]

The mist is lifting slowly
I can see the way ahead

---

[4] "I Know You're Out There Somewhere", written by Justin Hayward, performed by the Moody Blues, released 1988, http://www.youtube.com/watch?v=a97d5bUCFVQ

I Know You're Out There Somewhere

And I've left behind the empty streets
That once inspired my life
And the strength of the emotion
Is like thunder in the air
'Cos the promise that we made each other
Haunts me to the end

I know you're out there somewhere
Somewhere, somewhere
I know you're out there somewhere
Somewhere you can hear my voice
I know I'll find you somehow
Somehow, somehow
I know I'll find you somehow
And somehow I'll return again to you

The secret of your beauty
And the mystery of your soul
I've been searching for in everyone I meet
And the times I've been mistaken
It's impossible to say
And the grass is growing
Underneath our feet

I know you're out there somewhere
Somewhere, somewhere
I know you're out there somewhere
Somewhere you can hear my voice
I know I'll find you somehow
Somehow, somehow
I know I'll find you somehow
And somehow I'll return again to you

And the words that I remember

Missing Pieces

From my childhood still are true
That there's none so blind
As those who will not see
And to those who lack the courage
And say it's dangerous to try
Well they just don't know
That love eternal will not be denied

I know you're out there somewhere
Somewhere, somewhere
I know you're out there somewhere
Somewhere you can hear my voice
I know I'll find you somehow
Somehow, somehow
I know I'll find you somehow
And somehow I'll return again to you

Yes I know it's going to happen
I can feel you getting near
And soon we'll be returning
To the fountain of our youth
And if you wake up wondering
In the darkness I'll be there
My arms will close around you
And protect you with the truth

I know you're out there somewhere
Somewhere, somewhere
I know you're out there somewhere
Somewhere you can hear my voice
I know I'll find you somehow
Somehow, somehow
I know I'll find you somehow
And somehow I'll return again to you

Justin Hayward's haunting Moody Blues track became one of Heidi and Urban's favourite songs during their five month stay in New Zealand. And why not? They had wheels, they had the road unwinding in front of them, they had the wind in the hair and the sun on their faces. This was the summer of '88 and, for these northern hemisphere migrants, the year without a winter. The cold would come soon enough, but right now they had each other and they had an adventure to share. Returning home was for another day.

Heidi cranked down the window and wound up the volume just a little more as the small Subaru cleared the city fringes at Albany and headed north. Visions of her family huddled around the fire in a bitterly cold Swedish Christmas season came to mind. She just smiled, and joined in the chorus.

I know I'll find you somehow
And somehow I'll return again to you

CHAPTER 2

The Vanishing

"New Zealand is really a beautiful country. I don't know whether you, Mum, would really enjoy yourself on the roads here, some of the roads are narrow, curvy and steep… in the North Island we had rainy weather for a week. There has been a real storm in Auckland so they were forced to close the roads. We managed to get out of Auckland just before it started, otherwise we'd have been stuck there some extra days."

– *letter from Heidi Paakkonen, 6 January 1989*

While the Swedes made their way up and down the Auckland and Northland coasts over December and the New Year, another character in this Shakespearian tragedy was taking the stage on the Coromandel peninsula.

David Wayne Tamihere, a 36 year old unemployed steel worker, was on the run from police after jumping bail back in 1986 on a rape charge. One of twelve children, Tamihere's father was a miner at Waihi, at the base of the Coromandel ranges, and the family had ancestral Maori land on the peninsula.

After a troubled childhood, Tamihere left school to work in the construction and steel industries. At the age of 19, he committed his first major crime – the killing of 23 year old stripper Mary Barcham in 1972 with an air rifle butt. He was sentenced to two years' jail.

"I thought she had set me up with her minder," Tamihere explained to journalist Caroline Meng-Yee in 2012. "I went and grabbed the rifle and swung around to get to the door but the gun clipped her in the head and I shot through. That was accidental, rather than deliberate."

Top cop John Hughes would later note of the air rifle killing that he had a conversation with Tamihere where "he confided in me that it had had a distressing effect on him mentally, but he had come to grips with it as time passed."[5]

Jailed after being found guilty of manslaughter, Tamihere returned to police attention in 1986 when he invaded a 47 year old Auckland woman's home, raped and threatened to kill her after tying her up. For the victim, it was a six hour ordeal. Surprisingly, Tamihere coughed to the crime, pleading guilty, but while on bail awaiting sentence decided he could not face "doing the lag". He skipped and fled to the Coromandel bush, assuming a new identity under the name of "Pat Kelly".

In the meantime, given his confession, Auckland police wondered if the AWOL Tamihere was also their man for a 1985 home invasion and rape of a 62 year old Avondale woman. She too had been tied up. Police had good reason to find David Tamihere. He, on the other hand, had no desire to be found.

Keeping the home fires burning in Auckland was Tamihere's de facto wife Kristine, mother of his two sons, Jon and Blair[6]. By 1989, they'd been together 18 years, but she had seen him only occasionally since he'd done the runner back in 86.

Tamihere now says the attack on the 62 year old "was the worst crime I have ever committed. I spent three years not being sober. It was a bad crime and she didn't deserve it. It is something I am not proud of," he told journalist Meng-Yee. Nor did he enjoy having to reveal his crimes to his children.

"They went, 'Oh, Dad.' Yeah, they weren't impressed."

---

5   File note by Det. Insp. John Hughes, 27 July 1989
6   Aged 10 and 14 respectively by 1989

car sparks hunt

The abandoned car last night.

Nonetheless, you can see why police felt they had the right man for the Swedish tourist murders when they realised Tamihere had been in the same area. They didn't make the connection for quite a while however. By a strange quirk of fate, Tamihere had been arrested in Auckland on May 24, 1989 after being recognised by a police officer as a bail-jumper.

Thus, police didn't know Tamihere had been in the Coromandel; they'd found him in Auckland. His arrest coincided with an Interpol alert to Police National Headquarters in Wellington that same day about the missing Swedes, but of course no one made the connection. Why would they?

The first public inkling that Heidi and Urban were in trouble came in a front page *Herald* story on Friday, 26 May 1989. "A car belonging to a missing Swedish couple has been abandoned in Mt Eden for six weeks. The discovery worries Auckland police who were contacted by Interpol officers on Wednesday after a request from relatives."

The story featured a photo of a forlorn white Subaru with distinctive bullbars on the front, parked where it had been dumped in Watling Street, Mt Eden back on April 14. Neighbours had seen people coming and going, but the car itself had not moved. Its tyres were flat, its windows were down, and one window had been smashed.

Inside the vehicle, police found personal documents belonging to Paakkonen and Hoglin, including a travel itinerary suggesting they should have departed Auckland on April 20 for the Cook Islands. A quick call to Air New Zealand confirmed the couple had never made the flight. Interpol were telling police the regular letters home stopped coming – the last one received at this point was dated April 2, 1989. Everything pointed to something being horribly wrong.

The story featured on TV One news that night (TV3 did not begin broadcasting until November that year), and watching it was Detective Inspector John Hughes. "I was late shift DI that night," he later told journalist Carroll du Chateau,[7] "and they ran an article on TV talking about two missing Swedes and how Sergeant Colleen Mullins was making some enquiries on behalf of the family who had reported them missing."

Just after the news clip ended, the phone rang in the Auckland Police control room.

"We then got a call from the Thames Police," recalled Hughes, "which indicated to me that we should be looking at the matter more closely. It was about 9pm."

Hughes, a veteran cop with three decades of experience behind him, instinctively knew this was big, however it panned out. New Zealand was heavily pushing itself as a safe destination for overseas visitors, and suddenly two young lovers in their prime had dropped off the face of the map. By 11pm, the makings of a special task force were already in place.

---

7 "Auckland's Toughest Street Cop", Metro, November 1989

Missing Pieces

The heads-up that Hughes had received from Thames Police that Friday night was a solid lead. Forty-five year old farmer Edward Corbett had contacted his local police station that afternoon after hearing a radio news broadcast about a missing Swede named Heidi Paakkonen.

"I found a name tag with that girl Heidi's name on it, the one they're talking about on the radio," Corbett reported. Corbett's farm was at the top of Tararu Creek Road, several kilometres north of Thames township on the western flanks of the Coromandel ranges.

"The tag was hanging on the fence to the right of the stile at the top of the road. I can remember that it was on a bit of string, dangling on the fence."[8]

When he first found it, in mid to late April, Corbett had simply yanked it off the fence and thrown it on the ground. The name, "Heidi Paakkonen", had meant nothing at the time. It was distinctive enough to remember, however, and the news broadcast had sent him scurrying back up to the farm to see if he could find it again. It was a long-shot. He'd thrown it away late April. It was now late May. Nonetheless, Corbett struck gold.

"[I] found the ticket on the ground where I had thrown it, virtually. I was lucky that it was still there."

His luck was only just beginning, however. On a hunch that something else relevant might be lying around, Corbett climbed the fence and soon found men's and women's clothing. Again, he reported his discovery to police.[9]

Interpol's last known location for the missing Swedes was Rotorua – where the April 2 letter had been sent from. However, DI John Hughes now had a remote farm fence on the Coromandel range where Heidi's name tag had been located and secured.

As Saturday morning dawned, the *Herald* again front-paged the developing story, this time with an artist's sketch of Heidi and

---

8 Statement of Edward Charles Corbett, 27 May 1989
9 It later emerged at trial that Corbett had rifled through the bags of clothes around the time he found the label, pulling things out and putting them back.

Urban, and fresh details – probably sourced from DI Hughes, an astute massager of the news media. Hughes could always be relied on to slip a journalist an angle on the quiet, the news equivalent of a drug fix. Once hooked into the process, the journalist would do almost anything for future access and exclusives.

Hughes let slip to the *Herald* that the last known sighting of the pair had moved from Rotorua to Tauranga, where they'd stayed on April 4 at the Omokoroa Tourist Park camping ground. The wily detective did not disclose that he had Heidi's name tag on a Coromandel fence. That was a tip for a TV journalist.

By Saturday afternoon, thirty police and search and rescue volunteers had been assembled in Thames and briefed by Hughes in readiness for a Sunday operation. They were looking, he told them, for 21 year old Heidi Paakkonen and 23 year old Sven Urban Hoglin, and they were shown photos. They were also looking for a missing tent, backpacks, camping equipment and personal belongings including wallets and passports.

Among those initial searchers were Thames Search and Rescue leader John Cassidy and his mate Mel Knauf, men whose evidence would later become absolutely crucial to the Crown case.

Despite an extensive check of the seven kilometre long bush track at the top of Tararu Creek Road on Sunday, nothing of further significance was found. The media, however, were understandably out in force. By Monday morning, the *Herald* was announcing the "homicide base" was being established in Thames, and that Hughes would run it. "We are definitely dealing with a homicide inquiry", he told journalists.

The newspaper moved beyond "homicide" – which involves any suspicious death including unexplained accidents – it was calling the police operation a "murder inquiry team". Tararu Creek road resident Tom Thorley explained to the paper that the hills beside the bush track "are an absolute rabbit warren" of abandoned, decrepit mines. "It is no place for strangers to be wandering around in the bush. You could fall down a hole up there and never be found.

"There are a lot of vertical shafts that drop 30 or 40 feet into water and you would never get out."

Was that the fate of Heidi and Urban? No one knew.

On Monday and Tuesday, teams of detectives fanned out in what is known in police parlance as "area canvasses" – going door to door like Mormons with notebooks. Someone, somewhere, must have seen something.

Staff at a Thames hair salon were among the first to come forward. Sixteen year old Paula Johnson and her boss Merilyn Round were able to confirm that a couple matching the Swedes' description had been for a haircut on Friday, April 7.

"I cut his hair," Paula told detectives, "and he wanted it really short." The sixteen year old had three attempts before finally getting the famous mop that's appeared in all the photos cropped to the desired length. "He was really tall. I remember asking him to slouch down in the chair because the chair wouldn't go down far enough for me to cut his hair."[10]

Merilyn Round tackled Heidi's blonde locks.

"Her hair was about halfway down her back. When I had finished it was what I called a long bob, sitting on the shoulders."[11]

The way Round had cut it, Heidi's hair now "came down to about halfway over her ears". Round told the *Herald*, "she also had the front cut short." She remembered Heidi dressed in white, making her suntan stand out.

"I recall she had shorts on as her legs were quite eye catching, like a model", Round remarks in the police file.

This was crucial information for police, who could now place the missing couple in Thames township on the afternoon of Friday April 7.

A group of Air Training Cadets from Auckland were down at the Kauaeranga Valley campsite south of Thames on Saturday 8 April,

---

10   Statement of Paula Johnson, 29 May 1989
11   Statement of Merilyn Joy Round, 29 May 1989

and they reported a possible sighting of Heidi and Urban.

"We travelled in two Army trucks and an Air Force truck," Robert Owens, a service manager for Volvo who held the rank of Flying Officer with the air cadets unit, told police. "We had about 50 cadets and five instructors."[12]

At a camping area right at the top of the valley, Owens, driving an Air Force truck, came across a Subaru station wagon. "I noticed the back end of the car and remembered the registration number… began with an H, I can't recall the rest of the numbers. As I passed I looked down into the rear of the car and could see it was full of gear, neatly stacked and came up to just below the windows.

"As I drove further out I looked in the wing mirror of the truck as I went past and I remember seeing a bull-bar on the front of the car. I remember thinking it would have been a good car for camping, being a four wheel drive. It was a white car and was dusty up the sides.

"There was a yellow sticker on the left hand top side of the windscreen. I remember this because through my job we have involvement with the AA and I thought it was an AA sticker. The vehicle was closed up, all the windows were up."

This was at 2.45pm Saturday. At 3.30pm Owens returned in the truck and the Subaru was gone, but about 20 metres away was what he recalled as a green tent and what looked like a woman with blonde "collar-length" hair, about 5'9 tall. A man nearby was slightly taller. "He looked about 25 years old, he had fairish brown hair which was neat and tidy. The hair was down to about the ears and neat shoulder length at the rear."

The description matched the Swedes' car, right down to the AA sticker. It's hard to see how the people at the tent could be Heidi and Urban if their car was gone. He didn't see the Subaru again that weekend although he did hear a car "slithering and sliding" up the Valley road in the early hours of Sunday morning.

---

12   Statement of Robert James Owens, 31 May 1989

The Vanishing

At the same time, other Thames residents were coming forward with sightings of the couple's distinctive little Subaru.

On Sunday April 9, Harry Goodwin and Jennifer Gladwin drove up Tararu Creek Road sometime after lunch with friends Randal Cornish and Jackie Payne, who were looking to buy a property up in the hills there.

"I noticed a white Subaru station wagon parked at the right hand side of the turn [bay] facing back down the road," Harry Goodwin told police.[13]

The foursome had a house viewing appointment further up the Tararu track so didn't linger, but when they returned around 4pm, a couple of hours later, the car was still there. Approaching it from behind this time, Harry and the others noticed a "for sale" sign on the back. He was in the market for a new car and for the nearly $3000 asking price[14] this little unit seemed like a good buy. He pressed up and down on the front bullbars, testing the suspension.

"The thing which surprised me," he told police, "was the property left inside the car, because there was no one around and it would

---

13 Statement of Harry James Goodwin, 31 May 1989
14 As an example of how eyewitnesses can disagree on detail, Ed Corbett said the car's "For Sale" sign read $2,500; Harry Goodwin thought $2,995; Jennifer Gladwin thought between "$3,000 and $4,000"; and Randal Cornish felt $2,200

Missing Pieces

POLICE DEPARTMENT
JOB SHEET

Due _____
Record No. _____
P.N. _____
S.P.N. _____
S.L.P. _____

First plan your enquiry then set out the action taken, inquiries made, oral statements of persons seen and information gained, etc.

Typical Sunny Thames Day

...turn to Tararu Creek Road End - relieve Constable FREDERICKSON as Scene Guard.

IMPLEMENT SHED

FENCE LINE — STILE — FENCE LINE

× SILVER/GREY TENT BAG

HOUSE

GRASS
TURN AROUND

× ROBERT HARRIS LABEL
× BLUE/WHITE BRIEFS

× BBQ LEG
× BAG (1) M/CLTHG
× BAG (4) RUBBISH
× BAGS 2(a) & 2(b) F/CLTHG

BAG (3) M/F SWIM WEAR ×

BBQ LEG

BUSH LINE   BUSH LINE

Reg.No. 1420

Checked by:
Rank:
Date:

The Vanishing

have been very easy for anyone to break into the car. In the front seat I noticed at least one camera and possibly a camera carrying bag. I also noticed two or three dark coloured packs, the type used for tramping…in the back area of the car."

Randal Cornish also took a good look at the car and surroundings. "My impression when I saw the Subaru was that someone had gone for a walk into the bush but had left most of their gear in the car. I assumed they had only gone in for a day because they did not take their sleeping equipment with them."[15]

Their discussions were interrupted by the arrival of a local farmer from up the track, a neighbour of the property for sale.[16] Talk shifted again to the property, and it was around five pm by the time the Goodwins, Cornish and Payne had driven off. There had been no sign of the car's occupants for the whole afternoon, and for a day trip up the Tararu Creek track they were running out of time – sunset was due at 6:04pm and it would be dark by 6:30.

Armed with these statements, police had a time window to focus on. What had happened between the haircuts on April 7 and the appearance of their car at the end of Tararu Creek Road on April 9? How long had the car been there? When and how did it end up at Watling Street in Auckland, 200 km away late on April 14?

In the newspapers and on TV, an air of sadness was coming over the nation. Everyone feared the worst. Even their own families faced up to the realities early:

"We haven't given up hope, but it is hard to believe that they are alive," Juho Paakkonen and Hans Hoglin – the respective fathers of Heidi and Urban – said in a statement. The New Zealand sojourn, they said, was "the dream trip the couple had been saving for. They sent us letters every week with wonderful pictures."

---

15 Statement of Clement Randal Cornish, 1 June 1989
16 Police checks soon established this farmer was Ed Corbett, the man who had found the name tag. They re-interviewed him regarding the car and his conversation with the two couples, and he verified what they'd said. He wondered if he had also seen the car there on the evening of Friday 7 April, and again on the 11th, but he wasn't certain. Statement of Edward Charles Corbett, 4 June 1989

The family and police released a fragment of the latest letter to turn up, postmarked April 6:

"Here on Coromandel there are so many nice beaches and the weather is great so we spend most of the time on the beach. Most of the time we are alone, so there is no crowd. We still have the car, but it's getting time to sell it…"

On Thursday 1 June, police "sources" [read: John Hughes] were quoted in the *Herald* which ran a front page lead item:

"The missing Swedish couple may have died after stumbling upon a cannabis growing enterprise on the Coromandel Peninsula. A source close to the police said yesterday that a key witness, who claimed never to have seen Sven Urban Hoglin and his fiancée Heidi Paakkonen, had overheard an alleged Coromandel drug dealer talking about the missing tourists. The source said he believed the witness saw or overheard something vital to the police investigation into the Swedes' disappearance.

"The Coromandel countryside is renowned for its hidden crops of cannabis. The source said the key witness had told police of the activities of a drug dealer on the Coromandel, the Swede's campsite and their abandoned Subaru station-wagon. The cannabis-growing enterprise was described as 'elaborate'."

What you are reading is a classic example of Detective Inspector Hughes holding an informant's toes over a flame. If you don't believe that, read on and see how the "source close to the police" manages to positively identify their informant to the drug dealer:

"The source quoted the witness as saying the dealer was 'as big as they can get'. The plots, he said, would now have been harvested. He said the witness was afraid for his own safety. The witness was worried about a car left in the bush and mentioned it to the so-called drug-dealer. 'The car disappeared the following day and… [the witness] knew the cops had not been called'."

Just to make sure the relevant people in the underworld understood John Hughes' coded message, he also wrote it in plain English:

"Revelations about the couple's possible fate came to light yesterday. Police disclosed in the afternoon that they had located Mr Mark Tonks, a 21 year old itinerant, in Nelson, after publicity that they regarded him as an important witness in the investigation.

"Detective Inspector John Hughes, the officer heading the inquiry, said he understood Mr Tonks had confirmed seeing a white Subaru vehicle parked in Tararu Creek Road, near Thames, about April 12. Mr Hughes emphasised that Mr Tonks was neither a suspect, nor under arrest."

In other words, Tonks was an informant receiving a significant dose of pressure, Hughes-style.

In fact, there were other informants nominating a drug operation at the top of Tararu Creek Road associated with Tonks, but it was one Mark Shane Tonks taking the public heat.

By now, police also had information from two of their own Auckland officers who'd seen the distinctive white Subaru being driven by "hoons" in the Auckland suburb of Onehunga around 8pm on April 14. There were four men in the car, one appeared to have dreadlocks. Were they connected to the disappearance?

The officers who noticed the vehicle "QVR'd it" (query vehicle registration) but didn't pull the vehicle over. Had they done so back in the second week of April they might have been onto the murder mystery much sooner. By early June, however, that trail was cold. To be fair, the police patrol noted that the decrepit old Subaru was kind of in keeping with the four hoons driving it, in other words it did not look out of place. The QVR came back "no vehicle of interest", meaning it hadn't been reported stolen. Just some kids out joyriding, figured police.

Hughes, meanwhile, had scoured the Tararu track with search teams and found nothing further. Maybe the clothing and label finds were not as sinister as first thought.

"There is a growing belief among police involved in the case that the couple may simply have gone for a walk in the Coromandel bush at the end of Tararu valley and become lost in the maze of tracks that criss-cross the ranges," reported the *Herald*.

If that was the case, maybe the clothing had been ditched by opportunists who stole the Swedes' car.

"Mr Hughes appealed for whoever drove the couple's car in Auckland on April 14 or 15 to 'come clean'. Police could be saved many hundreds of hours of investigation if they could establish exactly where and when the vehicle was taken, he said."

Police now knew the car was mobile on the night of April 14, and dumped in Watling Street during that evening or the early hours of April 15.

None of this, however, changed Hughes' view on the ultimate outcome of the investigation:

"Nothing would please me more than to have the young couple turn up safe and well. But that is now virtually impossible, and the next best thing will be if we can find them and establish that they have died in non-suspicious circumstances," Hughes told the *Herald*.

To support their theory of accidental death and opportunistic car thieves, however, police still needed to find the bodies. If Heidi and Urban had died in an accident, a wider search should find them.

Search and Rescue coordinator John Cassidy briefed an 80 strong police and civilian search team on the hazards of the area. Old abandoned mineshafts from the 1870s gold rush were common, he said, and some were "hundreds of metres deep".

"Leave the mineshafts for the experts," police inspector Graham McColl cut in, telling the group they were bringing in a specialist team from the Huntly Mines Rescue unit to scour the many mineshafts for Heidi and Urban.

"It's incredible bush up there," added Hughes. "You could go 20m off the track and not be found. There are so many places in there that they could have gone in."

Needless to say, nothing was found.

A *New Zealand Herald* report from early June, at the end of the first week of the police operation, carried the first hint of what would turn into the Crown's "smoking gun" evidence against David Tamihere:

"The police also wanted to find a couple who had camped in

the Crosbie Clearing on April 8. The couple, believed to be from Auckland, are described as a part-Maori man of strong build, aged in his early 30s, and a woman in her late 20s with blonde hair."

CHAPTER 3

Forever Autumn

"How did it go for the Finnish couple who murdered the family up in the north of Sweden, and who stole the car?"
– letter home from Heidi Paakkonen,
29 January 1989, Murchison

The discovery that a part Maori man and a young blonde woman had been seen at Crosbie's Clearing, some three to five hours walk from the Tararu Creek Road carpark, on Saturday April 8, was initially little more than a tiny pebble thrown into the larger pond of incoming information. But the ripples from this pebble would spread.

The information had come early in the investigation from Search and Rescue coordinator John Cassidy, who made a statement to Thames Police just after 8 on the morning of Wednesday 31 May. Cassidy described how he and a friend, Mel Knauf, had gone hiking on the morning of Saturday 8 April, and that they had timed their tramp with a diary. They had entered the bush to the south at 5:59am, veering north on a route that would take them via Crosbies clearing eventually to the Tapu/Coroglen summit road. They estimated the trip would take them twelve hours.

Nine hours into their hike, at 3:12pm, they stumbled across a man and woman in the bush.

"We arrived at the Pines area of Crosbie's Clearing at 15:12 hours and we came across a couple whom we stopped and spoke to for 13

Forever Autumn

Thames Search & Rescue controller John Cassidy

minutes," Cassidy told police. "According to my diary we started walking again at 15:25 hours.[17]

"The couple had a tent and they indicated that they intended spending the night there. The guy actually pitched the tent while we were there talking to them. They said they had just walked in from the Tararu Creek Road. The guy appeared to be familiar with the general area from the way he was talking, because we explained where we had come from and he seemed to understand. They indicated that they were from the Auckland area.

"The guy was in his early 30s, part Maori, about 5'11, strong build, outdoor type, black hair, clean shaven although he may have had a moustache. He was wearing boots of some kind, denim shorts and I think a dark top.

"The girl that was with him was in her mid to late 20s, European, she had light blonde hair straight to the collar. She was seated on a piece of log or something when we arrived and she did not stand up or in fact say anything while we were there.

"She had a fair complexion and well-groomed appearance to the extent that she looked out of place in the bush setting. She was wearing a green shade of cape draped over her shoulders and it covered most of her. Light rain started falling while we were there.

"The tent which the guy was pitching was a bright blue hiker's tent with sewn-in floor and blue matching fly sheet. He had obviously had experience of pitching this tent before.

"I think from the conversation we had, the couple intended to return to Tararu Creek Road, the same way they had come up, because I presume they would have left their car there. The couple both had packs, but I can't recall just what they looked like.

"We got the impression that the couple were only going to stay over one night and then return to the Tararu Creek Road," Cassidy told police.

By the time he made this statement, on May 31st, John Cassidy had

---

17   Statement of John Thomas Cassidy, 31 May 1989

already been deeply involved in the search at the Tararu Creek track entrance for Heidi Paakkonen and Urban Hoglin since May 27. He had been briefed on the possibility of foul play, and he had studied photos of the missing couple. He had spent 13 minutes close enough to almost touch the woman in the green cape. He was not suggesting, however, that the woman he saw was Heidi Paakkonen.

Cassidy's tramping companion Mel Knauf made a brief statement to police the same morning. In it, he says he read and agrees with Cassidy's version of events, but just wanted to add:

"I thought the guy may have only been about 5'7" to 5'8" in height, but still with the strong athletic build, and he was very well spoken. The girl was attractive and I noticed her fingernails were painted. She did look out of place."[18]

Both men knew what Heidi Paakkonen looked like. Neither man was saying it was her. Nor did police take any action beyond issuing the one appeal for that mystery couple to come forward and eliminate themselves from the inquiry.

Instead, the Hughes-led investigation continued to focus on identifying the car thieves, and logging further sightings of Heidi Paakkonen and Urban Hoglin on the Coromandel Peninsula. One man to shed light on the Swedes' plans was local Four Square general store owner Graham Manning.

After buying some groceries, Manning says Heidi and Urban pulled out a book of local maps. "They asked me where the Tararu Creek was and how to get there. I told them they should be going into the Kauaeranga Valley [south of Thames]. I tried to persuade them to go to the Park Headquarters.[19]

"They were positive they wanted to go up the Tararu Creek. They saw it as a challenge. Their ambition was to go up to Table Mountain and down into the Kauaeranga Valley. They said it would be easier to get a ride in from there, than going the other way."

---

18 Statement of Theodore Melvyn Knauf, 31 May 1989
19 Statement of Graham Arthur Manning, 1 June 1989

This news gave the police fresh impetus. Clearly the Swedes had left their car at Tararu Creek Road deliberately for a planned day tramp, with the intention of hitching a ride back into Thames from a motorist on the well-travelled Kopu-Hikuai highway that crossed the ranges.

Such a journey, of course, exposed them to several risks. Firstly, it left their car full of belongings vulnerable at Tararu Creek, but they didn't really have an option on this if they wanted to do the tramp. Secondly, it left them open to misfortune on the tracks themselves, and thirdly, it opened up a risk at the end as hitchhikers on the main highway.

There is no indication in the police files that this particular analysis and option set with regards to the couple as victims of a hitchhiking gone wrong was actively considered by detectives. Yet if the attractive blonde and her fiancé had been picked up by the wrong kind of motorist at the wrong time, their bodies could be miles away from the police search area.

Not one news story pitched the angle of the Swedes as hitchhikers. Perhaps, because they had a car of their own it just wasn't on the radar.

In terms of the police investigation, clearly the first risk had materialised, as the couple's car had indeed been ransacked and stolen. The second risk was the one being concentrated on by police – extensive searches of the tracks themselves for any trace of the missing couple. The possibility of risk number three didn't seem to have occurred to anyone.

Graham Manning's testimony provided some more clues, however – the Swedes may have been intending to overnight in the bush, which could explain why their sleeping bags were never found.

"The map they had must have been an old one," he told police, "as it had huts marked on it that are not there now…I told them it was a two day walk through that track."

The visit to Manning's shop was timed to the late afternoon of April 6. Heidi and Urban had been seen in Thames on April 7 in what police and the media kept referring to as "the last official sighting of the pair".

Simple logic suggested a linear pattern to DI Hughes. The Swedes had talked of tramping Tararu Creek on the 6th, they'd been seen in the area on the 7th, and their car had been seen at Tararu Creek on the 9th.

When Heidi and Urban's families flew in to Auckland mid June, they were choppered over the Coromandel bush search area by police.

"This is not like Sweden – this is more like a jungle for us," remarked brother Stefan Hoglin sadly. His mind skipped to the many fishing and hiking trips he and Urban had made back home. Frankly, the occasional threat of bears and wolves seemed like a walk in the park compared with the blanket of rainforest, ridgelines and deep valleys below them.

Heidi's sister-in-law, 23 year old Cea Paakkonen, was equally taken aback. "They are like mountains, those hills, and Heidi was afraid of heights. I cannot believe she would walk there. They had just 14 days left before they were leaving New Zealand. I do not think they would take risks."

While police may have been attracted to the Tararu Creek car abandonment, they were not immune to chasing other leads. At

Missing Pieces

Forever Autumn

least, not at this stage of what was still a wide-open investigation.

"Police investigating the disappearance of the two Swedish tourists have been told the couple might have been walking on a Coromandel beach one or two days after the last known sighting of the pair," reported the *Herald* that week.

The newspaper detailed how police had heard from a man who'd been walking at Fletcher's Bay on the very northern tip of the Coromandel peninsula on either Saturday 8 April or the 9th.

"They had apparently told the man they were looking for a good place to go walking, and he thought they talked of going down to Colville," Detective Senior Sergeant Bruce Raffan told the *Herald*. "It is only a possible sighting at this stage but it coincides with another possible sighting of the couple's car at Colville and another in the Coromandel township."

This was a new direction for police, literally. Fletcher's Bay was around 120 km north of Thames. Raffan, however, pointed out that many of the April 7 sightings in Thames were "very vague".

"We have to remember that although the Subaru was seen parked by the bush behind Thames on April 9, and the couple told a local shopkeeper they planned to go walking up there, they were never actually seen up the Tararu Creek Road.

"It may be that something has happened to them further north on the peninsula and whoever took their car could have ditched it up the Tararu Creek Road."

The news reports that police were interested in sightings further north brought a fresh influx of information to the Operation Stockholm base. Police revealed they'd spoken to a 56 year old Auckland man who'd driven behind a white stationwagon on the road from Thornton's Bay to Tapu, where he was finally able to overtake. The car, he explained, was driving slowly and carefully as if by a foreign driver.

Additionally, a Whitianga farmer and his wife had been at the Port Jackson campground on April 8 when they "saw the missing couple in their car drive up from the beach into the camping ground and park at the ablution block," reported DSS Raffan to the *Her-*

ald. "They did some washing and dishes there, and that was between 8.30 and 9.30 in the morning.

The Swedes eventually drove off towards Coromandel, passing a red utility vehicle coming in with four Maori and European men inside, said police.

When police took the couple's Subaru on a display tour to Coromandel, suddenly even more people remembered seeing it and the occupants. For eleven weeks, two witnesses who were sitting on a sighting of Heidi and Urban at Port Jackson stayed silent, in the belief that police were only interested in sightings from Thames.

"Because there had been no other reports of the pair being so far north," explained Raffan to the *Herald*, "the couple decided their information must have been incorrect."

Another witness was the postmistress at Coromandel who remembered selling the couple some stamps on the afternoon of April 7. Their final letter was postmarked April 7.

On Tuesday June 27, DI Hughes signalled he was moving back towards a foul play scenario. A thorough search of mines and bush tracks had failed to find the couple. "Though a possible scenario for their disappearance has been that they went bushwalking, got lost and perished, our inquiries lean more towards the scenario that the couple met their deaths by unnatural causes – that they were murdered."

Ever cryptic, the enigmatic Hughes talked of "information privy to the investigation team" that indicated homicide, rather than accident.

With the power of hindsight, we now know a little bit more about the direction the police inquiry was heading. On 2 June, 1989, a 16 year old student named Jason Donald revealed how he'd stumbled across a campsite in Crosbie's Clearing while on a hunting trip with a friend. It was mid –March, he told police, the weekend before Easter. "I saw a blue tent, it would have been a three to four man one."

The embers of a fire near the tent were still warm, he remembered, but there was no sign of life. Unzipping the tent he found a note written in black pen: "I'm tired of waiting for you…So I have gone for a walk and will see you tonight or tomorrow. If anybody finds this tent, do not vandal it as it's all I've got."

The note was signed, "Pat Kelly", a pseudonym used by bail jumper David Tamihere.

Police searchers John Cassidy and Mel Knauf had, of course, mentioned a campsite at Crosbie's Clearing as well when they were there a couple of weeks later.

In the final week of May, another sighting of the white Subaru came into play that in turn pushed the "Pat Kelly" buttons. An informant named J A Benfield told police they'd seen the Subaru parked outside the Sunkist Lodge in Thames, described as "low budget accommodation". Benfield timed the sighting to the week commencing Monday 10 April.

This was dynamite! The first confirmed sighting of the car in the Thames region after April 9 at Tararu Creek Road. Police raced to the Sunkist Lodge.

Initially, on 31 May during preliminary police inquiries across Thames, lodge manager Wayne Stafford had told detectives he couldn't recall "a white Subaru being parked out front of my establishment." Nor had the missing Swedes stayed there, he confirmed.

Hughes had a hunch, however, and he very rarely let his hunches go untested. The Benfield statement about Sunkist hung around in the background, nagging him. Who stayed at the Sunkist that week? He wanted to know.

A break came in the final week of June 1989. Swedish journalist Peter Svensson, covering the search for the *Expressen* newspaper, received a phone call from a reader. Håkan Bokull told Svensson he'd just read one of the journalist's dispatches in the Swedish papers featuring a photo of the car, and that he had information about the missing Subaru to pass on.

Svensson, realising the information could be crucial, put Bokull in contact with police, who in turn arranged for detectives in the Swedish town of Norrköping to immediately interview him. Bokull told police he'd arrived in Thames on April 9 and stayed at the Sunkist Lodge. He and a Canadian backpacker, Anita Labrecque, had wanted to go on a Coromandel region tour but couldn't find anyone to take them. On the 10th, they met a man who volunteered, provided his room for the night and petrol were paid for.

The man, who gave the name "Pat", drove Bokull to a service station to fill up with petrol, and when they got back to the lodge a third visitor, a "Swiss girl" was asking to come along as well. Asked to describe "Pat", Bokull told Swedish police:[20]

"I'd say he was about 30 or 35, about my height, that is 180cm, perhaps a little shorter. Dark brown, almost black, a bit straggly but not untidy, thick hair, big bushy moustache curving down over the corners of his mouth."

Bokull said Pat was wearing a T-shirt and had no visible scratches, scars or wounds. "Mentally, he didn't seem temperamental or depressed or exceedingly happy or anything like that. Quite normal, I would say."

Did he make sexual passes at either of the two women, police wanted to know. The answer was negative. "So he was strictly the gentleman then, so to speak?" quizzed the Swedish detective.

"Yes, I found him quite nice when we travelled around."

Pat evidently made quite the tour guide when the group set off on April 11 in the white Subaru, and Bokull remembers being awestruck by their guide's explanations of Maori place-names. "I don't remember the name of the bay, but he explained it to us because it was very beautiful."

---
20 Statement of Karl Richard Håkan Bokull, 28 June 1989

The car, said Bokull, was definitely "a white Subaru, four wheel drive...and with kangaroo bars in front." Or, as Swedish police described them in their covering letter, "moose bars".[21] It's hard to envisage what possible help such bars might be if one's Subaru happened to whack into a Swedish moose on a remote country road.

"There was no luggage," said Bokull. "In the boot was a bucket with a fishing line in it and a telescopic rod, casting rod, which I tucked away because the roads are curved up there and this telescopic rod dangled this way and that."

Swedish police faxed their Bokull interview to the Operation Stockholm base in Thames, and by the afternoon of June 29 Sunkist Lodge manager Stafford was being asked to hunt back through the bookings records. A Swedish backpacker named Håkan Bokull had indeed checked in on the 9th and left on the 12th. Two carless kiwis named Kirstin Grant and Darcy Thrussell were staying there, along with a guy named "Pat Kelly" who'd checked in on the 10th and left on the 12th also.

You can tell this was no random fishing expedition by Hughes, because of all the people staying at the lodge, "Pat Kelly" was the only one for whom Stafford included a description in his police statement. Clearly, he'd been asked.

"I would describe Pat: male Caucasian, 35 years, dark complexion, dark jet black hair, moustache, 5'11", medium build. Very friendly."[22]

"Pat," he explained, "borrowed a friend's car and he took three people around the Coromandel. They were all persons staying at the lodge. I didn't see the car at all."

Several more paragraphs were devoted to this one "Pat Kelly" individual, including the names of those he was associating with at Sunkist. Police wasted no time in putting in some further groundwork. The net was closing on David Wayne Tamihere.

---

21 Contained in Briefing for Interpol by John Hughes, dated 18 July 1989
22 Statement of Wayne Stafford, 29 June 1989

CHAPTER 4

The Breakthrough

"You will have a lot of extra work when Fia has got another child...have you got any photo of the baby? It would be nice to see how he is looking. Maybe I should tell you that everything is well here, there's only one problem: time is flying too fast. We've been thinking about changing the tickets once again and staying here another week...

"Excuse me if it's a bit messy and bent in this letter, but it's because it's so windy. Most of it is probably because of the sandflies. These are the only animals that are really plaguing us, you don't have to think about snakes or spiders or other dangerous animals or plants, and that is nice.

"Now we are going to light a fire, and see if we can have some fried fish for supper."
— *Letter from Heidi Paakkonen, Cobb River, 6 January 1989*

What had Tamihere been up to? According to his version of events, he tramped up Tararu Creek Road in the early afternoon of April 10, 1989, with the intention of hiking up to Crosbie's Clearing. Instead, at the start of the track, he found a white Subaru station wagon, packed with camping gear and a camera on the back seat, begging for the taking.

He felt the exhaust pipe to gauge whether the owners were still nearby, and decided he had time to kill and a car to steal.

Looking around for something to break in with, Tamihere says he utilised some No. 8 wire from a nearby fence, bending it double for extra strength, twisting the end around the shaft for further rigidity and used it to flick the door toggle open. Quickly rummaging through the car he says he found a set of keys in the glovebox. Suddenly he had functional wheels.

After dumping some of the bags of clothing he found in the car, he says he fired the Subaru up and drove to the Sunkist backpackers' lodge, checking in under his man-on-the-run pseudonym, "Pat Kelly". Overhearing some fellow guests complaining that they couldn't get a car tour of the Coromandel peninsula the next day, Tamihere offered to take a Swedish man and two women – one Swiss and one Canadian – on a road trip around the region the next day provided they paid for petrol and his accommodation at the lodge that night – the princely sum of $12.

The tourists agreed, and the next morning, Tuesday April 11, the group set off on the tiki tour. Tamihere wanted to put some distance between himself and Thames and told the Swiss tourist, Gabrielle Staub, he could give her a lift to Auckland the next day. She accepted.

After dropping her off at a backpackers' lodge near Auckland Hospital, Tamihere says he drove the stolen car to the Railway Station, leaving it unlocked with the keys returned to the glovebox. He took with him the two packs belonging to Urban Hoglin and Heidi Paakkonen, as well as binoculars, some clothing and a telescopic fishing rod of Hoglin's.

He cashed in some of the gear at the Harmony House pawn shop on Auckland's Karangahape Road for a $100 cheque.

This, in a nutshell, is David Tamihere's backstory as told by him.

The police had not been slacking off over this time. They'd been trying to reach the other guests to see what they could add to the story of Pat Kelly, the tour driver. It was old-fashioned detective work that finally sprang the case open, however.

The breakthrough for police came on July 10, just after 6pm. It

The Breakthrough

was a Monday evening, three months to the day after Tamihere had stolen the Swedes' car, and a junior detective constable had been tasked with tracking through all the phone numbers that had been called by guests staying at the Sunkist Lodge in Thames.

At 6.20pm, David Tamihere's number was up, literally, when Detective Brown phoned an Auckland listing on his schedule. The police job sheet records what happened:[23]

"Speak with Jackie Jones, 231 Blockhouse Bay Road, Mt Roskill. She advises that she has been at the address after moving in last Thursday. She was not aware of the previous tenants. The landlord however said that the previous people had a boyfriend who was in and out of jail all the time."

A phone call to the landlord quickly confirmed "the address of 25 or 27 Victor Street, Avondale, for the previous tenants, the Tamiheres."

Game, set, match. Or, in Monopoly terms, "Go Directly To Jail, Do Not Pass Go". The name "Tamihere" rang every kind of klaxon horn, alarm and bell imaginable at Operation Stockholm. The police computer quickly threw up the recent arrest of David Tamihere at the Blockhouse Bay address, and the rap sheet confirmed a manslaughter conviction, rapes, robbery and indecent assault.

Within half an hour, detectives Brown and Devoy were disembarking from their squad car in the driveway of 27 Victor Street, to be greeted by an annoyed Kristine Tamihere.

"What is it this time, haven't you bothered us enough?"

Kristine told the officers it was nothing personal, but that last time police had visited they'd left the place in "a terrible mess".

Detective Brown replied he and Devoy were just making "routine inquiries" and would not be creating a mess on this visit. As she invited them in, Detective Brown's eyes were drawn to "a green jacket sitting on a chair...I immediately recognised this jacket as being the same as belonging to the Swedish couple."

---

23   Police Job Sheet of Det. Const. J E Brown, signed on 11 July 1989

While Detective Devoy ducked out to radio this bombshell back to base, Brown kept Kristine talking. Yes, she said, David had brought the jacket home with him recently and given it to one of their sons. Yes, there might be some other items and the police were welcome to take a look. Yes, she was aware he'd been staying at "some backpacker's lodge down in Thames" while on the run from the 1986 rape sentence.

"I questioned Kristine in relation to why she had stayed with David for this many years, and she indicated that he was a very kind person when he was sober," noted Detective Brown later. "She outlined that he was a totally different person when he had been drinking, and she had learned to stay well clear of him when he was drinking. She indicated that she had no problems with him sexually and he had never forced himself on her."

By this stage, police reinforcements including a crime scene commander had arrived – a total of seven detectives and uniformed staff by 9.20pm. Two more would arrive just before midnight to guard the scene overnight.[24] Among the items police picked up and took away were a group of photos of Coromandel bushland, several of them featuring a clean shaven David Tamihere, taken two years earlier.

So there it was. A phone call home from a man on the run was, at the end of the day, how police finally found their prime suspect in the murders of Heidi Birgitta Paakkonen and Sven Urban Hoglin.

The first David Tamihere knew of this new turn of events was the grating of steel as his Mt Eden prison cell was unlocked by a warder. "You've got some visitors," the guard grunted as he led the inmate to the prison's conference room. Seated inside to greet him were Detective Inspector John Hughes and three of his team. Detective Wayne Kiely leaned across the desk, offering the prisoner a cigarette. Tamihere declined, pulling out his own packet of Drum and rolling one.

"So," began the cop, "before we picked you up in May in Auckland, where had you been staying?"

"Around Waihi, Coromandel."

---

24 Police Job Sheet of Det. Const. J D Rinckes, signed on 11 July 1989

The Breakthrough

Photos of David Tamihere clean-shaven, 1987

When it came to his whereabouts, the prime suspect was utterly open.

"I walked all through the bush and around there."

"What, on your own?"

"Yeah."

He told them he'd been in Thames, "at the backpacker's lodge for a couple of days", and when police asked if he'd been to Crosbie's Clearing he answered, "yeah, about four times."

"When was the last time?"

"In April sometime."

"Did you have anyone with you?"

"No."

He told detectives he had a "blue, two man tent…an Igloo", with a silver fly.

"Bought them or pinched them?" asked the detective with a wry smile. "Pinched them," agreed Tamihere, "when I did the runner".

"Do you ever remember leaving a note?"

"Yeah, to say I was coming back."

"Did you put your name on it?"

"Yeah, Pat Kelly," replied Tamihere.

Honest so far, could Tamihere keep it up? Evidently not. Tamihere would later write of the next few minutes as a mistake on his part, "sheer bloody mindedness…wanting to make them work for their money". The police, understandably, saw it differently. Over coffee one morning, John Hughes once laughingly described such things as "failing the attitude test". Here's how it unfolded:

"Did you break into a white Subaru in Thames?", Detective Wayne Kiely wanted to know.

"No."

Instead, said Tamihere, he had borrowed a white Corolla station-wagon from a mate.

"Did you give your son a wet weather jacket?"

Tamihere knew from this question that his home had obviously been searched. "Yeah". He told police he found the jacket at Boom's

Flat, in the Kauaeranga Valley area south of Thames. "It was in a cardboard box," he added.

"Just the jacket?"

"Yeah, there was some food as well. I think there was little binoculars...little ones in a zip bag...green."

"Where are they?"

"Home."

"Is that all you found?"

"Yeah."

"Quite sure?"

"Oh, yeah. There were two packs as well."

"Where?"

"By the cardboard box, in the box."

The story was getting more ludicrous by the minute. Just how big was the box? Perhaps realising he was walking the credibility plank, Tamihere injected some reality back into proceedings.

"What did you do with them?"

"Sold them...Harmony House," replied the prisoner, telling the truth, and adding that the packs were green with metal frames, which of course they were. Aware he'd played a bad hand and was losing, Tamihere chose to make a confession after the lunch break.

"The car, I stole the car," he said as the interrogation resumed.

"Which car?"

"The Subaru."

"Where from?"

"Tararu Creek Road."

Tamihere gave police the version of events outlined earlier – that'd he'd intended to hike the four hours journey to Crosbie's Clearing on Monday 10 April when he stumbled across the unattended car full of gear, and broke into it using fencing wire. He told detectives he'd ripped out name labels from the jacket he found in the car.

"So you mean to tell me that a man who is on the run, broke into a car which was locked and full of property, then went through the property cutting out labels here and there? It was broad daylight and you hang around for 15 minutes?" Detective Kiely's eyebrows rose.

"Yeah, I had felt the exhaust pipe," Tamihere explained. "It was warm, not hot, so I figured they must have gone for a walk through the bush."

If the tailpipe was warm, it can only have resulted from the early April midday sunshine, as the car had been parked there since the previous afternoon, Sunday 9 April, and Tamihere's description of its location was identical to the witnesses who'd seen it the previous day.

Tamihere told police he'd found passports and ownership papers for the car in the packs. He'd thrown the passports and other contents in a rubbish bin in Auckland, but rifled through the bin when he realised he could retrieve and use the ownership papers as ID when he pawned the packs at Harmony House.

"What name did you use for ID?"

"The registration papers…Hoglin or something. The address was in Mt Eden."

Tamihere flicked off the two packs, the fishing rod and some binoculars. He told police he left "the cameras" in the car at the Railway Station. "They weren't much use to me at the time, even trying to flog them, they looked quite an expensive job."

After establishing that Tamihere had used the stolen Subaru, not a mate's Corolla, to escort tourists around Coromandel's northern tip, police were sceptical:

"Well Dave, you must have big balls. A guy that has been on the run for 2 to 3 years steals a car, then drives it around the area for another day or so. How do you know you wouldn't have got caught? The owners might have come straight out after you took it and reported it stolen."

"I had the ownership papers," retorted Tamihere. "I've done it before. I was in a stolen car once which had ownership papers. When I got stopped by MOT [Ministry of Transport traffic cops] I showed them and just said I had rung and told the Police I had found it. He believed me and I got away with it."

Detective Beard wasn't buying it, and laid an allegation that became one of the main themes of Tamihere's 1990 trial:

"Well Dave, I'm telling you the reason you knew the car wasn't going to be reported stolen is that you came across these people and you have done them in."

"No way! I have got nothing to do with that. If you want to charge me, charge me."

"Yeah, but Dave, you knew the car wasn't going to be reported stolen, didn't you?"

"Look, I stole the car," growled Tamihere. "I have never seen them or done anything to them. I don't know anything more about it…I stole the car and that's all."

To be fair, what you've just witnessed from police, and put to good effect in the trial, is a rhetorical argument. What Tamihere had coughed to was stealing the car from Tararu Creek Road and driving straight away to a backpacker's lodge in Thames where he parked the vehicle in a little-used side street. There was nothing of his in the car to connect it to him as such if it had been found that evening. The next morning, he took it on a 200 or 300km journey driving tourists around the northern Coromandel region, not returning to Thames until nearly sunset. Once again, the car was parked overnight, then driven to Auckland the next day. It wasn't as if he spent the whole time driving up and down Tararu Creek Road waiting to be discovered.

This caveat is written not to exonerate Tamihere, but merely to restore a sense of perspective – it's a weak argument when looked at logically. A car is stolen in New Zealand every 15 minutes. As many victims of such crimes know, it generally attracts a bored yawn from the front desk of the local police station, and a form to take to one's insurance company. People have even been known to give chase to their stolen car, only to have police respond, "we're too busy to send a unit".[25]

---

[25] Indeed, under cross examination at trial, Thames Police admitted that would most likely have been their reaction in 1989

"Did you have a poncho type cover?" police wanted to know. They were of course sitting on a description of a part Maori man and blonde woman in Crosbie's Clearing, where the woman was said to have been wearing a green cape or poncho, but their suspect didn't know that. Tamihere answered yes to the question, telling police the poncho would have been with him "all the time", and the garment was now at home.

"At 7.45pm the interview was completed and the accused Tamihere was advised that he would be charged with unlawfully taking the Swedish couple's vehicle and theft of the contents," the police file records. "At this he seemed quite happy, and shook hands with us. I asked him if he was willing to help us further with our enquiries into this matter and he said he would," added Detective Wayne Kiely.

It had been exactly 25 hours since police made the phone call that changed their entire investigation, but for most of July 11 the media were unaware of what was taking place. Instead, media reports that morning had noted that the number of people who'd seen the missing Swedes and their car at the top of the Coromandel peninsula on "April 7, 8 and 9" continued to grow rapidly, creating what Detective Senior Sergeant Raffan called "a lot of paperwork". More than 20 people, he said, had now reported sightings at Port Jackson.

As far as police were concerned however, all these sightings were about to become academic. They now had a suspect, and they began to build a case around him, rather than around the evidence. To John Hughes, it must have looked like a "gimme" dropped from heaven into his lap: a convicted killer, rapist and robber roaming the bush tracks behind Thames at the same time as the Swedes had gone missing. How could it not be Tamihere? He knew it, now he just had to prove it.

Naturally, the Hughes system of leaking strategic details to the media to keep them onside kicked in. As the morning of July 12 broke, a police car was sent to pick up David Tamihere from Mt Eden Prison and transport him to court, stopping en route at the rubbish bin in Karangahape Road opposite Harmony House so he

The Breakthrough

could show detectives where he'd dumped the Swedes' passports.

As he sat in the car, handcuffed to a police officer, Tamihere cannot have failed to see the newspaper billboards trumpeting another *Herald* exclusive, "Swede case breakthrough". If he'd had a chance to flick 50 cents into the honesty box, Tamihere would have read:

"Detectives investigating the disappearance of the Swedish tourists Heidi Paakkonen and Sven Urban Hoglin say they have uncovered evidence that significantly advances their inquiries. They have identified at least one of the men they believe is responsible for taking the couple's white Subaru stationwagon, and made a breakthrough in tracing the movements of the vehicle since the Swedes were last seen in April."

The newspaper revealed there had been "early morning raids" and said John Hughes had confirmed that evidence found during the "raids had substantially advanced the inquiry". If you could call being invited in by an Avondale housewife at 7pm an "early morning raid", then the leak was entirely accurate.

"Late last night," reported the *Herald*, "no one had been charged with theft of the car or any of Miss Paakkonen's or Mr Hoglin's belongings, but Mr Hughes said he expected further developments in the case today."

At about that moment, the police car containing the "further development" stopped – not at the secure back entrance to the Auckland District Court as is usual practice – but out the front where a huge media pack was waiting. As Tamihere stepped out, still handcuffed to an officer, he ran the gauntlet of photographers, journalists and TV crews for fifteen metres while being led into the court.

TV news played the footage that night, and Tamihere was immortalised in a front page *Herald* photo the next morning being paraded, cuffed, into court.

In cases where identification is critical, it is almost unheard of for police to muddy the waters by publicly showing off a suspect. The reason for this unwritten rule is simple: witnesses become tainted, and cases can actually fall apart. Did the witness really see the suspect at the crime scene, or has the witness subconsciously linked the suspect to the crime scene because he or she has seen them linked to the case on TV or in newspapers? Defence lawyers can have a field day with such things.

In 1999, the US Department of Justice and its Canadian counterpart published research into the accuracy of eyewitness testimony. The report, endorsed by Attorney-General Janet Reno, revealed that even the subtle body language of detectives can impact on identification:

"Similarly, investigators' unintentional cues (e.g., body language, tone of voice) may negatively impact the reliability of eyewitness evidence. Psychology researchers have noted that such influences could be avoided if "blind" identification procedures were employed (i.e., procedures conducted by investigators who do not know the identity of the actual suspect)."[26]

The decision to taint the witness memories was a deliberate one on the part of Detective Inspector John Hughes, and it is the first coded signal that Hughes had made his mind up already. The integrity of the evidence no longer mattered, he had a suspect, it had to be him, and making people subconsciously associate Tamihere with the Swedes as a "suspect" would pay dividends to Hughes as long as he could ride out the identification storm.

For the parents of Urban Hoglin and Heidi Paakkonen, July 12 1989 is the day their quest for genuine closure in the murders of their children began to run off the rails. From this moment forward, they too became pawns in a John Hughes game. A quick solution to a high profile murder of foreign tourists was going to make Hughes look good, make the police look good and, if he continued to schmooze the family, make the country look good. It would be a win all around, if you ignore the inconvenient possibility that Tamihere may not actually have been the killer.

---

26 Eyewitness Evidence: A Guide For Law Enforcement, US DOJ, 1999, page 9

The Breakthrough

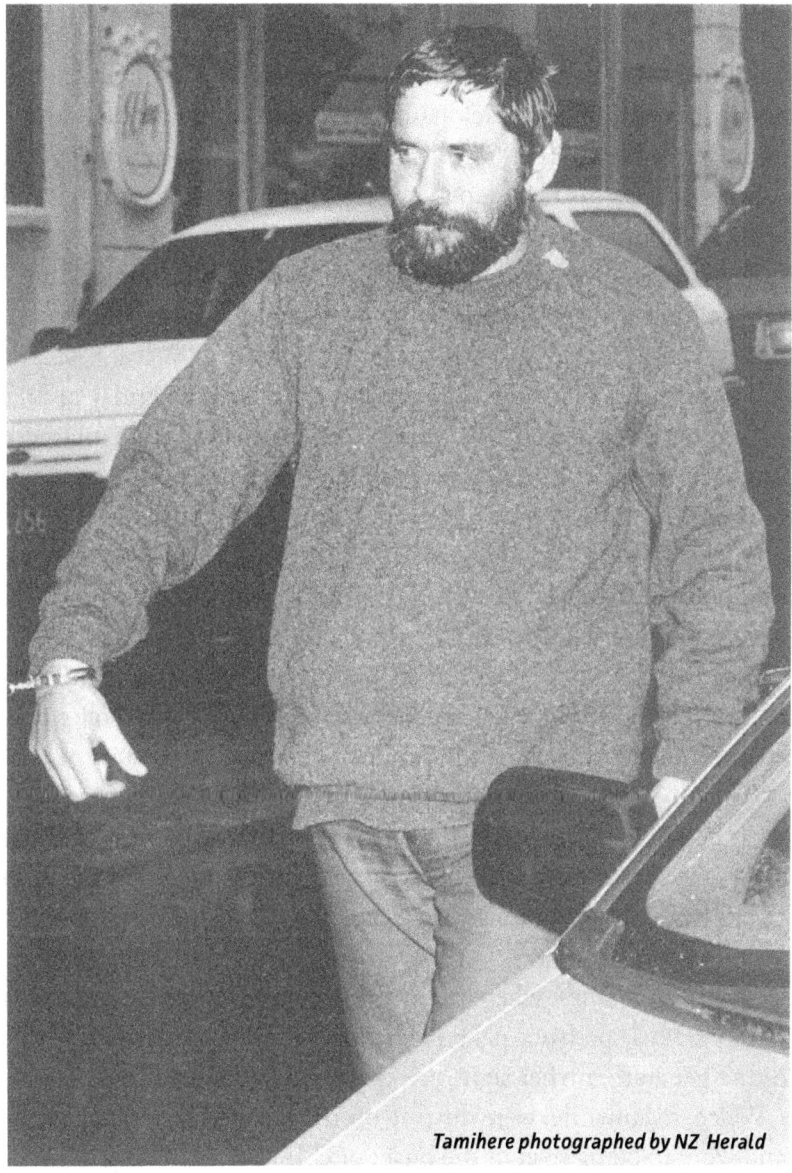

Tamihere photographed by NZ Herald

Tamihere made only a brief appearance in court that day. He entered no plea to charges of stealing the car and belongings, and was remanded in custody to reappear in the Thames District Court on July 26 – a fortnight away.

Detectives, meanwhile, were already at Harmony House even as Tamihere was waiting to appear. They recovered a pair of binoculars, and discovered Heidi's pack had only been sold just a week earlier, on July 4. Urban's metal framed pack had been sold on June 7. The fishing rod had also gone to a new owner. Efforts began to try and locate the purchasers of all the missing items.

The arrest on the car theft, and nationwide publication of Tamihere's photo gave the inquiry a massive new focus and PR opportunity.

"Police retrace man's travels," reported the *Herald* on Friday 14 July.

"We have reassessed the whole situation," Hughes explained, "and are going to canvass the whole of Thames and then every other town on the peninsula, from Kopu to Waihi…This is still a homicide inquiry and I believe the solution to the mystery is in the hills behind Thames." He added that revelations about "Pat Kelly… have given us a whole new direction…a tremendous boost".

Later that day, Hughes confirmed to the news media what many journalists had known since Tamihere's photo was published: "Police now confirm that Mr Kelly and Mr Tamihere are one and the same person.

"We are now concentrating on where he was, who he met and what he did while he was here on the peninsula. We know he often camped out in the bush, and that he walked extensively on the bush tracks throughout the area, and we want to talk to anyone who met him up there."

Down in Thames, where many of the witnesses were, Tamihere's photo graced the front page of the *Thames Star* newspaper. If this didn't generate further sighting reports, nothing would.

Police, meanwhile, were dusting off those earlier reports of a man and woman being seen in the bush, pitching a tent, telling journalists they were "anxious to speak to a couple tramping in the hills behind Thames in early April.

Detective Sergeant Bruce Raffan took the lead on this, explaining how the couple had been seen setting up camp in an area known as the Pines at "Crosbie's Settlement".

The Breakthrough

"They were seen on Saturday, April 8, by two Thames residents and were spoken to by them. The man appeared to be an experienced bushman and was putting up a light blue hiker's tent with a sewn-in floor and a matching blue fly-sheet."

Raffan described the woman as "European, in her mid 20s, with light blond collar length hair and painted fingernails.

"She was wearing a green cape or poncho, and the witnesses felt she looked rather out of place in the bush setting."

The man, he added, was part Maori, aged about 30, about 175cm tall, with black hair and an athletic build. "It is not thought they are in any way connected with the Swedes' disappearance, but they may be potential witnesses and we hope they will come forward to save inquiry time."

Just in case anyone thought police were implying Heidi Paakkonen was camping in the bush, police were keen to squash that rumour. "Police think it is unlikely that this woman was Heidi Paakkonen."

Heidi's missing backpack had, in the interim, turned up in Wellington. The woman who'd purchased it responded to the publicity and contacted police; the pack was flown to Thames. The second pack was located and retrieved from London, England.

Up at Operation Stockholm base, however, it was an extensive ground search of Crosbie's Clearing keeping them occupied. It wasn't the first search in the bush. Police had first recovered three plastic bags of what they called "soiled clothing" on 26 May, near where the car had been stolen from. The bags appear to have been clothes destined for laundering. One of the bags recovered that day was female underwear, which Tamihere had been colourfully questioned over:

"What did you turf out?"

"Mostly women's clothes."

"Did you sort them out?"

"I think they were in bags or something...I just grabbed them and chucked them."

"Did you go through them?"

"No, not the women's one. I had a look at some of the guy clothes but they were too small."

"How did you know they were women's clothes?"

"They were all women's clothes, mate. It was pretty obvious, there were panties, bras and all junk like that."

It's pretty clear from that exchange that Tamihere was making quick decisions about what to keep or throw before stealing the car. It's highly unlikely that he went to the trouble of finding clothing in the car, dividing it into men's and women's piles, with a separate pile for general rubbish, and then finding three plastic bags, bagging the stuff he wanted rid of, then finally throwing them into the bush. Commonsense suggests Tamihere grabbed laundry and rubbish already bagged, and simply tossed them over the fence.

When detectives mounted a larger scene search on May 27 and 28, they found a few more bags, including a clear plastic bag specifically containing four pairs of female underpants, and a soiled panty shield. Again, the idea that Tamihere had separated out clean and dirty underwear into different bags before throwing them away doesn't seem credible.

Inside the bag of soiled underwear was a pair of Heidi's briefs that had been cut. "The natural/pink/white pair appear to have been cut down each side of the leg on the outside (forming G-string type of shape)," records the police job sheet.[27]

The description of these cut briefs given to a jury at the trial a year later, would be dramatically different from the way they were initially described by police above. By the time DI Hughes and Crown Prosecutor David Morris – both of whom had featured in the Arthur Allan Thomas botched police investigation – had finished with the underpants, the initial description would be almost unrecognizable.

In addition to the specialist scene searches near the Tararu Creek Road parking area, police and search and rescue teams had of course conducted numerous searches of surrounding bush and tracks.

---

27   Job sheet of Det. Sgt D H Read, 29 May 1989

Thirty men had spent May 28 scouring the 4.6km road, adjacent Tararu stream, and bush between the road and the stream. A further team of six searched the Tararu track all the way up to a junction point known as the "Jam Tins".

Nothing was found.

On Queens Birthday weekend, the 3rd to 5th of June, a massive search team that included not just police and search and rescue but also Army troops from Papakura, covered "all tracks in the Crosbies and Kauaeranga portion of the Coromandel conservation park…the total distance of track searched would be in excess of 100 kilometres, plus numerous streams and untracked areas were also covered."[28]

Search teams were explicitly ordered to check not just the tracks but bush on either side of the track for things that may have been dropped or thrown, and to keep their eyes peeled for possible camp sites or off-track areas. They were told to go slowly and be thorough.

Again, nothing was found.

Now, after Tamihere's arrest on the car charge, 28 searchers had been sent back to Tararu Creek Road for a "close contact" search of "adjoining farmland and adjacent bush…nothing of significance was found."

Hence the decision to search Crosbie's Clearing yet again. The order came through on July 19, and on Saturday 22 July a team of forty police and S&R personnel gathered for airlift up to Crosbie's Clearing at 7am.

"Searching was done to a grid pattern using string lines," S&R coordinator John Cassidy – the man who said he'd seen a man and woman putting up a tent at Crosbies – later testified in court. There'd been brief excitement over the discovery of a mound, but instead of a grave police found only litter buried by a tidy camper. The team continued their sweep on Sunday 23 July.

"Despite the thoroughness of the searching, there was no trace of the Swedish tourists detected."

---

28   Brief of Evidence, John Cassidy, Depositions hearing May 1990

It's not the first time in New Zealand police history that major searches have failed to find anything. Famously, during the 1970 Crewe murders investigation, repeated searches of the garden and lawn around the Crewe farmhouse failed to find any shell casings from the double homicide, until detectives with a suspect in mind (Arthur Allan Thomas) stole a used shell casing from the suspect's farm and buried it in the Crewe's garden where a new "search" suddenly found it.

Detective Inspector John Hughes knew the Crewe case well, he'd worked on it. David Tamihere would later tell journalist Carolyne Meng-Yee, "Hughes had a bad reputation. His nickname inside was 'The Gardener' among the crims – he had a bad habit of planting things."[29]

The Gardener wasn't feeling very perky after the latest Crosbie's search came up empty-handed.

"I am satisfied there is nothing up there. It is better to be thorough than be unsure, and have that nagging thought at the back of our minds that there may still be something up there," Hughes told the *Herald*.

Instead, the police PR guerrilla campaign to imprint Tamihere as the killer in the eyes of the public continued behind the scenes. Opposition MP and National's spokesman on police issues, John Banks, used parliamentary privilege to reveal Tamihere's previous criminal record to the public, ahead of his looming court appearance in Thames.

"David Wayne Tamihere, charged with stealing the vehicle driven by two missing Swedish tourists, was on bail at the time on a serious rape charge…Mr Banks said in Parliament," reported newspapers up and down the country.

"Mr Banks also said Tamihere had a previous criminal record which included a charge for 'a brutal killing'."

Listening to all this unfold were two crucial police witnesses, John

---

29 "The Man Who Wasn't There", Carolyne Meng-Yee, Metro, March 2012

The Breakthrough

Cassidy and Mel Knauf – the two men who'd reported seeing the couple at Crosbie's Clearing – the girl with the painted fingernails and the blonde hair falling down her cheek to her shoulders.

As we begin to analyse the strength of the case against David Wayne Tamihere in the matter of the murders of Heidi Paakkonen and Urban Hoglin, it is time to assess the Crown's most important strands of evidence. These strands, Justice Tompkins would eventually tell the jury can be considered this way:[30]

"There is no direct evidence to prove that the accused killed the Swedish couple. The Crown is asking you to infer that he did, from facts that the Crown claims have been properly proved, and thus the Crown is relying on what is called 'circumstantial evidence'.

"When proved circumstantial facts connect themselves with each other in such a way that results in a strong body of evidence that carries conviction to the mind of the jury, that can result in proof beyond reasonable doubt.

"Taken separately, each fact may not amount to proof," Justice Tompkins told the jurors. "But if taken together you find such a series of undesigned, unexpected coincidences that you find you are compelled to come to one conclusion that of guilt then you are entitled to find the accused guilty.

"But if the cumulative effect of all the relevant, proved facts fall short of that standard, if it leaves some gaps, it has failed to prove guilt beyond reasonable doubt.

"It is like a rope made up of a number of strands. One strand may not be sufficient to sustain a weight. But sufficient strands working together may do so. So it is with the weight of evidence. There may be a combination of circumstances, no one of which would raise a reasonable conviction, but the whole taken together may create a strong conclusion of guilt."

That's the test the judge laid down to the jury: the Crown case is woven from a number of strands. Do those strands of evidence

---

30 Summing up of Tompkins, J, R v Tamihere, 3 December 1990, page 5

have sufficient integrity on their own that, when woven into a rope, they are strong enough to hang Tamihere on?

    Let's find out.

CHAPTER 5

Eyewitness Evidence

"Maybe I told you in the last letter that we were going for a tramp with a Canadian couple...We started Friday the 13th (can you imagine how lucky that day went?)...The first night we didn't come to a hut but had to sleep on a big rock that was leaning a bit. Ron and Sharon had a tent they could put up everywhere, so they slept in that. Urban and myself slept under the sky with only our sleeping bags and the outer tent if it should rain.

"It started to rain, of course, in the middle of the night and the outer tent didn't keep us dry, we were soaked wet...The next day we went on. We had to climb (or rather, we had to pull ourselves up by small bushes and grass) up the mountain that was about 1,500 metres. It was really hard and in some places it was soaking wet and there were rivers you could fall down into as well...it was foggy on the other side so you couldn't see the path.

"We had to wait there for some minutes and luckily enough the fog went away. Urban's and my tennis shoes started to fall apart so we were a bit worried that they wouldn't last all the way...At the end...they told us that we've been tramping one of New Zealand's hardest hikes...we managed the whole thing in a week with heavy backpacks on our backs and we calculated that the total distance was some 85kms.

> *"Maybe I should tell you that I have become an Aunt to a little girl, her name is Anna and she was born on 11 December."*
>
> – **letter from Heidi Paakkonen, 29 January 1989, Kaikoura**

Stripped of its uncontroversial elements, the Crown case that convicted David Wayne Tamihere in December 1990 of double murder essentially came down to four elements:

- The Crosbie's Clearing sighting of Tamihere with Heidi Paakkonen after 3pm on Saturday April 8, 1989
- The secret witness testimony
- The impossibility of stealing the Subaru using No. 8 wire, and Tamihere's 'blatant' use of the vehicle
- Tamihere's links to the couple's belongings, including Urban Hoglin's watch and Heidi's slashed panties

We'll start with the Crosbie's Clearing sighting. It hinges on eyewitness evidence and it's worth bearing in mind this recent story from the *New York Times*:

"Every year, more than 75,000 eyewitnesses identify suspects in criminal investigations. Those identifications are wrong about a third of the time, a pile of studies suggest."[31]

As US Supreme Court Justice William Brennan once noted cynically about the power of eyewitness testimony: "There is almost nothing more convincing than a live human being who takes the stand, points a finger at the defendant, and says, 'That's the one!' "[32]

In submissions to the US Supreme Court, the American Psychological Association reported that a staggering one in three eyewitness identifications of offenders have turned out to be wrong:

"The risk of inaccurate eyewitness identifications is not merely a theoretical possibility. Controlled experiments as well as studies of actual identifications have consistently found that the rate of incor-

---

[31] "34 Years Later, Supreme Court Will Revisit Eyewitness IDs", NY Times, 22 August 2011
[32] Ibid

rect identifications is approximately 33 percent."

These are the cautions that readers are invited to bear in mind as we examine the integrity of the only eyewitness sightings of "Tamihere" and "Paakkonen" together.

Search and Rescue personnel John Cassidy and Mel Knauf had on 31 May 1989 first reported seeing a couple at Crosbie's back on April 8. It was just after 3pm. Mel Knauf told police then that the man he saw was about 5'7" to 5'8" and that the "girl was attractive and I noticed her fingernails were painted. She did look out of place".

Cassidy told police "the girl was in her mid to late 20s…light blonde hair straight to the collar". Paakkonen, for the record had only turned 21 during her holiday down under. "She had a fair complexion and well groomed appearance to the extent that she looked out of place in the bush setting," said Cassidy originally. The man, he said, was 5'11, "clean shaven although he may have had a moustache. He was wearing boots of some kind, denim shorts and I think a dark top…the couple both had packs, but I can't recall just what they looked like."

Those were the first statements, taken seven weeks after the sighting in question.

Fast forward a month or so. On 11 July, the same day police were interviewing Tamihere about the stolen car, detectives had gone back to Cassidy to get another statement. Cassidy had not seen a photo of Tamihere at this point as none had been published. He told them he couldn't add much to his original statement, "I am not sure if he was part Maori or not". He did remember the woman had "brown boots, or tan, similar to Paraflex, with a rubber sole".[33]

Back in the day, Paraflex made a "lightweight" tramping boot suitable for an afternoon stroll in the bush.[34] There's no evidence Heidi Paakkonen ever owned a pair of the NZ-made boots. Not one single photo from their New Zealand trip showed her wearing those boots.

---

33   Second statement of John Thomas Cassidy, 11 July 1989
34   Paraflex today make a wide range of good industrial, army and hiking boots

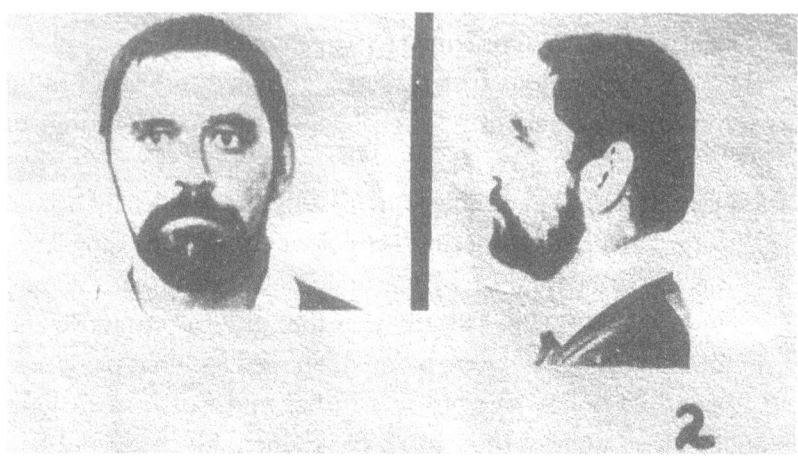

"I have been shown some colour photographs of the missing Swedish girl, and the one I saw was thinner in the face than her," Cassidy said in his second police statement. Given that he'd spent nearly 15 minutes standing near her, watching her, there's not a hint that the woman was Heidi. In fact, given the explicit opportunity to make that link, he rejected it.

Desperate for something, anything, that would turn the couple into Heidi and Tamihere, police returned to Cassidy the following day, July 12, this time with a photo montage that included the prime suspect.

"Cassidy did not identify anyone on the montage," Det. Sgt Sanderson noted for the file.[35]

Sick of hearing about this witness who couldn't take a hint on identification issues, Detective Inspector John Hughes stepped in personally, as Cassidy revealed:

"Over the weekend of the 22nd and 23rd of July 1989, I was asked by Detective Inspector John Hughes to go to the Thames District Court at about 10am on Wednesday 26 July," Cassidy wrote in statement number three.[36]

---

[35] Job sheet of Dt. Sgt. C R Sanderson, 12 July 1989
[36] Third Statement of John Thomas Cassidy, 27 July 1989

"Det. Insp. Hughes had asked me to view the people there and see if I could identify the person I had seen at Crosbie's Clearing. I was aware that David Tamihere was appearing at the Court in relation to the Swedish inquiry.

"I got to the courthouse just before 10am. Mel Knauf was already there. When I arrived, there were television crew member and possibly other reporters on the street outside. By the entrance doors to the court were Mel and another person.

"At sometime around half past ten a red car pulled up and I saw Tamihere alight, handcuffed to a detective."

If Cassidy had not already known it was Tamihere because of the photos in the local papers and on TV over the previous week, the media scrum as journalists flanked Tamihere on his way in would have been a dead giveaway.

Detective Wayne Kiely testified, "We drove around the back of the court to try and avoid the media. However, as we pulled up the TV cameras approached and a female television news reporter came up to Tamihere and asked him several questions."[37]

Kiely may have thought he was avoiding the media, but former TV1 news crime reporter Pauline Hudson says she too had been tipped off by police to be at the court, and she knew where her cameras needed to be.

"I definitely knew I was going to get a shot of him. We knew he was going to be there, and we knew we would get video footage of him. Where I did get in trouble later with John Hughes was for asking questions of Tamihere as he walked past.

"I got a real bollocking later. The police were paranoid about me asking Tamihere 'did you kill the missing Swedes?', but I think I only asked 'did you see the missing Swedes'."

Possibly, the reason for that paranoia was because Hughes had so many irons in the fire, with two key witnesses standing beside Hudson, unbeknown to her, whose already questionable identifica-

---

37 Det Wayne Kiely, Brief of Evidence, Depositions, R v Tamihere, May 1990

tion could have been thrown out by this contamination. He hadn't anticipated that journalists might try asking questions. Perhaps that's why Cassidy later denied hearing Tamihere speak during the 20 second interview.

Cassidy and Knauf went into the courtroom and watched as Tamihere was called up on theft charges. "I didn't hear him speak at all," said Cassidy in his statement.[38]

Nonetheless: "Having seen Tamihere I am now positive that he is the male person I met at Crosbie's Clearing on the afternoon of the 8th of April last."

Normally in any investigation, the first witness statement taken closest to the events in question is the most accurate. That's because, over time, memories can fade or become corrupted. The only exception to this general rule is traumatic events, where initial shock may need to be overcome first. Meeting a couple pitching a tent, however, doesn't count as traumatic. Of course, skilled neutral questioning can tease out greater detail, but leading questions can instantly contaminate the evidence. John Cassidy was now at statement three.

Mel Knauf, meanwhile, was under intense police pressure to amend his statements as well. On 12 July he was shown the photo montage featuring David Tamihere but, like Cassidy, drew an identification blank: "I do not recognise anyone in it as the man I saw with a woman at the Pines area at Crosbie's." This, despite Tamihere's eyes.[39]

Three days later, on the 15th, Knauf was again at the Operation Stockholm base at Thames Police Station:

"I've been thinking about the sighting that John Cassidy and I made on the 8th of April 1989, at Crosbie's Clearing, of the guy and girl. I have been shown the photos of Pat Kelly in black and white and colour, and I can't be sure whether he was the male person or not."[40]

---

[38] Knauf, on the other hand, admitted at trial he heard Pauline Hudson's Q&A: "Yes, he replied to that question".
[39] Second Statement of Theodore Mel Knauf, 12 July 1989
[40] Third Statement of Theodore Mel Knauf, 15 July 1989, found in Job Sheet of Det. Sgt. Del Read, 24 July 1989

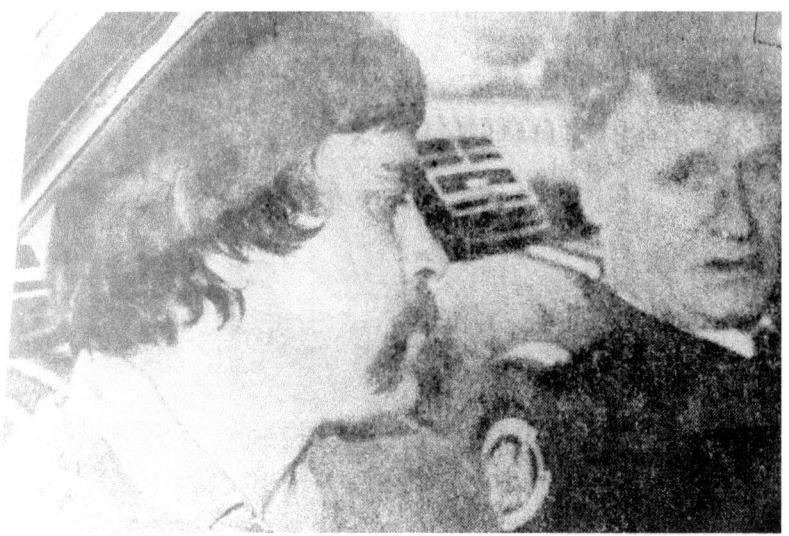

Evidently police had abandoned all pretence of a lineup – the witness had now clearly been shown photos and told "this is Pat Kelly". Even then, Knauf wasn't sure.

"One thing I am sure of now," he added, "is when we first arrived the guy was clearing the long grass and fern from where he was going to pitch the tent. He was using a little tomahawk which had a small head. I think I would recognise the type of tomahawk again if I saw it."

This was new, not in the original statement at all, and Knauf was suddenly "sure" of an event that he had not even listed as a mere "uncertainty" previously. It also just happened to have emerged four days after police first learnt from Tamihere himself that he carried a small tomahawk around with him.

Knauf appears to have been invited as well[41] to witness Tamihere being paraded via the media circus into court on 26 July, and on the following day he made his fourth statement to police.

"At the Thames Court I observed a person who I know now as David Tamihere. I saw this person on three occasions and was able

---

41 Although Knauf has told the court on oath that he couldn't remember why he went there, he later admitted on oath that John Hughes had asked him to go.

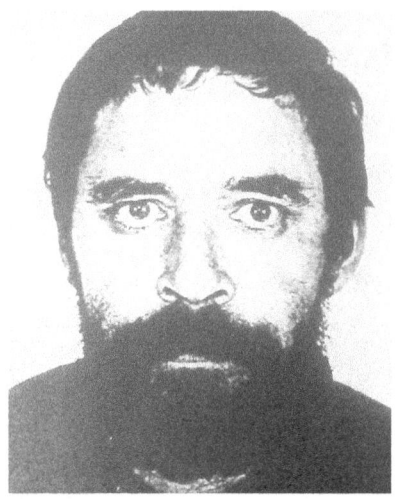 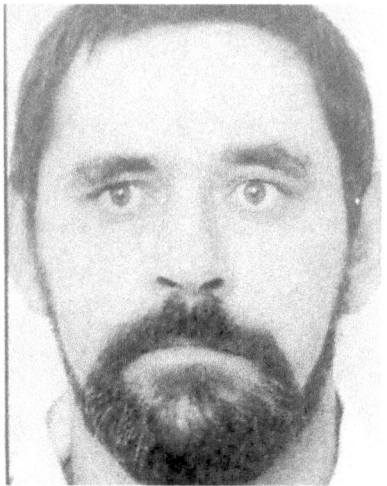

to draw a conclusion that David Tamihere was the same person who both myself and John Cassidy had spoken with at Crosbie's Settlement area on April 8."

Knauf was basing his identification not on a positive facial recognition, but because Tamihere was consistent with the type of man he saw – olive skin, "half caste", height, build, and "his eyes – the colour and the prominent eyes was something I noticed the first and second meeting.

"The only feature that is different is the beard. When we spoke with him at Crosbie's Clearing he had a two day growth."

Even so, when push came to shove you could see Knauf still wasn't sure. He pulled together all these ingredients saying they "lead to my belief that he was the same person". At the end of his statement he couldn't resist adding: "After seeing the person I am 90% sure he was the man at Crosbie's."

In their first statements, Cassidy had described the man as "clean shaven", possibly with a moustache. Knauf had never mentioned a moustache but was now talking of a two day growth. He had also suddenly remembered "prominent eyes", yet had also made no mention of those in the initial statement. Nor had he recognised Tamihere's "prominent eyes" from the mug shots.

But still John Hughes was not satisfied that his two main witnesses were properly up to brief. Cassidy made another statement, dated 10 August 1989. This one contained yet more new information. Now Cassidy remembered "Tamihere" doing things to the ground as well:

"The male, who I have since identified as David Tamihere, was removing some small bumps on the ground in the area where he was going to pitch his tent. He did this using either a small tomahawk or machete. He was using this in his right hand."

For the uninitiated, the purpose of this massive evolution of evidence was to work in the key identity features John Hughes knew he would need if he wanted to get a conviction. He had to transform the mere "man" seen in Crosbie's Clearing on April 8 into an unmistakable identikit of David Tamihere, based on the gear *police knew* he had with him. Tamihere, for example, was asked on July 11 1989:

"Describe your blue tent."

"It's just an igloo tent with a silver storm cover".

"What colour blue?"

"Dark blue."

"What shape?"

"It's a rounded one."

Tamihere added that he had a second, larger A-frame tent, which was the one seen by trampers at Crosbie's earlier.

For the objective reader, however, it is always worth taking a step backwards and considering the bigger picture. The police had several witnesses – not Cassidy or Knauf – who'd seen Tamihere's regular "Pat Kelly" campsite in the Crosbie's area only a couple of weeks earlier. Cassidy and Knauf say no one else was in Crosbie's Clearing the 13 minutes they were there, so why wouldn't Tamihere have pitched his tent in its usual position, instead of clearing fresh ground? And who cuts long grass with a small tomahawk? Really?

What was originally a "hiker's tent" in the early statements turned into a "hoop tent". In fact it even turned into the exact brand that Tamihere used, an "Igloo":

"From memory," Mel Knauf wrote in yet *another* statement, "I classified the tent as being similar to a 'Fairydown Igloo'."

Cassidy, meanwhile, was waxing lyrical with screeds of never before revealed information:

"I think Mel asked something about the tent which prompted Tamihere to invite us to look inside and see how roomy it was. I bent over and had a look inside."

When Cassidy had given his first statement, back on May 31st, police had not yet interviewed the hairdresser who cut Heidi Paakkonen's hair into a bob. After her haircut, only her hair at the back reached the top of her shoulders; her hair at the sides was cut short, just over the top of her ears, and her fringe was shorter as well.

Bearing that in mind, Cassidy originally told of a woman who had "light blonde hair straight to the collar". In his new statement, Cassidy now said, "The woman I saw with the poncho had the hood of the poncho pulled up over her head when I saw her. At no stage can I recall seeing her without the hood on, however I could see some blonde hair on the left side of her face."

If she had truly worn a hood the whole time, he could never have seen her hair reaching all the way to her collar – not if it really was Heidi – because the back of the woman's neck was not visible to Cassidy, and Heidi's hair no longer reached her collar at the sides, but only just over her ears. This latest statement, two and a half months after the initial statement, was the first of Cassidy's to suggest the woman was now hooded.

Entirely coincidentally, Mel Knauf's new statement, also dated August 10 1989, now also revealed for the first time that the mystery woman "had the hood up covering her head".[42]

There are two rational explanations for this escalation of detail with every new statement. Explanation one is that the boys had been standing down-wind of a Coromandel police cannabis burn-off and inhaled too deeply whilst making their statements. Explanation two

---

42 Fifth Statement of Mel Knauf, 10 August 1989

(and in reality the only one) is that Cassidy and Knauf were sincere about what they were saying, but that Hughes had played so many mind games he had corrupted their memories. There is excellent expert opinion to support this latter contention.

In 2010, the University of Sydney published research showing how easily witnesses' memories can be wrecked.[43]

Memories can't be trusted and become contaminated when people discuss their memories of an event with others, explained the University of Sydney study. Lead researcher, Dr Helen Paterson said sharing memories can contaminate people's recollections and create false memories.

"A false memory is the recollection of an event, or details of an event, that did not actually occur," she said. "My research focuses on how people can contaminate each other's memories for an event by discussing it with one another."

Dr Paterson said a key finding of the research was that misleading information presented through discussion with another person who observed the event can also lead to memory distortion. "That is, witnesses who discuss an event with a co-witness are very likely to incorporate misinformation presented by the co-witness into their own memory for the event," she said. "Once their memory has been contaminated in this way, the witness is often unable to distinguish between the accurate and inaccurate memories."

Witnesses like Cassidy and Knauf could easily go their whole lives genuinely believing what they've said in the collector's edition set of altered statements, all because they were allowed to keep comparing notes, and a wily detective inspector who was an acknowledged expert in mind games – and proud of it – planted suggestions in their brains that grew into the strands of evidence he needed. Picture Hughes as Obi-wan Kenobi on Tatooine in *Star Wars* – "These *are* the droids you are looking for" – and you have a pretty good analogy.

---

43   See "Sydney study finds false memories are common", University of Sydney news release, 9 August 2010

The US Department of Justice report on eyewitness evidence stresses how important it is to make sure witnesses never speak to each other: "Separate witnesses and instruct them to avoid discussing details of the incident with other witnesses."[44]

Yet New Zealand Police had taken the highly unprofessional approach of allowing Cassidy and Knauf to read each other's statements:

"I have read the statement made by John Cassidy to Detective Sergeant Read on the 31st of May 1989 regarding our trip and agree with what has been recorded," wrote Mel Knauf in his own statement.[45]

The US DOJ report also stresses how important it is to try and prevent witnesses seeing media coverage that could contaminate their memories:

"Encourage the witness to avoid contact with the media or exposure to media accounts concerning the incident."

Cassidy and Knauf both say they were aware of Tamihere's arrest before trying to identify him – another no-no in US law enforcement:

"Ensure that no writings or information concerning previous arrest(s) will be visible to the witness."

And of course the policy manual instructs police to "Avoid saying anything to the witness that may influence the witness' selection."

Yet Cassidy, as we have seen, says "Det. Insp. Hughes had asked me to view the people there and see if I could identify the person I had seen at Crosbie's Clearing. I was aware that David Tamihere was appearing at the Court in relation to the Swedish inquiry."

According to the US Department of Justice, police should never ask leading questions like, "is this the man you saw at Crosbie's Clearing?" The correct phrasing would have been neutral: "Do you recognise any of these men?...Where do you recognise him from?"

Another report notes:

"Eyewitness misidentification is widely recognized as the leading cause of wrongful conviction in the United States, accounting for

---
44   Eyewitness Evidence: A Guide For Law Enforcement, US DOJ, 1999, page 15
45   First Statement of Mel Knauf, 31 May 1989

more wrongful convictions than all other causes combined."[46]

"Studies have shown that information provided to an eyewitness after an identification can influence the witness's level of confidence, and thus skew a juror's assessment of the accuracy of the identification. For example, if an eyewitness makes an identification of a suspect, and that same witness later learns that the person identified also has a criminal record, the witness's confidence level may become artificially inflated.

"Confirmatory feedback oftentimes occurs without the knowledge or intent of investigators in the case or even the eyewitness, and if a confidence statement is not taken directly after the identification, the window of opportunity for protecting the integrity of the identification evidence as an indicator of accuracy is lost.[47]

In this case, Cassidy and Knauf were wallowing in "confirmatory feedback" which, in contrast to the above report, was ladled on *with* the knowledge and intent of investigators.

In essence, the new research shows Cassidy's and Knauf's memories of the Crosbie's Clearing encounter were by this point utterly wrecked; munted beyond all hope of recovery. Quite frankly, if John Hughes had softly planted the idea by this stage that Heidi Paakkonen had been kidnapped by hobbits, we quite possibly would have seen statements to that effect complete with suspected hobbit sightings, particularly from Cassidy, down the track, and Peter Jackson in handcuffs.

Knauf and Cassidy are not to blame, they are victims. Their lives were turned upside down by what police did to them on this case.

If you think this was the pinnacle of the psychological warfare being waged, however, think again. John Cassidy made a new statement to police on 30 November 1989, exactly six months after making his first.

The new statement concerned the tent he saw at Crosbie's Clearing on 8 April 1989:

---

46 "Eyewitness Identification – A Policy Review", The Justice Project,
47 Ibid

"I can only recall seeing a tent pitched in that position at Crosbie's once before. That was a bit over two years before. It wasn't the same tent but the person with it was Tamihere. I talked with him on that occasion too."

Yes, now Cassidy had suddenly remembered having a chin-wag with David Tamihere in *exactly* the same spot in 1987. He had overlooked this encounter in all his previous statements and dealings with the case despite its uniqueness. If he had only ever seen a tent pitched in that exact space once before, you would think that upon seeing one there a second time he'd think, "this looks familiar". Apparently not. Nor did he remember seeing the man before when he came across him on April 8 in exactly the same spot.

As if to add a sense of drama, Cassidy added:

"While I was there, there was a cloudburst. Thunder and lightning and torrential rain fell."

So now he's ducking lightning bolts, getting drenched to the skin while talking to David Tamihere who had the only tent in the entire area, and he forgot about this first encounter entirely?

CHAPTER 6

Seven Habits Of Successful Witnesses

"Yesterday we went to the foot of Mt Cook, New Zealand's highest mountain, 3,746 metres[48]. The snow covered tops were glimmering magnificently in the sunshine. We even managed to see the kea, a very funny and clever parrot that lives up in the mountain. They can be a real nuisance because they tear apart the tents and steal things that they come across.

"We got some nice trouts, two of them were between 2.5 to 3kg. In one of the lakes I saw an incredible amount of trouts. It was sunny and calm and you could see them sitting there and swimming around in water only half a metre deep.

"The car is working well, almost anyway, and it seems as though the money will last the time remaining. We are sleeping in our tent for nothing and the foot is not expensive...it's going to be really exciting when we are coming home..."

– letter from Urban Hoglin, February 1 1989, Tekapo

To give you an idea of how this played out in the court hearings, at Depositions in May 1990 Cassidy made no reference whatsoever to seeing Tamihere two years earlier with his tent on the same patch of ground.

---

48 Sweden's highest peak is 2,104 metres

After Depositions, however, Cassidy returned to the issue like a dog with an old bone, signing his *seventh* statement for police:

"I am making this statement to Detective Sergeant Sanderson to put in order the times I believe I saw David Tamihere and the matters that led to my identification of him.

"The first time I saw the person I believe to be David Tamihere was at Crosbie's Clearing. I was up there on my own checking the track from Kauaeranga to Crosbie's. I arrived at Crosbie's just before midday. A man was camped at The Pines at Crosbie's, with a small tent. I think the tent was blue or grey. It was an 'A' frame tent.

"The man was clean shaven although he may have had a moustache. He was wearing a charcoal coloured bush swanndri and shorts. He had heavy boots, they were thick-soled and steel capped. They were more like heavy work boots than bush boots…He told me that he was doing a five day hike in the area and he was going to go to the Kaueranga. He had an orange book written by a guy, Hildreth. It is called *How To Survive In The Bush, On The Mountains And On The Coast In New Zealand*. I have a copy myself and I recognised the book.

"He said he had read the book and he had doubts as to the accuracy of some of the information in it…he told me that he had two sons and he told me he wanted to introduce them to the bush. He said that he was going to take three months off work and teach them bushcraft.

"He told me that he was a highly paid rigger who had worked on the big construction jobs such as the steel mill and Marsden Point. He said he was one of a group of selected or elite riggers who got called first to that type of highly paid job.

"While I was talking to him a thunderstorm developed and a cloudburst and torrential rain fell. He suggested that I shelter in his tent. I said I was going to get wet regardless and that I might as well head off. I left at noon or a few minutes after.

"About three months later I went to the Moss Creek hut in Kauaeranga. In the hut log book there was an entry signed by the same name as I had been given by the man at Crosbie's. The entry was dated about four days after I had seen him. The entry made reference to the book he had and that he had checked it and some of the information was incorrect.

"I checked all the log books available from the Conservation Department for that hut, but there wasn't one available for that period.

"The next incident was on the 8 April 1989 when Mel Knauf and I saw a man and a woman at Crosbie's. I believe that man is the same person I had met there in 1987," wrote John Cassidy in his seventh police statement.

Again, look at it objectively for a moment. He remembers all this, in excruciating detail, more than a year after giving his first statement where he remembered none of this. Even his previous statement carried virtually none of the detail listed above.

In his first statement regarding the 1989 sighting just seven weeks prior, Cassidy wrote that the man "was wearing boots of some kind". Yet in this latest statement, dealing with a supposed sighting two years in the past, Cassidy could remember the boots almost down to the shoelace brand.

The description of the alleged 1987 man: "Clean shaven although he may have had a moustache".

The description of the 1989 man: "Clean shaven although he may have had a moustache".

The tent: suddenly it was an A-frame, like the one all the other witnesses had seen him with. Which raises something else to consider: all of the biographical information allegedly given by Tamihere to Cassidy had – by July 1990 – appeared in other police witness statements.

Take Cassidy's July 1990 testimony: "He had heavy boots, they were thick-soled and steel capped. They were more like heavy work boots than bush boots."

Now compare it with this from witness David Reid dated 4 August 1989: "He was wearing a heavy pair of boots, they did not seem to be ordinary tramping boots, they were more like work boots, possibly with steel caps…"

To understand how this happens, you first need to be familiar with the police interrogation process back then. Interviews were generally not tape-recorded in those days, and statements were written up by a police officer based on the answers the witness gave during questioning. The statements never recorded the questions asked, so you could never be certain precisely what the question was that led to a particular answer.

This covered a multitude of sins where police officers asked leading questions designed to get a particular answer. Essentially, witnesses were spoon fed.[49] An example might be:

Q: "Now that you think about it a bit more, do you think the swanndri could have been blue and black check?"

A: "Yes, that might be right, now that I think about it."

Statement: "The man I saw was wearing a blue and black check swanndri bush shirt."

In other words, Cassidy was effectively drawing a word portrait of every identifying feature being fed to him.[50] His heavily evolved statement was not the product of him simply sitting down with a pen and paper and jotting down what came to mind; his statement was manufactured, constructed, elaborated on to incorporate everything Hughes felt he needed to prove it was Tamihere.

Two sons? Check.

Glenbrook Mill and Marsden Point? Check.

Book on bushcraft? Check.

TV1's crime reporter Pauline Hudson remembers the Hughes

---

[49] I am not saying this was the case with most of the grass roots work done on this case. Ordinary coppers, not part of the inner circle, were simply doing their jobs the way they always had, and the job sheets and interview statements of most reflect that. But Cassidy and Knauf were "special" for John Hughes' case, and Hughes had no qualms about making evidence fit if he had to.

[50] And Cassidy won't have been the only witness John Hughes pulled this stunt on. His willingness to engage in manipulation has already been established by the identification fiasco and will later be canvassed in the chapter on the secret witnesses. Unfortunately it taints the credibility of the evidence generally.

methods well. "He was the orchestra conductor, his cases always came together in a grand symphony."

Even so, it seems even Crown solicitors Meredith Connell & Co eventually balked at humming this particular tune at the October trial as, once again, Cassidy's earlier meeting with "Tamihere", although raised, was downplayed at trial.

"At any stage during that 13 minutes when you were talking with him on the 8th of April," asked Colin Nicholson QC, "did you recall that you had met him before?

"No."

"Did you get a niggling feeling that you had met him before?"

"Not that I remember."

The main trial, however, shows just how dangerous these memory issues for Cassidy and Knauf had become. A case in point is the colour of the tent. In his first statement, the one taken only seven weeks after the encounter, Cassidy said the tent was "bright blue" with a "blue matching fly sheet". Note that: matching bright blue.

By statement four, in August 1989, Cassidy's memory was fading. The colour of the tent was now "mainly blue" with a "definite dark blue floor…the tent had a fly. I had the impression that this was blue but I'm not sure."

At Depositions in May 1990, Cassidy admitted he had said the tent was "bright blue" with the matching fly: "Yes that is what I recalled at the time."[51]

Yet at trial, in summing up Justice Tompkins told the jury:

"Mr Nicholson [Tamihere's lawyer] raised the issue of the fly. Mr Nicholson I think said to you that Mr Cassidy said that the fly was blue. Well, not quite, what he said was this, 'There was a tent fly that went with the tent, yes…I'm not sure, I don't remember what colour it was, I thought it was a blueish colour'."[52]

In other words, because of Cassidy's memory fade on what had

---

51 Page 201, transcript of evidence, Depositions hearing, R v Tamihere, May 1990
52 Judge's summary for the jury, R v Tamihere, 3 December 1990, pages 23-24

originally been a bright blue matching fly, suddenly the judge was criticising Tamihere's QC for putting the jury wrong.[53]

It wasn't the only major memory fade. In his July 1990 statement, just three months out from the murder trial, John Cassidy suddenly remembered another new "fact" – that he had alerted police only "a week or two" after giving his very first statement, that he had previously met Tamihere.

"Shortly after the enquiry into the missing couple began I made a statement to Detective Read about seeing the man and woman at Crosbie's. I still did not recall seeing him earlier, in 1987. I believe it was about a week or two after I made that first statement that I recalled the first meeting with the man in 1987. I don't know what it was that made me recall it. I recall advising the Detectives of what I had recalled but I think it was a few days before a statement was taken off me."

In fact, as the record above shows, Cassidy suddenly "remembered" this earlier meeting not a week or two after the first statement, but a full six months later on 30 November 1989!

If Cassidy and Knauf had not been crucial witnesses for John Hughes, and if they had not been members of the official search squad set up by police, it is highly likely their evidence would have been discounted as near worthless after going through so many revisions. Police files show a couple named Bill & Sybil Lawrence were questioned in 1989 about a sighting of the Swedish tourists, and questioned again in 1991. In their second police interview the couple were categorical: "Sybil Lawrence is convinced the girl was Heidi Paakkonen. Bill Lawrence is convinced he saw David Tamihere. Both were not so strong when they were spoken to in 1989. *They have convinced themselves over a period of time*," wrote Det. Sgt. Knight. "Conclusion: no weight can be placed on any of these sightings."[54]

Given that you now have clear documented evidence in just a

---

53   To be fair to Justice Tompkins, he later called back the jury and told them he'd put the wrong spin on the colour
54   Job sheet of Det. Sgt. R A Knight, 23 October 1991

couple of easy examples, of memory fade for tramper John Cassidy over time, how likely is it – really – that his memory for detail in a whole range of areas improved the more that time slipped past? How reliable was he, really, as a witness?

Let's continue with another bombshell from his July 1990 statement, however:

"The first identification I was asked to do was when a number of photographs were brought around to me at work. I was not able to identify the man I had seen amongst the group of photographs.

"A few days later I was at the enquiry base and I was shown a group of photographs of bush scenery and I was asked if I could identify the places or if they could be of relevance to the searching. There were 20 or more photographs in the pile. Some of the photos had writing on the back describing where they were.

"As I was looking through the photos I saw one showing the head and shoulders of a man standing outside, I recognised the man as the person I had seen at Crosbie's Clearing on the two occasions…this photograph showed the man clean shaven as he was when I saw him at Crosbie's. The police photographs showed the men with beards.

"During the weekend 22-23 July 1989 while involved in searching I was asked by Detective Inspector Hughes to go to court at Thames on 26 July 1989 to see the person appearing on a charge of stealing the Swedish couple's car to see if I could recognise him or not."

In case you missed it, John Cassidy was now saying that he positively identified David Tamihere from photos he picked up off a desk, *and did nothing about it!* At no point did he rush to DI Hughes and say "This is the guy! And guess what, I saw him two years earlier there as well!"[55]

Much has been made of the fact that Cassidy says the man at Crosbie's on April 8 had a "moustache". But just how big was that moustache?

---

55 Cassidy told the court he'd mentioned "these photos look like the man I'd seen at Crosbie's" to police and got "not a great deal of response at all", but he did not mention the earlier meeting at this time.

"Possibly a small moustache," Cassidy told a pre-trial hearing. Yet here is how Swedish tourist Håkan Bokull from the Sunkist Lodge described Tamihere's facial hair when he met him the same day the Swedes' car was taken:

"[A] big bushy moustache curving down over the corners of his mouth."[56]

Mel Knauf says of the man he spent 15 minutes talking to at Crosbie's: "I do not recall him having a moustache."[57]

Fifteen minutes, and he never saw the trademark Tamihere mo? On the one hand, Cassidy doubts there was a moustache and if there was it was only a "small" one, whereas Knauf couldn't see one at all. Yet they both claimed, after police pressure, that it was definitely Tamihere they saw.

The sequence of moustache growth is important here. If the Crosbie's witnesses had seen a big bushy moustache curving down over the corners of his mouth at 3pm on the Saturday afternoon, and Håkan Bokull had seen Tamihere clean shaven 48 hours later, you could explain it. But there's nothing on earth outside of Bugs Bunny's ACME Hair Restorer lotion that would turn a non-existent or small mo into the full "gringo" in 48 hours.

Bruce Dittmer, a tramper who met Tamihere in the bush at Easter two weeks before the Swedes went missing, remembered "he had a moustache" and told police "I didn't think much more about him, until I saw him on television. I recognised him straight away although it was only a short glimpse."[58]

Canadian tourist Anita Labrecque, who met Tamihere the same day he stole the car, recalled "a big moustache towards the corners of his mouth". Swiss tourist Gabrielle Staub, when shown the photos of "Pat Kelly", said "he did not have a beard then, only a moustache".

There seems absolutely no doubt, then, that Tamihere was fuzzed

---

56   Statement of Karl Richard Håkan Bokull, 28 June 1989
57   Testimony of Theodore Mel Knauf, Transcript of Evidence, Depositions May 1990, R v Tamihere, p210
58   Statement of Bruce Gregory Dittmer, 26 July 1989

Seven Habits Of Successful Witnesses

up at all crucial times, including when he was allegedly seen by Cassidy and Knauf. The rest of their description of the man they saw was, with respect, pretty general. It could have applied to virtually any dark-haired male in his mid thirties in the bush. The one standout feature that differentiated Tamihere, his gringo moustache, was something the men never remembered.

The man they saw was wearing a "top garment...made of woollen material similar to a bush shirt...blue and black check with the squares being about two inches each way. I can remember that it was short-sleeved or had no sleeves because his biceps were showing," Cassidy told the Depositions hearing in May 1990.

Police have found no such garment, and Tamihere told them "I had a red swanndri jacket".[59] Another witness who saw Tamihere around March and April 1989 reported:

"He was wearing a red check swanndri."[60]

"When I am tramping, I don't wear f*** all," Tamihere told police at one point. "It gets too hot. I might have had a T-shirt on and that would have been about it."[61]

Remember, the test we are applying to these strands of evidence is to see whether they are sound enough to be woven into a rope of conviction, or whether they disintegrate under their own weight long before they can be woven.

Justice Tompkins instructed jurors that "It is the Crosbie's sighting [that is] probably one of the most important, or the most important, issue. This, of course, is an absolutely crucial issue in the case.

"The issue is, has the Crown proved that the man seen at Crosbie's was the accused, that the young woman was Heidi?

"If the Crown has proved that the man was the accused and the woman was Heidi, then that is very strong evidence in support of the Crown case that the accused is responsible for Heidi and Urban's death. If the Crown has not proved that the woman there is Heidi,

---

[59] Det Wayne Kiely, Brief of Evidence, Depositions
[60] Statement of Kevin Massey-Borman, 3 August 1989
[61] Statement of David Wayne Tamihere, 11 July 1989 to Det. Wayne Kiely

then the Crown case is very much weakened. If it has not proved that the man is the accused, then that is even more so."

Tompkins was in a tough position. At a pre-trial hearing in September 1990, he had ruled the identification evidence of Cassidy and Knauf was tainted. He ruled that the two men could not say at trial that the man they saw on April 8 was definitely Tamihere. The evidence in regard to the 1987 sighting was ruled inadmissible.

The jury was not allowed to know about this argument, so it is worth revealing what the trial judge thought.

Crown prosecutor David Morris argued the evidence should be permitted, because one of the secret "jailhouse confession" witnesses would testify that Tamihere had told him of "nearly being sprung" by two people who came across him and Heidi in the bush. Justice Tompkins raised an eyebrow doubtfully:

"If the identification evidence is questionable, and if the inmate's evidence is to be challenged as being unreliable, so that it too may be found to be questionable, each may tend, possibly unjustifiably, to corroborate the other.

"The danger of doubtful evidence being used to support and corroborate doubtful evidence is obvious."

"The importance of this identification evidence is obvious… If the identification evidence is in any way suspect, but yet was accepted by the jury, the consequence to the accused would be highly prejudicial."[62]

Of the failure to hold a formal identification parade, Justice Tompkins said he simply could not understand why Hughes had taken the "dangerous" steps he had. "If a suspect is available for an identification parade [as Tamihere was] or informal identification, photographs should not be shown to a witness. These instructions were not followed in the present case, when Mr Cassidy and Mr Knauf were shown the folder of three photographs, all being photos of the accused…that procedure is unacceptable.

---

62   R v Tamihere (No 2) (1990) 7 CRNZ 594

"The Police instructions set out procedures for an informal identification. But those procedures require the Police to ensure that nothing is done to suggest to the identifying witness which of the persons in the informal identification is the suspect. Those instructions clearly were not followed.

Tompkins, working through the complete list of altered statements and police nudging of Cassidy and Knauf that you've read highlights of here, ruled that the police identification process was "so unsatisfactory" that it would be unfair to justice to include the evidence.[63]

The Court of Appeal, however, overruled Tompkins at the Crown's request and allowed the disputed identification evidence back in. In doing so, the Court was utterly scathing of the police for turning the identification process into a farce, with its President, Sir Robin Cooke, warning:

"Irregular identification techniques by the police can jeopardise the course of justice.[64]

"The failure to offer an identification parade was regrettable and not adequately explained...indeed, the Defence is able to make the point that at no stage has Mr Cassidy or Mr Knauf identified the accused, from a photograph or otherwise, in circumstances where it has been necessary to single him out among others without any form of tacit prompting or clue."[65]

Nonetheless the Court held that the balance should go in favour of allowing the evidence in if it was "quality" evidence from "careful...reliable" witnesses.

"They are witnesses evidently used to noting detail," said the Court of Appeal. "Their accounts of what they observed on their tramp are likely to be especially reliable."

The court also took into account the "cumulative effect" of other evidence in the case, such as the alleged admissions made to secret

---

63   R v Tamihere (No 3) (1990) 7 CRNZ 221
64   R v Tamihere [1991] 1 NZLR 195, 197 (CA), n 3, 203 per Cooke P
65   Court of Appeal, ibid

witnesses. When we get to the chapter on secret witnesses, you will be able to decide whether the Court of Appeal was right to place any weight on their testimony, or whether the High Court's Justice Tompkins was right about the dangers of dodgy evidence being used to corroborate other dodgy evidence.

Readers can make their own minds up about the separate and cumulative weight of each of these strands of evidence, and also of the reliability of the witnesses involved.

Where the Court of Appeal's usual commonsense evidently hit the rocks was its faith in the reliability and confidence of the witnesses, as if those factors compensated for the flawed process. The problem the court appears to have overlooked is that the perceived "quality" and "reliability" of the witnesses' evidence may have been reinforced by the flawed process itself.

"Traditionally, a witness's self-reported degree of certainty in an identification was considered a good indicator of accuracy. Unfortunately, a great deal of research in recent decades has proven this intuitive assumption false," reported researchers recently.[66]

"The level of certainty a witness expresses in her eyewitness testimony does not necessarily correlate with the level of accuracy of the identification. An eyewitness's confidence that she has identified the culprit can fluctuate as a result of factors that occur after the identification and have little to do with memory. This is what is referred to as confidence malleability.

"For example, experiments have been conducted in which witnesses were shown a staged crime and asked to identify the culprit from a lineup. The lineup they were shown, however, did not contain the culprit. After the witnesses unknowingly made false identifications, they were then asked their level of confidence. Before doing so, however, some of the witnesses were given various types of reinforcing feedback.

"Those witnesses who received some confirmation of their false

---

66 "Eyewitness Identification: a Policy Review", The Justice Project

identification, whether the information that a co-witness identified the same individual or some other confirming feedback, were far more confident in their identifications than other witnesses who were given no feedback–despite having given false identifications. These witnesses also distorted and exaggerated certain details, such as how good their view was, how much of an opportunity they had to view the culprit, etc.

"Our new and better understanding of the influence feedback plays on a witness's self-described level of confidence strongly suggests that measures that control for this influence be adopted in our identification procedures."

In simple terms, the dog's breakfast of hints, clues and pats on the back for Cassidy and Knauf so convinced them of the truth of what they were saying that their evidence took on an aura of quality and reliability, even though it may have been false.

Let's see what prosecutors made of Cassidy and Knauf's crucial evidence.

CHAPTER 7

To Hell In A Handcart

"We are still going south and we've been driving some 5,000km with the car. It has gone well except for once, we were on our way down a mountain on a narrow serpentine road and suddenly the brakes didn't work. I had to use my handbrake, and it turned out that something on the brakes were gone on the left front wheel. It smelled like hell, and sulphur and a lot of other stuff. I had to phone some breakdown service."

– letter from Urban Hoglin, February 1989, South Island

When John Cassidy finally took the stand at the murder trial, he was asked by assistant Crown Prosecutor Paul Davison if he recognised the man he saw in Crosbie's Clearing on that April afternoon with the woman. "That's him over there," Cassidy stated loudly and confidently, pointing to Tamihere in the dock.

"I'm not sure if he did have a moustache," Cassidy told the court. "If it was, it would be a very small bristly one."

"I don't recall any moustache," testified Mel Knauf.

How long had they watched this man?

Thirteen minutes.

Shown a photograph of Heidi, Davison asked Cassidy: "Could the girl in the photograph have been the woman that you saw wearing the poncho at Crosbie's?"

"She could be," Cassidy hesitated. "She looks something similar in features…although the girl in the photo looks a little more rounded in the face."

Given how much the rest of Cassidy's evidence slid around, at least on this point he was consistent. He had after all declined to identify Heidi Paakkonen as the woman way back in his second statement to police: "I have been shown some colour photographs of the missing Swedish girl, and the one I saw was thinner in the face than her".

The woman, he told the court, looked around 24 or 25 (he had originally estimated late 20s in his first statement) and had a "shock of blonde, shoulder-length hair" visible on the left side of her face beneath the hood of the green poncho. "It went down to where I could see which was below her chin."

Could Heidi have had a "shock of blonde, shoulder-length hair" in such a place, after receiving a haircut one day earlier that shortened the hair on the left side of her face to "about halfway over her ears"?

From the jury's point of view, such subtleties were in one ear and out the other, hair today, gone tomorrow. To them, if the man was Tamihere, as Cassidy and Knauf testified it was, then the blonde woman at Crosbie's Clearing *must* have been Heidi, regardless of the inconsistencies. In the jury's minds, it was literally that simple. Even though neither of the men remembered Tamihere's huge moustache, the jury bought the positive identification.

Look back above, however, at the identifications made, and the men's inability to pick Tamihere out of a photo montage even with his moustache.

There were other aspects of this 13 minute meeting the reader should note, mainly those relating to the blonde woman.

Cassidy's first statement to police on May 31 1989 was limited to "fair complexion and well-groomed appearance to the extent that she looked out of place in the bush setting. She was wearing a green shade of cape draped over her shoulders and it covered most of her."

Knauf on the same day wrote only, "The girl was attractive and I noticed her fingernails were painted. She did look out of place."

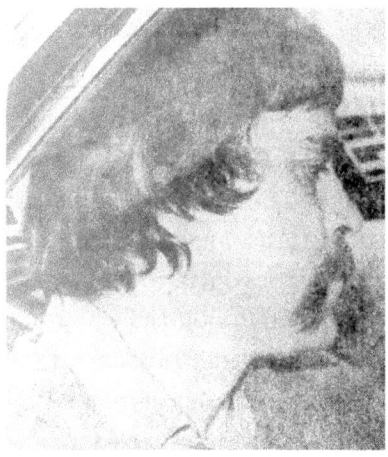 

By the time these men testified at the Depositions hearing in May 1990, the story had grown in leaps and bounds:

"I sat to her right and partly forward of her. She was wearing a poncho garment with the hood pulled over her head and pulled forward on her face. The garment had provision for her hands to come out because her hands were held or clasped on her lap most of the time that I saw her. Her feet were out fairly straight in front of her.

"She seemed to be very much out of place where she was. She seemed to be uneasy that we were there. She did not sit in what I would call a normal or natural manner. It was almost as if she was posing. It seemed as if she was trying not to attract attention but was doing just the opposite."

The prosecutor showed Cassidy the green rain cape that belonged to Tamihere and which he had used in the Coromandel. "How does that article compare to the one that you saw this female wearing?"

"It looks exactly like it. I don't remember the toggle in the front. I don't remember the sealing compound on there."

Asked to describe her, Cassidy told the court:

"Possibly in her mid-20s and European. The hood of the cape was quite well forward on her face but on the left side of her face I could see some very light honey-blonde hair that went about to her shoulder…I never saw her ears. When I looked at her I thought that she had in the last few hours or that day sometime had applied makeup to her face.

"I wondered what a girl like that might wear for footwear to the bush and I purposely looked at her boots, her feet, and she was wearing a pair of light tan or beige coloured boots. They looked very similar to a pair of boots that I have myself that are Paraflex brand."

The poncho, said Cassidy, covered all of her down to four inches above her boots – no mean feat if it was Heidi Paakkonen who stood as tall as many men. He could see she was wearing "black trousers".

"She never said one word while we were there, to us or to her companion…Here was a couple who had arrived at a camping spot and she was making no attempt at all to do anything to assist with setting up the camp. She did not assist her companion with the tent. She had not opened up her pack to get anything out, perhaps something for them to eat or whatever and this was unusual. I thought even a novice tramper would be probably wanting to do something at the campsite and because of this at one stage I made a humorous but probably frivolous remark and watched the girl to see what reaction there was. When I made the remark the rest of us, including her companion, laughed a little at what I had said and I observed that she smiled, but it looked like perhaps a forced smile or a polite smile."

Cassidy confirmed there was no sign her ankles or wrists were tied up, "I did not see anything like that."

For his part, Mel Knauf didn't think the woman's legs were out straight in front of her:

"She was sitting…with her knees together and the lower part of her legs to one side."

Knauf also saw her in the dark green poncho raincoat with the hood up, but admits that may have been because it was starting to rain and "somebody who was sitting still and not walking may well have put a coat on at that stage, yes."

Knauf said the woman did not appear to appreciate him and Cassidy being there, "I had the feeling that she would be just as happy to see us move on."

"Was she crying?" asked Tamihere's lawyer Colin Nicholson QC.
"No she wasn't".
"Did she have reddened eyes?"
"No she didn't."
"Is there any dissimilarity between the woman you saw at Crosbie's and the woman shown in the middle photograph [Heidi Paakkonen]?"

"Yes there is. "The woman in the photo has no make-up on that I can see and the woman that I saw at Crosbie's did have make-up… predominantly lipstick…face powder and fingernail polish."

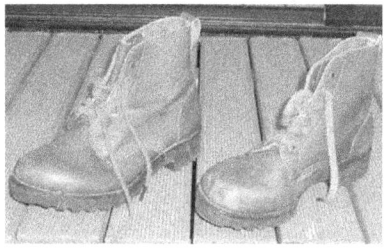

At the actual murder trial in November 1990, Knauf testified he knew what Heidi Paakkonen looked like before he gave his first statement on 31 May 1989, because he had seen photos of the missing couple as part of that first search operation.

"You didn't link her by recognition with the lady that you had seen at Crosbie's in early April, did you?" asked Tamihere's lawyer.
"No."

Knauf repeated his claim that the woman was well "made-up", including a "shade of red lipstick".

Naturally, police had tried to firm up the make-up evidence, but they drew a blank. "I think I would have noticed if she had nail polish on," remarked hairdresser Merilyn Rounds, "because I did manicures as part of my business. I certainly cannot recall her having any polish on."[67]

Heidi's sister in law, Cea Paakkonen, confirmed to the court that while Heidi had worked in the cosmetics section of her local supermarket back home, and sometimes wore make-up, "she didn't like bright colours". It was unlikely, therefore, that she would be carrying red lipstick.

Canadian tourist Sharon Stray, who spent 17 days with Heidi

---

67 Job sheet of Det. P J Devoy, 15 August 1989

and Urban in various places around the country, said she never saw Heidi using or in possession of make-up or nail polish.

The Crown suggested at one point that Tamihere may have been touring the Coromandel with his own supply of women's cosmetics.

She may have looked "out of place" in the bush, but the blonde at Crosbie's on April 8 had a counterpart in the same clearing a week later. Toyota engineer Colin Louden told police he and his nephew were heading into Crosbie's Clearing on Saturday 15 April when they passed a blonde woman wearing tan or beige light tramping boots, on her own, coming out.

"She looked like a lady who should have been on the street as opposed to being in the bush. She just didn't look like a tramper."[68]

More significantly, however when they got into the clearing the men saw a tent pitched. "It was a blue tent with a fly over it which was the same colour blue."

This tent had the infamous "Pat Kelly" note inside, which read:

"Please don't touch this tent, it's all I've got. Got sick of waiting. Gone walkabout. Pat Kelly."

Surprisingly, the witness appeared to have been given the 'Hughes' treatment, because by the time of Tamihere's trial the brief of evidence was almost identical, except the tent had mysteriously changed to the green and yellow one owned by the Swedes. The implications of that in a sighting a week after the murders are obvious:

"I recall the tent as being a green roof with orangey-yellow ends insides. It was an A-type tent...there was no fly over the tent."[69] Pressed further at trial, he called it an "old tent" and described it as "very, very faded green and orange."

Colin Louden insisted at trial that describing the tent as blue was a mistake: "I was in a room with about six people and everyone was talking." Louden said he called police and changed his tent description in August 1989.

---

68 Statement of Colin Edward Louden, 14 July 1989
69 Brief of Evidence of Colin Edward Louden, R v Tamihere, October 1990

By the time of the murder trial, however, police had the missing Swedes' tent as an exhibit. The implication – that Pat Kelly's famous note was seen inside the Swedes' tent – was left hanging in the air for the jury to assume. You can bet your bottom dollar that it was not Heidi and Urban's tent, however, otherwise the Crown would have nailed it by inviting Louden to compare it to the Swedes' shelter. The fact that Louden was not asked to identify that exhibit for the jury shows police knew it was not related.

In closing the Crown's submissions to the jury, prosecutor David Morris waxed lyrical on the credibility of Cassidy and Knauf and their identification:

"Juries must be warned of the risk of convicting on the basis of eyewitness identification," admitted Morris. "A brief glance at a person's features might be the basis of a mistaken identification. Mr Cassidy has supported his impressions by photos he has seen. The reason for the warning is that a convincing witness might still be wrong. There are a number of things to consider, witnesses may make the same mistake.

"His Honour will talk to you about such things," explained Morris with a passing nod to Justice Tompkins. "The purpose of it all is so that you appreciate the quality and reliability of identification is governed by a lot of things. For example, a witness may be a child, a young man. The identification might be affected by lighting or cover. It might be a fleeting glimpse or a longer look.

"What you have to go and do," urged the prosecutor in his distinctive Scottish brogue, "is look and see the situation which existed when Mr Cassidy and Mr Knauf came into Crosbie's Clearing…look at first of all the quality of the people and secondly their maturity. They are not young, not irresponsible. They are people who take note of things…solid types…they were observing and used to the bush…they were there for 13 minutes."

Thirteen minutes, and not one of them remembered a long droopy Mexican moustache.

"This is not a sighting from 50 yards away, or the length of the courtroom. It was man to man and face to face. Thirteen minutes by responsible and senior people.

"It took place at 3pm in the afternoon. Not dusk or dawn. In the middle of the day in late summer or autumn. There is no question of bad light. Nothing to detract from the ability of the man to know who he is talking to. You might in fact be surprised if he couldn't identify him," said prosecutor David Morris.

If so, then re-read above Cassidy and Knauf's failure to recognise Tamihere until their arms were practically twisted by police, then ponder on how "surprising" that must be.

Morris was a skilled orator. He could sell Koolaid to a Jim Jones congregation. He could certainly sell Cassidy and Knauf's questionable identifications to an unsuspecting jury. It is stunning that his construction of the prosecution case was so good that no one ever bothered to ask the obvious question: If David Tamihere had just killed Urban Hoglin, what the heck was he doing sticking up a tent with Heidi Paakkonen in the Coromandel bush track equivalent of Grand Central Station? Crosbie's clearing was the central transit point, and one of the main camping spots. It was three o'clock on a Saturday afternoon, others were bound to come through and perhaps even camp there that night. There was no sign that this woman was tied up. Of all the issues with the Crosbie's Sighting, this is perhaps the biggest, and it went unasked and unanswered. The jury was being asked to believe that Tamihere was superman, capable of overpowering and controlling a Swedish soldier whilst at the same time holding his girlfriend hostage without making it look that way, and setting up a tent in effectively the middle of the main road during rush hour – a weekend on a hiker's track.

If you were the killer, is that what you would have done?

In fact, here's a piece of evidence the jury never got to hear that is directly relevant to this Crosbie's sighting. As predicted, someone did come to Crosbie's that day. Two young men, a seventh former from Thames High School, Andrew McLean and his mate Tony Goonan, took their dogs on a tramp to Crosbie's Clearing on Saturday 8 April.

"We entered the bush off the Tapu-Coroglen Road and walked through to Crosbie's," Goonan told Detective Wayne Kiely. "It took us quite a while. We lost our dogs for four hours. At Crosbie's we camped in front of the old broken down shed."[70]

"We didn't see or hear anyone else camping in the area. The next day we left Crosbie's and went down the Long Shute track which takes you out at Puru. We never saw any other people the whole trip. I have been shown photos of Pat Kelly. I have never seen him before."

The police file doesn't note the timings, but Tapu-Coroglen up to Crosbie's would normally be a two and a half to three hour hike. If they'd started at nine am they should have been there by midday, except their dogs went awol for several hours. Even so, an arrival at 3pm or 4pm appears possible.

Goonan's friend McLean told police the same thing – Crosbie's Clearing was empty. "We never saw any other person. There was not ever any signs on the tracks."[71]

No signs, no noise, no screams, nothing to get the dogs going. Saturday night was very quiet up at Crosbie's. If Tamihere was slaughtering people and burying them or – as prosecutors would later allege – making multiple trips back and forward to their car from Crosbie's on Saturday evening and Sunday – Goonan and McLean never saw them.

And the jury never heard them say that.

Let's turn now to the evidence Tamihere's defence counsel *did* put up against the Crosbie's Clearing identification.

The key point about Crosbie's is the timing. If true, it placed Paakkonen on the Tararu Creek track from at least midday on Saturday 8 April, if you work back the minimum three hours it would have taken to get to Crosbie's from where the car was left parked.

The first problem is, however, that no one saw the Swedes' car at Tararu on the Saturday morning or afternoon. The police have

---
70 Job sheet of Det. Wayne Kiely, 16 August 1989
71 Job sheet of Det. Wayne Kiely, 16 August 1989

no reports of the car being there then. The earliest appearance of the car at the Tararu track carpark is one report from dusk on the 8th, and several more from 12.30pm onwards on Sunday April 9th.

What do we really know of the Swedish couple's movements?

Early in the police investigation, detectives became convinced that Heidi and Urban had travelled north around the tip of the Coromandel Peninsula, after getting their haircuts in Thames, probably around 12.30pm or 1pm on Friday April 7.

In support of this is hairdresser Merilyn Round, who says Heidi told her "they intended to visit around the area, that is – go further afield than Thames." The other hairdresser, Paula Johnson, cut Urban's hair and she remembers him saying "they were travelling around the Coromandel Peninsula, I thought he said something about staying in a camp because they had tents."

Thames shopkeeper Mavis Wilson is another who remembered the Swedes, and their travel plans. She ran the Salvation Army Thrift Shop in Thames and says Heidi and Urban came in on the morning of Friday 7 April, around 10 or 11am.

"I am sure that they said that they were going to Coromandel. I don't know how they were travelling."[72]

Detective Robert Mills, a police intelligence analyst, wrote in a "Probability Assessment Report" submitted to John Hughes:

"Following the re-interview of all persons who claim to have seen the Swedes' 4WD Subaru stationwagon on Tararu Creek Road I have completed a probability assessment report.

"My inference – concluded through five supporting premises – is that there is a 65% probability that the Swedish couple Hoglin and Paakkonen drove their vehicle to the end of Tararu Creek Road on late Saturday afternoon the 8th April 1989 *after completing an overnight trip to the top of the Coromandel Peninsula.*"[73]

The Mills report is hugely problematic for the Crown, which is

---

72   Statement of Mavis Joy Wilson, 17 August 1989
73   "Subaru/Tararu Creek Road – Probability Assessment", Job sheet of Det. R J Mills, 31 July 1989

probably why it was buried unceremoniously.[74] If the Swedes' car did not arrive at Tararu Creek Road until at least "late Saturday afternoon", then how could Heidi Paakkonen have been with David Tamihere at Crosbie's Clearing – three hours into the bush – at 3pm that same day?

The question of where Heidi and Urban stayed the night of April 7th – Friday night – has never been definitively answered, but they must have stayed somewhere. Whitianga farmer Albert Bowers has a fair idea. He and his wife were holidaying at the Port Jackson campground on the tip of Coromandel when a white Subaru station wagon pulled up on the morning of Saturday the 8th, sometime between 8.30am and 9.30am.

"I saw a Subaru station wagon pull into the camping ground," Bowers told police. "It had come from the Fletcher Bay direction. This car went direct to the ablution block. This manoeuvre gave me the impression they knew where to go, had possibly spent the night on the beach a short distance away.

"When the car pulled up I was approximately 20 metres away. They stopped 6ft from a tap, the hatch was opened up and things placed on it.

"Two persons got out of the car, one male and a female. They washed dishes, thoroughly brushed their teeth. Then she washed the male's hair, he had stripped his shirt off. After he had finished with his washing the girl began washing herself.

"I know at one stage she was bare to the waist (I could see all of her back). She stood between the fence and the Subaru. The male stood at the rear of the car, seemed to be guarding the girl."

Without labouring the point, this was a farming man watching an attractive young blonde woman wash herself. He had reason to be paying attention to the couple, making his testimony more credible because he was more engaged in the event.

---

[74] Under cross examination at the murder trial, Mills was asked if he had changed his opinion in the year and a half since. "No sir, I haven't," he replied. "I am more firm now that this inference was, in fact, correct."

"I would describe the Subaru as a white station wagon, with the name Subaru written on the side, it was pretty dusty so I didn't notice whether it was pin-striped on the side. I had a look at the registration number but I can't recall what it was. I have viewed the Swedish couple's car today in the presence of Constable Breach and I am certain it is the same make/model of car as I viewed in Port Jackson. I was mainly looking at the side of the car and couldn't say whether it had bullbars to the front.

"I noticed the following gear belonging to the Subaru: cardboard box which all the dried dishes went into, an aluminium pot with a handle, which also went into the box, a blue-green cover (like a tarpaulin). The car appeared to contain a large amount of gear to the rear."

Albert Bowers' description of the Subaru and its contents is almost identical to that of witnesses Goodwin, Gladwin, Cornish and Payne, who examined the vehicle at Tararu Creek Road on the Sunday afternoon with a view to possibly buying it. It also matches what Tamihere said he found when he broke into it. The car did have the word "SUBARU" in a decal on the side rear doors, above a black stripe that ran the length of the car.

"I would describe the woman from the Subaru as blonde with a yellowish tinge to her hair, hair was down to her shoulder."

This description matches that of hairdresser Merilyn Round, cited by police as the last person to have seen Heidi at Thames the day before. "Her hair was streaky blonde and sun streaked…sitting on the shoulders," Round told police.[75]

Albert Bowers stated the woman he saw was "about 5'6 tall" – in other words, above average height for a woman, "slim build, long legs, early 20s Caucasian. At the time they left she was wearing light shirt and shorts, shoes of some type." Again, a description entirely consistent with documented sightings of Heidi Paakkonen.

"I would describe the male as having a darker shade of hair

---

75   Statement of Merilyn Joy Round, 29 May 1989

(browny), hair came down to collar, covered ears, did not look untidy, clean shaven, fresh face, medium build, approx 5'9" (taller than the girl), 25 or so years. Wearing light T-shirt, possibly khaki coloured shorts, sandshoe type shoes, he was doing the driving."

Again, textbook description of Urban Hoglin, right down to the fact he was around three inches taller than his fiancée. She was actually 5'9", and Urban was 6'.

It would appear almost certain that Albert Bowers and his wife saw Heidi and Urban Hoglin and their car on the morning of Saturday 8 April at Port Jackson campground near Cape Colville. There's only two roads in and out of Port Jackson. One goes east to the dead end of Fletcher's Bay further around the tip of Coromandel, and the other road heads back to Coromandel township along the western perimeter. The Swedes, says Bowers, took the Coromandel township road, as if heading back down towards Thames.

Bowers was not called by the Tamihere defence team at trial.

Instead, Colin Nicholson QC relied on Vern McDonald and James Gray, up from the Manawatu to visit a holiday house one of them owned at Oamaru Bay, just north of Coromandel township. The two men saw what appears to have been the Swedes' Subaru at

Wilson's Bay, around 40 minutes north of Thames, and 25 minutes south of Coromandel.

"It was one Saturday April 8 1989," McDonald told police. "It would have been between 4.30pm and 5pm that we went past a lookout, because when we got to Coromandel the shops had just closed. I saw a white Subaru wagon with a big bull bar on the front. It was parked on the left-hand side of the road – going up – and was facing south.[76]

"I had just made a bull bar for my Landcruiser, the day before we went up, and James Gray owns a Subaru station wagon. I commented to James that I could make bull bars for his Subaru. That was as we came around the corner and saw it there.

"I saw a very blonde female standing in front of the vehicle, taking a photo of the view. I remember that the camera had a neck-strap. I can't remember any more about her. I didn't see anyone else there.

---

76 Statement of Vern Scott McDonald, 28 June 1989

"The back of the Subaru was open and there appeared to be a lot of stuff in the back."

Echoing that was James Gray, who told police:

"As we descended from the lookout past Wilson's Bay – at the top of the hill Wilson's Bay – I saw a white Subaru with bull bars on…parked facing towards us. I own an old Subaru, and I noticed the bull bars. Vern said, jokingly, that he'd build a set for mine and that it'd look smart.

"There was a girl standing about 5 or 6 feet away from the Subaru, parallel with front, by a fence. She was facing out towards the islands, taking a photo. She had really long white blonde hair, and I think she had a white top on.

"The back of the Subaru was up. It was full of gear, you could see that they were on holiday. I couldn't say exactly what any of it was."

In court at the murder trial, Gray said the woman had blonde, "shoulder-blade length hair". The Crown made much of the fact that it was long hair, but the relative length would appear different depending on how far back she was tilting her head to take the photograph. Try it at home.

By the time Gray and McDonald reached Coromandel, the shops had just closed, so they estimate their encounter with the Subaru was around 4.30pm.

We don't know where Heidi Paakkonen or Urban Hoglin spent the night of Saturday 8 April, but they were only 40 minutes away from Thames and there were plenty of areas they could park-up and camp on the roadside.

There are strong, credible sightings then that place the Swedes in Coromandel's far north on the morning of the 8th, consistent with their stated intention of seeing the rest of the peninsula. Albert Bowers spent more than half an hour watching the half-naked Heidi (she rarely wore a bra, according to her family) bathing and washing dishes at the Port Jackson campground.

Gray and McDonald's sightings, while fleeting, are nonetheless consistent with Bowers' sighting and the travel direction he said the

Subaru headed off in, and consistent with the Swedes closing in on Thames by the evening of the 8th.

Did they, in fact, spend the night camped at the Tararu Creek Road carpark? Witnesses Ed Corbett, Harry Goodwin and others all reported seeing the remains of a fresh campfire close to the Subaru.

"Someone had lit a fire in the turnaround which had stones around the edge of it," local resident Corbett told police. The fire looked as though it had only recently been burning and it was the first time I had seen the fire in that position."

Randall Cornish was another to remark on the fire:

"About 10 feet away from the car was a circle of stones where someone had obviously had a campfire. By the look of the ashes I would have thought it was a recent fire."

The fire could have been lit by anyone, but locals had never seen anyone light a fire in that location. It had stones around it, campfire style, and was close to the Swedes' car. Could they have arrived there from Coromandel on Saturday evening? One police witness says yes.

John Kennedy, a resident living further down Tararu Creek Road, "saw a white station wagon drive up his street with two dark-headed people in on Saturday 8 April about 7.30pm," recorded a police job sheet.

Kennedy was interviewed on 8 August and confirmed: "Yes I am certain that the date I saw the vehicle was Saturday 8 April. I know this because on that particular day I did part time work for Deka painting some shelves.

"I saw the station wagon about 7.30pm. I was standing on the decking and admiring the job I had just done in the front garden. I am not sure whether the vehicle I saw was the same you are inquiring about. I am definite it was a white Subaru station wagon.

"The occupants of the vehicle were European, male and female. I don't know how old they were. I couldn't even describe them."

Kennedy told police he never saw the car drive down the road again past his house that night.

At first glance, you might look at the description of two "dark headed people" and say, "nah, not them". If you check the sunset times for that date, however, you'll find the sun went down around 6.06pm over Thames, and it was all dark at 6.40. He could not have seen them at 7.30.

This mystery is solved when you go back to his first contact with police back on 17 June 1989 when he first tried to report it.

"We haven't spoken to police yet," he said then, "but I thought I would mention that I saw a white station wagon go up our road at about dusk one evening…The vehicle I saw had bullbars at the front…the car drove up the road but I didn't see it come back down." Kennedy talked of sunlight glinting off the tailgate.

Now, if it was dusk the timing fits perfectly with Heidi and Urban returning from their northern trip. They would have arrived anywhere from 5.20pm onwards, depending on whether they stopped to take more photographs or diversions. The low angle of the sun also accounts for why they may have seemed "dark headed" – they were silhouetted in the dusk. Kennedy says the occupants were a male and female.

The police established there were four white Subaru wagons with bull bars in the Coromandel region during the relevant week, but unless there were two old white Subaru wagons with bull-bars, driven by couples, both frequenting Tararu Creek Road in the space of 24 hours, it's a fair bet to say this Kennedy sighting was most likely the Swedes, and that is where they camped the night which is why nosey neighbours never saw the car drive back down.

What is screamingly significant about all this?

If these numerous witnesses are correct, then Heidi and Urban were still alive until at least 6.40pm on the night of Saturday 8 April, and Heidi had been nowhere near Crosbie's clearing at 3pm that afternoon.

So why didn't the Tamihere defence team win points for all this in court? Because they didn't pull the evidence together in quite the same way.

Primarily, Tamihere's lawyers anchored their defence on a couple named Anne and Peter Novis who ran the Stony Bay campground for DOC. The Novis' were certain they had rented Heidi Paakkonen a cabin around lunchtime on the Friday or Saturday, after the Swedish couple had tramped in from Fletcher's Bay, three hours west.

The only problem with that is if the Novis' were right, then Albert Bowers could not be right. They could not have stayed the night at Stony Bay, and been able to turn up at Port Jackson at 8.30 the next morning. The legal team tossed a coin and chose to go with the Novis sighting, backed up by McDonald and Gray, and supported also by a BMW parts manager named Stephen Waters who believed he'd seen the couple and their car at Fletcher Bay, either late Saturday afternoon or Sunday morning.

Crown Prosecutor David Morris had a field day ripping into the timing problems caused by the witnesses Tamihere's team had called.

"I will deal with the defence sightings," thundered the dour Scotsman to the jury. "These are inconsistent among themselves and irreconcilable with the account given by the Crown witnesses. They conflict with each other and independently verified sightings of the car.

"We know that they were in Thames on Friday. They had a haircut after lunch. It took about half an hour. The car was at the top of Tararu Creek Road according to Mr Cornish at about 12:30 to 2pm on Sunday. The times should be noted.

"Mr and Mrs Novis, they are honest witnesses – say they saw them on the Friday or the Saturday. They are unsure of the day, but they stayed at Stony Bay. It is a three hour walk there and back from Fletcher's Bay. If it was the Friday, then they would have had to drive from Thames and walk for three hours and get there by lunch-time. Mr and Mrs Novis are wrong.

"If it was the Saturday, and they left on Sunday about 'eightish' then it's a three hour walk back. They would have to get to Tararu Creek Road in time for the sighting of the car at about 12:30 or 1pm so they are still wrong.

"The actual sightings are of little value," claimed Morris. "Urban

Hoglin – little was seen of him at Stony Bay or Fletcher's Bay. At Fletcher's Bay he was not seen there by the man from Fletcher's Bay, Mr Waters. He was not there Friday, so that puts the lie on Mr and Mrs Novis.

"Mr McDonald and Mr Gray – the fishermen. They saw the car at about 4.30pm on Saturday. If he's right, then Mr and Mrs Novis are wrong," argued the prosecutor triumphantly.

You can see, then, how difficult eyewitness testimony can be. McDonald's and Gray's testimony is entirely consistent with Bowers', but not with Novis and Waters. There may be an explanation for that.

Both the Novis' and Steve Waters reported Heidi or the couple wearing light tramping boots. A "fairly expensive variety of tramping boot with the visible eyelets and two sets of hooks at the top, and a commando type sole," conceded Peter Novis under cross examination. Yet Heidi was not known to own a pair. Anne Novis provided

a clue in her police statement, however. The girl she thought was Heidi Paakkonen "had really muscled legs…that made one think she had done a bit of tramping". The photos of Heidi don't disclose the level of muscle suggested.

Another giveaway is that Peter Novis told the trial the woman he saw was "medium height". Yet Heidi Paakkonen, at 176 cm or 5'9", was almost as tall as an average man. She would almost have eyeballed Novis. He never saw the face of the man he later assumed was Urban Hoglin. In fact, the closest Novis got to him was about 50 metres. Novis believed the man was less than average height for a male, where in fact he stood 183cm tall, or 6'.

Anne Novis told the court the woman was "about my height".

Steve Waters said the hair of the woman he saw was "long, partially down her back."

"So very long?" queried assistant Crown Prosecutor Paul Davison.

"Yes, longish hair."

The young man he saw had "scruffy" hair which, given that Urban had just had three haircuts in Thames to get it absolutely short, doesn't seem to fit his description. The closest the couple got to Steve Waters was 50 metres.

Waters, a BMW parts manager from Auckland, knew his cars and recognised this particular couple's car as a white Subaru with bull bars. But go back to that earlier point: police established there were four of these cars on the peninsula at this time. This could have been one of them.

Is it possible that another foreign blonde woman and her boyfriend were hiking in the area at the time? Stranger things have happened. This may explain why Novis and Waters, each at different ends of the same track, reported seeing a blonde in tramping boots, at times that conflict with the Bowers and McDonald/Gray sightings.

Finally, of course, only the Bowers/McDonald/Gray sequence gets us back to Tararu Creek Road on Saturday at sunset where Kennedy sees the distinctive Subaru with bullbars.

It is timely to remember that the Bowers/McDonald/Gray/Kennedy sequence is in full accordance with the police intelligence briefing which concluded:

"My inference – concluded through five supporting premises – is that there is a 65% probability that the Swedish couple Hoglin and Paakkonen drove their vehicle to the end of Tararu Creek Road on late Saturday afternoon the 8th April 1989 *after completing an overnight trip to the top of the Coromandel Peninsula.*"[77]

But there's another potentially massive hole in prosecutor David Morris' compelling legal rhetoric. His entire speech attacking the Novis/Waters/McDonald/Gray sequence was devoted to showing how the Tamihere defence timings were inconsistent with the appearance of the Swedes' car at Tararu Creek Road. However, there may be another twist to this story, and it is one the jury never got a chance to hear.

Buried deep inside the police files are a large number of interviews with members of the St James Union Church at Thames. There were 140 or so people in the congregation on the morning of Sunday 9 April 1989, and many of them say they saw, and spoke to, Heidi and Urban.

If what you are about to read is correct, it lends even more weight

---

[77] "Subaru/Tararu Creek Road – Probability Assessment", Job sheet of Det. R J Mills, 31 July 1989

to the already compelling evidence showing Heidi Paakkonen cannot have been at Crosbie's Clearing on Saturday 8 April, and it would also explain why their car was not seen there earlier that day, where it would have had to be for her to be at Crosbie's.

"She said her name was Heidi, and I can't recall his name, and they said they were from Sweden," parishioner Juanita Bridgeman, who was manning the door to the St James Church to greet people, told police. "They said that they were enjoying themselves and were going to do some more hiking. They didn't say where they were going to go."[78]

Given that their car turned up at Tararu Creek sometime later that same Sunday morning, it's not hard to guess what "hiking" Heidi was talking about.

"I have looked at the photos and I am certain that it was her at church."

Allowing for all the problems with eyewitness identification and photos, in this case the apparition had introduced herself as "Heidi".[79]

Elderly parishioner Roald Barthow told detectives, "I remember Reverend Glen coming and making note of two Swedish visitors that were in the congregation. I mentally resolved that I would like to speak with them because I have a Swedish grandfather.[80]

"I have difficulty remembering people's names, and she repeated her name to me a couple of times, at which time I reflected the name was the same as the series of books popular with my children, the *Heidi* books.

"The only recollection I have of the person with Heidi is that he

---

78 Statement of Juanita Bridgeman, 10 June 1989
79 As a check and balance, I searched out the top 100 girl's names in Sweden for the years 2008 and 1998, which was the oldest top 100 list I could find. The name "Heidi" did not make the top 100 girl's names in either of those years in Sweden. http://www.thinkbabynames.com/popular/0/sweden/1998 A check of Statistics Sweden shows Heidi did not make the top ten girls names for either the 1960s or the 1970s http://www.scb.se/Pages/TableAndChart____286720.aspx In nearby Norway, only one in every 150 women alive in Norway today is named Heidi: http://www.ssb.no/navn/.
80 Statement of Roald Eyuind Moeller Barthow, 12 June 1989

was fairly slight and somewhat taller than myself at five foot seven." [Urban Hoglin was six foot, and slim]

"I remember that day there was a white vehicle parked adjacent to my car, in the carpark, when we left at about 11.45am. I couldn't be certain the white Subaru in the photos shown to me by police is the one, but it looks similar."

Tui Caird was aged 81 back in June 89 when she spoke to police, calling herself a "senior elder" of the church. She remembered Reverend Frank Glen mentioning the Swedish visitors, and told police, "after looking at the photographs I am sure the girl is the one I met..they sat on the left hand side of the church, as you go in, about halfway down."[81]

A local doctor, Ian Hamilton, was another of those there that morning. A police job sheet records he was vague about the date but "was definite about the couple being in the church. He did say the girl had a mauvey pastel coloured top. The snap shot shown had Hoglin wearing a similar top. Hamilton, I feel, is fairly credible".[82]

When police took Dr Hamilton's statement, he told them:

"The girl I would describe as slim in build, fit looking and good looking. She had a light complexion. She was about 5'8" – 5'9", tallish for a girl. [Heidi Paakkonen was exactly 5'9", or 176cm in today's numbers] I don't recall what colour her eyes were. I think she had blonde hair...I know she had shorts on, but I don't know what colour they were. I would say her hair was shoulder length.[83]

"The guy was about the same height as her [Urban was six foot, or 183cm]. He had brownish hair. It wasn't long... He was slim and fit looking too...they would have been in their early 20s.

"I have been shown a snapshot of a couple, the guy is in a purple t-shirt. It looked a lot like them but I can't be 100% sure.

"I can't remember if Lyn introduced them to me but she must have because I remember the name Heidi. I don't recall the guy's

---

81 Statement of Tui Caird, 10 June 1989
82 Job sheet of Det. Const. G J T Kaye-Ivitu, 7 June 1989
83 Statement of Ian Sinclair Hamilton, 7 June 1989

name…I vaguely remember them asking where the Kauaeranga Valley was."

The Kauaeranga Valley was one of the areas Heidi and Urban had discussed with shop owner Graham Manning the previous Thursday.

An 80 year old churchgoer named Mary Milne told police a young foreign couple had helped her get down the stairs as she was leaving the church. "The male I spoke with was about 20 years of age [Urban had just turned 23], 6', skinny. He had on a pair of skin tight trousers. They were either dark navy blue or black.[84] They made him look very skinny."[85]

Mary told police showing her the couple's photos that "the male in the photo is the person I spoke to outside the church." She thought the couple was leaving for Auckland soon. She didn't see their car.

To top it all off, the pastor of the church, the Reverend Frank Glen, was the official police chaplain for the Waikato region, and he'd seen the Swedes as well.

Glen, now a respected military historian living in the South Island, says he was later told by police that the couple were probably a man from the Swedish navy and his wife, aged in their mid to late 30s.

"After I consulted with the inquiry team it was looked into and reported to me there was an 11% chance it could have been them. Within hours I was told the couple were likely a Swedish naval officer and his wife who were also in the district and who had an interest in attending Divine Worship. I reported it because the lady was blonde, both were tall, but after careful reflection they were older. She was at least 35 and he could well have been late 30s or 40."[86]

There is no doubt that's what Glen was told and what he now remembers, 23 years later. Intriguingly, however, no statements from such a couple appear in the police file released to Tamihere's lawyers, no police job sheets mention this couple, and the "complete list" of all people spoken to during the missing tourists investigation –

---
84   Hoglin's skeleton was found with the remains of dark Lee jeans.
85   Job sheet of Const. C I Dobson, 13 June 1989
86   Email correspondence with author, December 2012

several hundred – does not contain anyone named "Heidi". Nor did the other witnesses report them as aged in their 30s.

Now, it could of course be that there were two more Swedish tourists – one named Heidi – who were the same size, build and hair colour as the tall Heidi Paakkonen and Urban Hoglin, visiting Thames on the very day the missing couple's car was last seen. And it may also be that this other blonde, shoulder-length haired Heidi and her 183cm boyfriend were also planning on hiking and visiting the Kauaeranga Valley as well. But if there wasn't a Doppelganger Swedish couple in town[87], then the simplest explanation might be that Heidi and Urban visited a quaint old church service on their final Sunday morning in Thames, before driving back up to Tararu Creek Road to begin that final trip up the track they'd told Graham Manning about.

If that's the case, it makes the entire Crown argument about Tamihere and Paakkonen being seen in Crosbie's Clearing on the 8th, based on two "tainted" witnesses, utterly irrelevant. Trampers John Cassidy and Mel Knauf had kept a diary note: whoever they met at Crosbie's was there at 3pm Saturday. It can't have happened. Not if the multiple witnesses at the church are correct. Nor if Albert Bowers, Vern McDonald, James Gray and John Kennedy are correct about seeing Heidi and Urban and their car at Port Jackson, then south of Coromandel on the road to Thames, and finally driving up Tararu Creek Road around sunset on the Saturday evening.

And if they are correct, what is the scenario?

One possibility is this. Urban and Heidi finally entered the bush at the Tararu track late on the morning or early afternoon of Sunday 9 April, after church. It is highly unlikely they entered on the Saturday night, and the campfire by the car is circumstantial evidence that they did not. They knew the track was too long to do in a day, they had discussed the location of huts with Graham Manning, and

---

87 The other couple seen by Novis/Waters would still have been right up north on Sunday morning

they had taken their sleeping bags, cooking gear and a tent with them. If they were not at St James Church, then the earliest they could have entered the Tararu track was after breakfast on Sunday morning, 9 April.

Their stated plan to Manning was to loop across to Table Mountain, then down into the Kauaeranga Valley and then out to the highway, where they hoped to hitch a ride back into Thames and from where, presumably, they would walk back up and retrieve their car.

For several reasons, that never happened. Firstly, David Tamihere stole their car on the early afternoon of Monday 10 April. Secondly, there is no evidence the couple ever made it out of the Kauaeranga Valley, however. At least, not together.

We are not required to examine this aspect in detail yet, however, because the next major strand of the Crown case hinged on secret jailhouse witnesses who all claimed they knew how the Swedes had met their fate.

CHAPTER 8

The Secret Witnesses

"I have a lot to tell you, but I'll save it until we come home again. Everything is OK otherwise, now I can feel the sun burning my back. It's nice to be able to sunbathe a bit because often there's been a lot of sandflies around and you wouldn't dare think about taking the clothes off and just wearing shorts and a t-shirt. If you did that you would be eaten – I, anyway, because they seem to love my blood.

"Did you recognise the titles of the songs that I sent in the last letter? There's some of them that I have to buy and I wonder if they are available at home.

"Now I have to stop writing this because I think I hear some footsteps coming closer; it may be Urban."
— *letter from Heidi Paakkonen, January 1989, Twizel*

Secret Witness A [SWA] was a convicted heroin trafficker. At the time he first began talking to Tamihere in Mt Eden prison, he had not yet been convicted, but he knew he would be. The charge – importing millions of dollars worth of heroin in one of the country's biggest drug hauls at the time – carried a possible life sentence in jail. SWA didn't like the sound of that.

He figured he would plead guilty in the hope of getting a lesser penalty. His lawyer discussed with him the prospect of becoming a jailhouse informant for one John Hughes, detective inspector. SWA admitted he hoped that would count for a much lighter sentence indeed:

"I do know incidents where people have been given full immunity on drug cases," he testified. He added that he knew that option wasn't open to him in New Zealand, but he'd done time in Australia for murder and robbery – he knew how to cut deals and he was aiming for a "lighter sentence".

"It might help me, yes," he told the court.

Nor was this the only case he had turned 'supergrass' on in order to reduce his sentence. "From the time of my arrest I did assist the drug squad to apprehend the rest of the syndicate that I was involved with, yes," SWA confirmed, saying he had worn a concealed recording device.

In total, SWA was a secret witness in three cases, two of them run by John Hughes.

His first meeting with Tamihere came when Tamihere was suddenly transferred to an adjacent cell in Mt Eden, around 24 hours after being charged with stealing the Subaru. Over the preceding 24 hours Tamihere had been extensively interviewed by police about his movements. It's impossible to know or prove that police leaked basic information from their inquiries to SWA, but it is entirely consistent with John Hughes' proven modus operandi.

On the one hand SWA claims Tamihere didn't tell him key information, such as the fact that Cassidy and Knauf claimed to have identified him. "No, he never said that part. When he said the police spoke to him he did not go into detail, sir."

On the other hand, he says Tamihere sang like a canary:[88]

"Dave said…he met them on the Saturday up in the bush. He said they met on the track. After exchanging hellos he said they were very friendly, that's when they agreed to let Dave and his mates act as their guides. That's when they told Dave about their car being parked down the road.

"I said to him 'when did they rape them, attack them and rape them?', he said that was Saturday afternoon, up in the bush."

---

88 Gratuitous sexual detail has been edited out of this.

SWA asked where they'd met, and Tamihere allegedly told him about 5km up the Tararu track, 2km before the turn-off to Table Mountain. "He said it was Saturday before lunch, about 9.30am…I asked him if he took them straight to where he raped them and he said no, he'd showed them around first. I asked him where he raped them and he said it was up further in the bush in an area the locals call The Pines.

"I asked him how he rooted the girl with her boyfriend there. He said well, the boyfriend was tied up, his mates had him and he smashed the girl in the stomach, she fell on her arse. She was really scared. He dragged her trousers off…I said how about the boyfriend? He said he belted the boyfriend on the side of the neck first before he hit the girl, and when the boyfriend fell down that's when his mates took over."

"Did he say anything to you about what he used when he hit the boy on the neck?" asked assistant Crown Prosecutor Paul Davison.

"Yes, he said he hit him with a lump of wood on the side of the neck. I asked him if he tied the girl up. He said no, he only tied the bloke up. He said he gagged them with a t-shirt from his pack. I asked him if he killed them when they finished their orgy. Dave said he couldn't kill them there because there is nowhere to hide their bodies. After they raped them they took them to where he killed them.

"I asked him if he was worried about other people seeing him. He said no, because where they were they were under the trees, covered in by undergrowth and that.

"I asked Dave if she was a good root, he said, oh yes, she was. I said to him if she is such a good root, why did you root the bloke? Dave says, 'I'm a slut, I'll f*** anything', and he explained to me that when he got off the girl one of his mates took over, started rooting the girl and one of his mates was rooting the boyfriend, so Dave decided he wants to try the boyfriend too.

"He told me that when he was rooting that young girl, he rooted her for ages."

In the courtroom you could see the jurors examining Tamihere with absolute loathing and disgust, especially the women, when one of the secret witnesses claimed Tamihere was boasting about Heidi responding sexually during the rape. There were more explicit and degrading details delivered in the courtroom that don't bear repeating. One juror became physically ill and the hearing had to be adjourned.

These were emotional bombshells, and Detective Inspector John Hughes knew it. He just had to get the jury to hate Tamihere enough to convict regardless of the quality of the evidence.

All of this sexual violation, supposedly, was taking place in Crosbie's Clearing, supposedly around an hour before trampers Cassidy and Knauf walked in and found a perfectly-groomed woman wearing well-applied make up, fingernail polish and red lipstick, who even managed a "polite smile" when they attempted humour and moved her legs out of the way when Cassidy walked past.

In contrast to his denial that Tamihere had told him about the Cassidy/Knauf sighting, SWA then told the court, "Dave said that the police said that some people saw them in that area on that weekend, but according to Dave he said that was bullshit."

All this, supposedly, was also taking place around the time young trampers Goonan and McLean walked in with their hunting dogs and began setting up their tent "in front of the old broken down shed".

Now, here's an interesting little twist. SWA was asked where the rape and attack actually took place:

"Under the trees there below the hill where he has got the remains of forestry hut pulled down, in the back of those trees…that is where they attacked that couple and raped them."

This would be the same broken down forestry hut that Goonan and McLean were camping beside with their dogs that afternoon. They and their hounds failed to hear or see any signs of a woman being pack-raped, her boyfriend being pack-raped, or Tamihere and his "three mates" dragging their two prisoners away.

When he asked Tamihere if the police would find the bodies, SWA claimed he responded, "they are looking in the wrong place". Asked why he killed them, Tamihere allegedly said it would be too easy for the Swedes to recognise the mug-shots of him and his mates, and additionally, "he wouldn't be able to stand the shame of being charged with f***ing a bloke."

According to SWA, Tamihere told him the best place to hide a body was the edge of a bluff or a cliff, because pig-hunters were worried their dogs might plummet off the edges of bluffs and so stayed away from them.

"If you want to hide something in the bush, always be careful of pig-hunters and never leave it out in the open. Bury it by a bluff because pig hunters don't go near a bluff."

"Did he say anything to you about the Swedish couple's car and his movements?" prosecutor Davison wanted to know.

"He said that on the weekend they were up in the bush he made a few trips to the Swedish couple's car. He said, 'I'll tell you something'. He said, 'nobody knows this, not even the police'. He said that he used the car on that Sunday and he came back on the Sunday to get his things and do some things, then he left that area on the Monday afternoon altogether...he didn't take his mates with him, they stayed back in the bush."

Contained in SWA's taped statements to his lawyer, but not given in evidence at the trial, was a claim that Tamihere had marched the Swedes to their final resting place.

"I said surely they must have protested or something, he said how could they, because I had them gagged."

"So he walked them?" asked SWA's lawyer Chris Reid.

"Yeah, he walked them while they were gagged, they were gagged from the word go."

"Well he took a bit of a risk with someone seeing them like that."

"True, that's his area, that's the bush he knows."

"But if he had walked them gagged from the Pines and he had punched her in the stomach and dropped her, she'd been raped and goodness knows what else, how far could he have taken them from there?"

It's a really good question, because as you will see shortly, Urban's body turned up an incredible 73 km away, and the tragic group of six – attackers and gagged prisoners – would have had to be frog-marched across a major state highway as part of that journey, let alone past numerous other trampers.

We will come to that in due course. Firstly, let's examine the obvious bits. If SWA is telling the truth, then Heidi and Urban had to have entered the bush sometime around 7.30am Saturday morning, and their car must have been parked at Tararu Creek Road from at least that time. Yet, no one saw it there until John Kennedy saw a white Subaru with bull bars being driven by a male and female arrive around sunset on Saturday.

If SWA is telling the truth, then all those who saw Heidi, Urban and the car up north on Saturday are wrong. If SWA is telling the truth, Heidi and Urban cannot have attended the Sunday morning church service at St James.

If SWA is telling the truth, his evidence conflicts with trampers Cassidy and Knauf. Now, they testified they had walked into the Pines and heard a man making noise sometime before they cleared the bushline. They didn't want to startle the man so they actually yelled out a greeting before they emerged. The noise they had heard continued unchanged, and they found the man allegedly clearing the ground with a tomahawk as he put a tent up.

The significance of this is that Cassidy and Knauf appear to have heard the man before he realised they were there. Yet there was no sign of anyone else, no "mates" scurrying for the trees dragging another prisoner behind them.

If Heidi had endured all this on Saturday afternoon, why was there not a trace of it in the eyes of the woman the trampers claimed was Heidi:

"Was she crying?" Tamihere's lawyer Colin Nicholson QC asked tramper Mel Knauf.

"No she wasn't".
"Did she have reddened eyes?"
"No she didn't."

Then you have the problem of two trampers and their dogs who actually spent Saturday afternoon setting up camp at the very same broken hut that SWA claims the rape was taking place behind. The trampers and their dogs saw no one. Heard nothing.

There's also the difficulty of the apparent multiple trips back and forth to the car and driving around in it on Sunday.

Really? Because five witnesses came upon the car from 12:30pm Sunday afternoon and spent most of the afternoon around it. The car was untouched and did not move anywhere. If it had, it had to have done all of its movement before midday.

SWA's final morsel: the bodies will be found buried at the top of a cliff, where pig hunters never go.

For his troubles, SWA was sentenced this way:

"Mr [SWA], you appear today for sentence after pleading guilty to one charge of importation of 2kgs of 80% pure heroin and one charge of possession for supply of the same material. You already have one conviction for dealing in heroin in a substantial way, that having been entered against you as recently as 1985.

"The size of the operation and your previous conviction would in the ordinary way have justified the imposition of a maximum penalty. However I am told by Crown counsel...most particularly that you have assisted the police on this and other matters....It is appropriate that something less than a maximum penalty be imposed."

SWA was jailed for 12 years, but got it reduced to eight years on appeal when the Court took into account a letter from John Hughes praising him, supported by Crown lawyers. The Court of Appeal noted the starting point for his heroin crimes as 18-20 years. Interestingly, the Hughes/Crown Law intervention came in May 1990 just as he was testifying at Tamihere's depositions. Had SWA threatened not to testify if the Crown didn't support his urgent bid for a lighter sentence? He'd been jailed in Australia in 1976 for 13 years for the manslaughter of his Lebanese girlfriend, reduced to eight years on appeal. By 1980 he was out deported back to New Zealand, but he hopped back on a plane to Sydney four days later. In 1985 he was caught heroin trafficking, for which he received another 12 year sentence in Oz. By rights he should have been nowhere near New Zealand where he was arrested only four years later on the latest heroin trafficking charge. He'd served three years and three months in Australia.

This strange situation of committing major crimes then having the sentences slashed seemed to be developing into a suspicious pattern.

In slashing his sentence from 12 years to 8, the Court of Appeal specifically noted, "his evidence for the Crown in the case against Tamihere is viewed as crucial."

Presumably only if it was true, which we will come to in due course.

So that's Secret Witness A.

Now let's hear from Secret Witness B (SWB). SWB claims to have met Tamihere outside the prison chapel to smoke marijuana joints and the subject of the Swedish tourists came up. SWB's evidence was that Tamihere boasted the police would never find the bodies because "I cut the f***ers up".

The inmate said this conversation took place after the cannabis had been smoked.

"You were having psychiatric problems then, weren't you?" asked Tamihere's lawyer.

"Yes," confirmed SWB.

"And you found you were having nightmares, didn't you?"

"Yes."

"And you spoke to a social worker about the problems, didn't you?"

"Yes."

"And you told her your eyes were yellow, didn't you?"

"Yes."

Always a good sign.

It was the testimony of Secret Witness C (SWC) however that the Crown argued supported Cassidy and Knauf's identification. He too, was a desperate man.

"I am currently serving a sentence of life imprisonment on two charges of murder. I started this sentence in 1983 and I will be going before the Parole Board next year."

According to SWC, he met Tamihere in Paremoremo and happened to see a large map of Coromandel on Tamihere's cell wall. "The bloody clowns are searching the wrong f***ing area! They won't find the bodies there!" Tamihere allegedly broadcast.

SWC's police statement is worth a good read, although once again the most graphic detail is edited out:

"Between now and then we have spoken on a large number of occasions, usually in his cell. He has told me various things over that time, but I could not put a date to particular conversations.

"He told me that he had met the couple and I think he said it was at a camping or picnic area. He said he had bullshitted them about how well he knew the area and talked them into letting him show them around the area.

"He told me about the attacks that he made on both the girl, Heidi, and the man. As far as the man is concerned, he said that he had tied him up while he had attacked the girl, but he also told me that he had 'Donald Ducked' the man. That is a prison slang for a sexual assault. I didn't really believe him when he told me that, but I do know that he is an animal.

"He told me that he killed the man by smashing his head in with a piece of wood. When he was talking about the attack on the girl, Heidi, he said that he had raped her several times….he said that she was terrified. The first time he raped her was in the bush and that the man had been tied up when this happened.

"He told me that he had pinched a tent from a farmer's shed and had kept it for several days. He said that the other attacks on Heidi had taken place in the tent and that he had killed her by strangling her in that tent. He told me that he had then put the tent back in the shed.

"He didn't tell me exactly where the attacks took place, but that it was in the search area. He said that they had almost been sprung by a couple who had come across them. He didn't say what they were doing when this couple came across them, except that the girl was sitting down. He didn't say what the couple were, I just thought he was talking about a man and a woman.

"At the time this couple came across them he said Heidi was too terrified to say anything because the man was tied up to a tree nearby.

"When he talked to me about disposing of the bodies he told me that he had got rid of the two bodies at different times. The man first and Heidi a day or two later. He told me that he had kept Heidi for a day or two after he killed the man.

"He told me that he had stolen an aluminium boat with a motor from a motor camp opposite the pub at Tapu. He said he had kept the boat for several days and used it to dispose of both of the bodies. He told me that when he had finished with the boat he washed and scrubbed it and put it back.

"The area where he got rid of them is between Tapu and Wilson's Bay on the Coast Road. There is an area where the road in from the main road loops around. Between the main road and the loop road is a grass area, and between the loop road and the water is a grass area. He said that he took the bodies about 15 minutes straight out from the shore at that point.

"He never said anything about wrapping the bodies up, but he did say that he had stolen some scrap metal from a yard or factory in Thames and had used that to weigh the bodies down.

"He did tell me that he had brought the car up to Auckland and used it for several days before dumping it at the Auckland Railway Station. He gave that mad laugh of his and said that a Police car had driven right past him in the couple's car when they were looking for the car…he also told me that he had given the man's watch to his son."

One can imagine Detective Inspector John Hughes rolling on the floor with laughter as he drafted all the main points he wanted his third secret witness to hit. Virtually every plank of the prosecution case that needed shoring up had received testimony he could feed to the jury, along with plenty more doses of lurid sex and violence to shock the innocent jurors.

It was this testimony above that the Court of Appeal relied on, and treated as credible, because it supported the Cassidy and Knauf sighting by saying Tamihere had confessed to nearly "being sprung" by a couple who saw him with Heidi, who was sitting down.

What was it that trial judge Justice Tompkins had said when throwing the Cassidy/Knauf identification evidence out?

"The danger of doubtful evidence being used to support and corroborate doubtful evidence is obvious.

"The importance of this identification evidence is obvious… If the identification evidence is in any way suspect, but yet was accepted by the jury, the consequence to the accused would be highly prejudicial."[89]

But of course, the Court of Appeal had allowed it back in, and Hughes and David Morris must have been doing hi-fives in the corridor. SWC's statement had also drawn on another ingredient from their time together on the Arthur Allan Thomas case – scrap metal to weigh down the bodies at sea, just as Harvey and Jeannette Crewe supposedly had been.

It was almost as if the top cop and the top prosecutor had simply dusted off the stunts that were pulled in the Crewe murders debacle, and put them all into play again.

As you can read in the book *Inside Story*:

> It was only later that I discovered some equally dodgy jailhouse secret witness testimony had been trumped up against Arthur Allan Thomas as well, as Hughes and the rest of the police team attempted to fit the farmer up for the Crewe murders. You could

---
89   R v Tamihere (No 2) (1990) 7 CRNZ 594

say there was a little bit of a pattern to John's cases.

Ivan the Insane, a mentally-ill prisoner, was wheeled in by police at the Thomas Royal Commission hearings with testimony supposedly proving Thomas had confessed to him while they were in jail together. The Royal Commission, after hearing from psychiatric experts, told Crown lawyers the man was clearly barking mad and they were wasting the Commission's time. The police refused to take the hint and kept asking questions of the inmate.

Where to begin with Secret Witness C, then?

Why would Tamihere care if police were "searching the wrong f***ing area!", if in fact he had dumped them miles away out to sea? For that matter, why would he care at all? Wouldn't he be very happy they were searching in the wrong place?

Why would Tamihere, who carried and had two tents of his own with him and who, according to the secret witness testimony, had come across Heidi and Urban by accident several kilometres into the bush, have "pinched a tent from a farmer's shed", staged a rape and murder inside that tent, and then "put the tent back in the shed"? What did he do at first, see them in the distance, think to himself, 'cor, she's a looker, I must get that tent', and then make a 10 km round trip to steal the tent before locating Heidi and Urban again and attacking them?

If Tamihere killed Urban and "got rid of the two bodies at different times", how exactly did he manhandle a dead weight of 75kg while still maintaining control of Heidi for "a day or two later". More to the point, how exactly did he manhandle a 75kg dead weight 12km out of the bush to Tararu Creek Road on a busy tramping weekend?

What use was a little aluminium boat to him when the Subaru had no towbar, or did Tamihere putt-putt 30 km up the coast and then head 15 minutes out to sea? How long did that take again? Was Heidi still minding the tent back at Crosbie's for this whole time, with instructions not to remove the make-up while Tamihere was gone?

Apparently so. Under cross examination, SWC embellished this story even further:

"Did he tell you that after killing the man he had the girl in a tent for two or three days having sex with her?" asked Colin Nicholson.

"That's right."

"So he killed the man, took his body and dumped it at sea, and during this time was he having the two or three days sex with the girl?"

"That's what he said."

"So he dumps the body at sea, comes back and he has sex with the girl in the tent, is that what he told you?"

"Yes, over a period of two or three days."

"And he kills her and takes her and dumps her at about the same place as he had dumped the guy, is that what he said?"

"That's right."

"And so was it after he dumped the girl's body that he took these tourists on the Tamihere tiki tour?"

"That's right."

If you feel a Homer Simpson head-smacking 'doh' moment coming on, you are probably not alone. This is what passed for "credible" testimony, according to the Crown.

The reference to "Donald Ducking" Urban Hoglin – a repeat of SWA's claims – was probably John Hughes' code to other prison inmates that Tamihere would be up for a bit of Donald Ducking himself if the opportunity arose in the cells or the prison showers. Just another Mickey Mouse aspect to the case. A bit of psychological warfare. As *Metro* magazine's Carroll du Chateau noted in her profile of Hughes in 1989:

"I remember Hughes telling me how he liked someone in charge of witnesses 'who'll shake the shit out of them…scare them witless'. For this case," she wrote, "that will probably mean Hughes himself."

The saddest and most cynical thing about the secret witness testimony is the hell it put Heidi and Urban's families through. How many nightmares have they endured over the years in the darkness, wondering if one of the witnesses was telling the truth? The most lurid details have been edited out for the purposes of this book, but they were stated in open court. Did John Hughes engineer that, knowing their evidence was false?

These 'Devil's Advocate' questions are taken to provoke the minds of readers, to invite you to see the holes in the Crown case. They are not here as part of a position for or against the guilt of David Tamihere, but merely to throw a blowtorch on the story as presented to the jury. In all murder cases, it is for the Crown to prove the Defendant did it. It is not the Defendant's job to prove he did not, although that usually helps.

If Tamihere is lying about walking up Tararu Creek Road on the 10th, and in fact he was still on the track heading south towards Thames, it is possible that he met the couple at the Jam Tins as they hiked up from Thames on the afternoon or evening of Sunday April 9. The problem with this scenario, however, is that it further slashes the time window available for Tamihere to have done anything.

Let's assume for a moment he did kill the Swedes, not on the 8th as the Crown alleged, but on the 9th. How does he manhandle two bodies 12km out of the bush, back to the car and have disposed of them by 2pm the next day when he drove to the Sunkist Lodge? Given that we now know Urban Hoglin's carotid artery had been slashed open, causing him to die almost instantly, how much blood would have spilt, and how much blood would be in the car if Tamihere then drove the body 73km to where it was found?

Why was no blood found in the car?

Of course, when David Tamihere was convicted of the murders, Urban's body had not been found. Certainly no one expected it to be far, far away. We will come to that shortly, but first let's examine the actual forensic evidence found by police, because in 1989/1990, that's all they had to build a case on.

Their biggest leads turned out to be a bloodstain, and a watch.

CHAPTER 9

Don't Pay The Ferryman

"Cities here are rather different from the cities at home. There's not any high houses and we haven't seen one single boring block of apartments. Most of them seem to live in villas, even in Auckland. The city is bigger and there's more shops.

"Marika, how did you celebrate the "valentine day"?...the shops here in New Zealand seem to earn good money on this day. They have a lot of signs with hearts on them in almost all the windows and on the radio they are talking about it all the time, that you are supposed to buy a flower (maybe a tulip or rose) for someone that you like a lot.

"We haven't got a tape recorder here. When we come home I may have to spend days and nights by the stereo. Please play all the songs for me when we come home. I heard a song with Chris de Burgh right now, it was really good, I think it was something with "Missing You" in it, about a guy who said goodbye and when he discovered after that that he still loved the girl it was too late because she'd found another. The song is starting with him sitting by a table with some roses and wine on it, all by himself, thinking back..."

– letter from Heidi Paakkonen,
February 14 1989, Invercargill

Often crimes these days are solved CSI-style, with forensics teams and DNA scientists crawling over the evidence and nailing someone on a microscopic flake of skin transferred during a touch. As you might have guessed by now, this wasn't one of those crimes.

Apart from the clothing and rubbish that Tamihere had admitted discarding at the Tararu track carpark when he stole the Swedes' car, initial searches of the track, the junction area known as the 'Jam Tins' and Crosbie's Clearing had turned up nothing.

As we noted earlier in the book, thirty men scoured the 4.6km Tararu Creek Road, adjacent Tararu stream, and bush between the road and the stream. A further team of six searched the Tararu track all the way up to a junction point known as the "Jam Tins".

Nothing was found.

On Queens Birthday weekend, the 3rd to 5th of June, a massive search team that included not just police and search and rescue but also Army troops from Papakura, covered "all tracks in the Crosbie's and Kauaeranga portion of the Coromandel conservation park…the total distance of track searched would be in excess of 100 kilometres, plus numerous streams and untracked areas were also covered."[90]

Search teams had been expressly asked to investigate bush and ground on either side of the tracks for things that may have been dropped or thrown, and to keep their eyes peeled for possible camp sites or off-track areas. They were told to go slowly and be thorough.

Again, nothing was found.

The July 11 arrest of David Tamihere on the car theft charge provided a new impetus, and John Hughes sent 28 searchers back to Tararu Creek Road for a "close contact" search of "adjoining farmland and adjacent bush…nothing of significance was found."

Crosbie's Clearing, where Cassidy and Knauf had reported their controversial sighting, was again gone over with a fine toothed-comb, literally, when a huge squad was helicoptered in at dawn from the Operation Stockholm base at Thames, on Saturday 22 July.

---

90 Brief of Evidence, John Cassidy, Depositions hearing May 1990

```
                    LEGEND
    ■ A    MINE SHAFTS SEARCHED
    ━━━━━  SEARCHED  28/5/89   Sunday
    ━━━━━            29/5/89   Monday
    ━━━━━            3/25/6/89 (Queen Birthday w/e)
    ▨▨▨▨             15/7/89
    ▨▨▨▨           · 21-23/7/89   (......  gullies.....)
    ▨▨▨▨           · 29/7/89   (Pearce found jacket)
    ▨▨▨▨           "  2-16/8/89
    ▨▨▨▨           "  21-28/9/89
    •----•         "    4/3/90
```

"Searching was done to a grid pattern using string lines," S&R coordinator John Cassidy – the man who said he'd seen a man and woman putting up a tent at Crosbies – later testified in court. There'd been brief excitement over the discovery of a mound, but instead of a grave police found only litter buried by a tidy camper. The team continued their sweep on Sunday 23 July.

"Despite the thoroughness of the searching, there was no trace of the Swedish tourists detected."

The trail seemed to have gone cold, until search and rescue volunteer Graeme Pearce made a personal pilgrimage back into the area the following weekend, Saturday 29 July.

"As far as I was concerned, all the searching was officially called off the weekend before that," Pearce later testified. This trip was done on his own initiative.

"I said to my wife, 'I feel I have to go up there and have another look and get it out of my system'."

Pearce ferreted around the Jam Tins area, having taken around an hour and a half to get there from the end of Tararu Creek Road. It was towards the end of his search – he was anxious to get home to

Missing Pieces

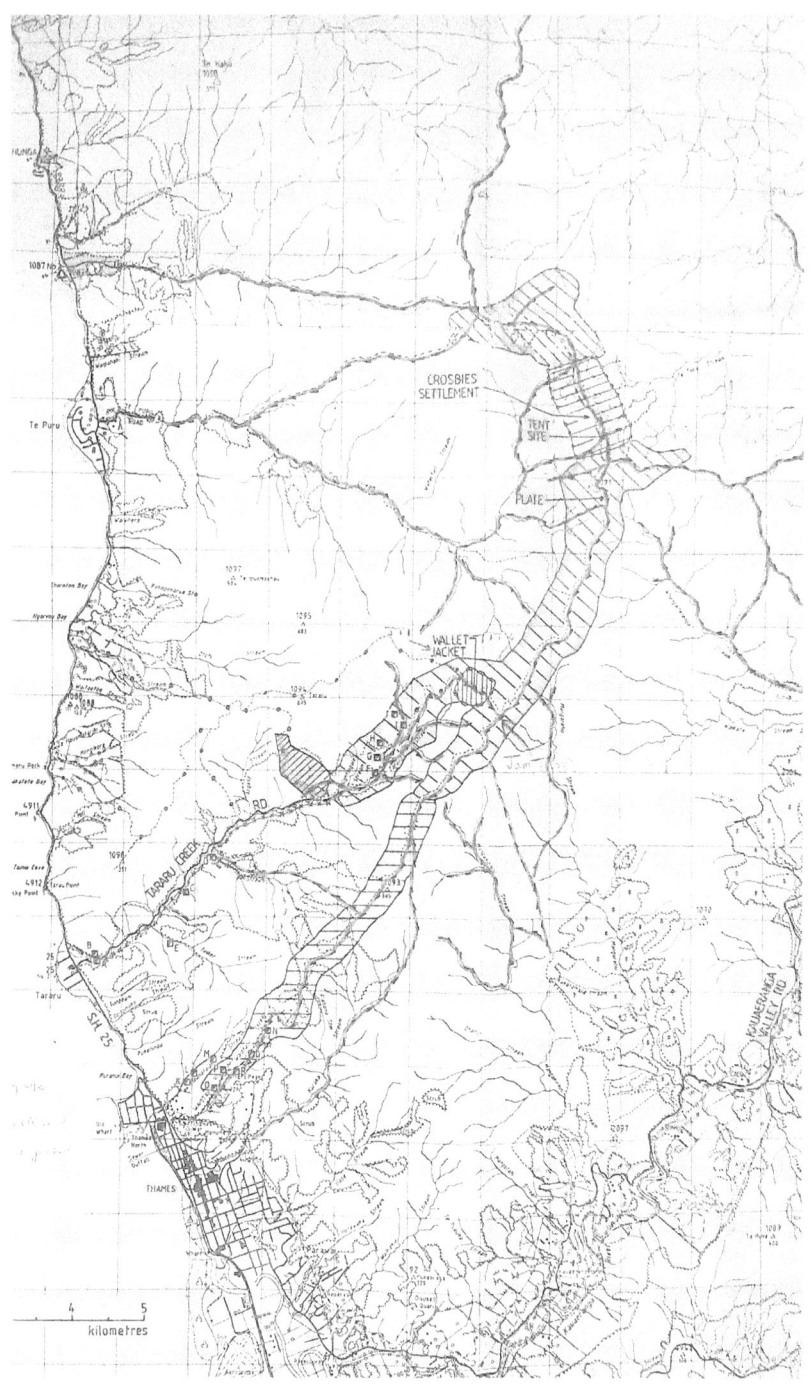

watch an All Blacks test – that he chanced down an animal track, "very small trail" on his left just as he was leaving the Jam Tins on the Tararu track. He told the court he went maybe three metres down the track but couldn't see anything else and turned around to come back. As he did so, there it was, a neatly arranged blue jacket:

"It was just sitting there, it was about so square," he indicated with his hands, "folded up, and it was sitting on the ground."

"When you say 'folded up'," asked the prosecutor, "describe to us whether it was lying in a crumpled state or otherwise?"

"No, it was folded into a square, about 12 inches, it wasn't crumpled or anything, it was as you would find something folded in someone's pack or similar."

Checking the label and finding it was Italian-made, Pearce realised it could be evidence. He placed the neatly folded garment into a plastic bag, marked the spot he'd taken it from with some of his own rubbish, and hightailed it back to the Operation Stockholm base.

"When you lifted the garment from the ground, what was underneath where the garment had been?" asked the prosecutor.

"Only just dead leaves and the normal things you find in the bush. There was no plants growing in that area, just dead leaves and humus or whatever they call it, the thickness of leaves on the ground...there were a couple of dried leaves on top of it and it was quite damp, but nothing else to indicate anything."

Police immediately dispatched Det. Sgt. Derek Read and Detective Devoy, along with some members of the volunteer search and rescue team, and they tramped

Heidi Paakkonen wearing the jacket found the weekend.

back into the area with Pearce. As police sniffed around the area where the folded jacket had been, Devoy noticed a nearby photo on the ground, and beside it a "black, fold-over wallet". The photo, and another close by, were of Urban Hoglin and one of Heidi's family. The wallet was Heidi's. Missing from it was the remainder of $150 she'd withdrawn from the BNZ Waihi the week before she disappeared.

More searchers were brought in, including the Army, who, making their way further up the track – an hour ten's tramp – towards Crosbie's Clearing, discovered cooking utensils and plastic plates and a Woolworths label for a bag of red delicious apples. All of these items had been missed during the earlier grid searches. These items were only a metre or two to the sides of the track.

In December 1989, Randall Cornish, one of the men who'd been tyre-kicking the Subaru on the afternoon of April 9 at Tararu Creek Road because of the for sale sign on the car, returned to the road and ended up exploring a barn up the track.

"In the rear room, in front of a pile of old sofas and chairs, I found a nylon tent…and took it outside and unrolled it and saw Tysklind Sweden written on it."

The tent was wrapped up in its silver fly…it was just bundled up and had been stashed in the shed. Police had searched the barn in June 1989 and found nothing. David Tamihere was already in custody in Auckland by that stage – although police had not yet linked him to the disappearance of the Swedes. Police returned to the barn on 20 July to conduct forensic tests at the barn. Still they did not find the tent that Cornish located five months later.

In true CSI style, police had a humdinger of a case to try and unravel.

Lisa Melia was the DSIR forensic scientist attached to the Operation Stockholm investigation. With no bodies, police effectively had no crime scene. Or to be more accurate, they had a very large crime scene in which finding clues was like searching for the proverbial needle.

One of the first tasks Melia had was to conduct Luminol testing on a number of possible crime scenes and items. The large barn near the start of the Tararu track, for example, had to be checked.

"Screening for blood involves spraying 'reagent' on the area to be examined," Melia explained to the court. "This is done at night in total darkness. Areas of blood – and especially old blood – will fluoresce. I sprayed the walls, floor and all objects present in the shed with the reagent. The reagent also causes items like lichens or in this case bailing twine to fluoresce. Generally this non-specific fluorescence can be differentiated from fluorescence which blood may give.

"The test actually works better when the blood stain is up to six months old, rather than new blood, and blood up to three to five years will still fluoresce."

The only thing glowing in the barn that night, however, was the lichen and the twine.

A bigger challenge was Luminol testing of the open countryside. When Heidi's jacket and wallet were discovered in the area up the Tararu track known as the Jam Tins, Melia and her team were brought in the next day.

They sprayed areas of the clearing including bush and foliage, in the dark winter night, but the only things lighting up were pockets of native glow-worms.

Testing of Heidi and Urban's backpacks was more promising, but only slightly. One of the packs had a small bloodstain on the lower right outside of the pack. "The blood was of human origin," Melia testified. Significance? There was insufficient blood for scientists to discover the blood group, and given that Heidi and a fellow tramper had been injured in the South Island after slipping down a bank, any blood from that could have been accidentally transferred. Given that the packs appear to have been untouched in the back of the car when witnesses saw it at Tararu Creek road, it's highly unlikely to be related to their murders. Melia testified the small size of the bloodstain on the pack was consistent with a scratched arm brushing the pack while it was being carried.

The blue and white track suit jacket of Heidi's found at the Jam Tins yielded no blood, just heavy soiling from mud and it had started to rot after four months in the open. An old black wallet, thought to be Heidi's had begun to go mouldy. It contained a "card advertising a backpacker's hostel in Brisbane and a receipt for the purchase of a car, written on a Postbank withdrawal form. No blood was found on any of these items. The letter 'H' was embossed on the inside of the wallet."

From the couple's tent, mysteriously recovered from that barn on Tararu Creek Road in December 1989, the silver tent fly had "a lightning bolt-shaped cut at the apex of one flap. The cut was recent in appearance." Strangely, the green loops at the base of the fly, used for securing it with tent pegs, had been cut off, and again the damage was recent, in the sense that the fly probably had not been used since.

Melia told the court three loops on each side of the fly had been cut off, either with a sharp knife or heavy duty scissors. It is very hard to find an innocent explanation for why six metre-long tent strap loops had been lopped, given that the tent fly and the tent were found rolled up in the barn. Nor is it easy to explain a jagged zig zag rip in the main tent opening flap. But it does raise a glaring possibility that was never raised at trial: Heidi and Urban were attacked while asleep in their tent, not while they were walking. Why else would the tent be damaged? What better way to strike terror, than a knife blade suddenly ripping through the tent entrance? And if Heidi and Urban were in their sleeping bags in a cramped tent, they'd have been defenceless.

Lisa Melia found bloodstains on two places of the tent equipment. In the first instance, one of the tent guy ropes had blood on it, but this was found to be of animal origin. Precisely how animal blood got onto a tent guy rope will never be known. The couple's tent also contained a bloodstain on its roof. "The bloodstain appeared to penetrate the fabric from the inside," reported Melia. The patch was about 8cm square, but it was a smear rather than direct staining. "The blood had penetrated through to the other side of the fabric," explained Melia, "but I would still consider the stain to be a light stain given that the fabric itself is quite fine." The scientist testified the amount of blood was consistent with something like a cut thumb rubbing the fabric.

Of significance to the tent find is that no blood was found on the floor of the tent, which one would expect, nor were there any spots of blood consistent with those from a stab or a blow found in the tent. The blood was A+, consistent with Urban Hoglin's blood type but not David Tamihere's, who was type O.

In regard to the pair of Heidi's underwear briefs found cut on each side, which detectives initially noted turned the garment into a G-string design, the scientist commented: "The cuts in the panties were possibly cut by a sharp edged instrument such as a knife but no further specific information could be obtained…if the cut was made by one action using scissors, as opposed to several chops, this could be a possibility." Based on microscopic analysis of the ends of the fibres, Melia said she did not believe the garment had been worn or washed since it was cut.

Despite the wallet having been in the open for months, forensic scientists were able to lift four fingerprints from the wallet and its contents. Two of those fingerprints belonged to Heidi Paakkonen, the other two fingerprints were unidentified, all of them from pieces of paper in the wallet.

"Clearly you would have compared them with the prints from Mr Tamihere?" queried Colin Nicholson QC.

"I did, there were no matches," confirmed Kevin Sturgeon, a police fingerprint analyst. "None of the identifiable prints belonged to the accused."

In her examination of David Tamihere's property, including the two knives and tomahawk many Crown witnesses had seen with him in the bush, no blood was found on the weapons.

"In the course of your experience as a forensic scientist," asked Nicholson, "have you examined knives which appear to have been washed and yet have found that some minute traces of blood still remain?"

"Yes I have," confirmed Melia.

"And could you find even minute traces of blood on that knife or its pouch?"

"No."

Of the bone-handled hunting knife with the brown sheath, there was no blood on either the knife, the handle or inside the sheath. Likewise a Swiss Army knife. Did you find any blood in any of the traverses of the pocket knife, Nicholson wanted to know.

"No."

"Are there any surfaces," queried Nicholson, looking at the tomahawk, "on that which are particularly receptive to retaining blood?"

"The handle itself has a pattern of grooves marked on it, I would expect blood possibly to be trapped in those," she answered, "also the area where the handle of the tomahawk meets the blade is an area where blood is often located."

"And any even minutest particles of blood found there?"

"No."

Which brings us to the Subaru car.

Lisa Melia was tasked with finding any evidence in the vehicle. The first thing she checked for was blood. If the bodies of Heidi and Urban had been transported in the car, traces of blood from them should have glowed in the dark under luminol testing. Nothing was found.

The big issue with the car was whether Tamihere was telling the truth about breaking into the car with a length of No. 8 fencing wire, and whether Tamihere was stretching coincidence too far by claiming to have found some car keys in the glovebox.

On the keys, the testimony was interesting. The Crown's case is that Tamihere must have opened the car door with "the" key obtained from the dead Swedes.

Per Eric Andersson, who sold the couple the Subaru in December 1998, gave them only one key and warned them it had a crack in it, "but it should be OK".

What would you do if you'd just spent your life savings on a car you planned to travel to the back of beyond in, in a strange country, and you had only one, cracked, key between you? What would happen if you planned to go tramping in the South Island somewhere and you took a fall down a bank or into a river and lost "the" key?

Absence of evidence (the lack of definitive proof that the couple got more keys cut) is not evidence of absence. In other words, it's possible and some would say probable that prudent tourists – like Urban and Heidi – would have ensured they had a spare for all contingencies.

Sharon Stray, a Canadian tourist who hiked around the South Island with the couple, wasn't aware of a cracked key, and told the court the couple's key ring had up to four keys on it when she saw it.

Tamihere needed a key to drive the vehicle, because even this 1976 model Subaru had a steering lock that couldn't be bypassed without smashing the ignition column open, which had not been done.

Tamihere claimed he initially only broke into the car to grab some food, but realised he'd lucked out when he stumbled across a set of two keys in the glovebox. Had Urban and Heidi split the set of four into two sets of two? We simply don't know. Would the couple normally leave a spare set in the car, or would they carry a set

each? Again, we simply don't know. We don't even know what other things they had keys for, if any, and whether they would want spare sets of those.

Stray and her partner Ron Lewis testified they normally saw Urban with the keys as he did most of the driving.

Much was made at both depositions and trial of the fact that the Crown had been unable to break into the car using a piece of wire.

Among those consulted by police was Graham Doggett, Subaru NZ's National Service Manager. He spent an afternoon under police supervision trying to break into the Subaru using wire passed down through a 2cm gap in the window, but simply couldn't do it.

"In my professional opinion," he wrote in his statement, "it would not be possible to unlock the driver's door of Subaru HF8593 using a piece of No. 8 wire placed through a 2cm gap in the window. The toggle switch is too stiff for this to be successful."[91]

Next batter up was Bruce Hing, a Ministry of Transport vehicle inspector and qualified mechanic. "The wire wasn't strong enough to activate the lock and it just merely slipped off." He told the court at Depositions that it would be "impossible" to open the door using No. 8 wire through the window. He told the jury in the murder trial that his opinion had not changed.

The final Crown witness, forensic scientist Barry Axon, had a dif-

---

91   Statement of Graham David Doggett, 31 July 1989

ferent story to tell – he had indeed broken into the car, in a scenario with similarities to Cinderella's slipper. His colleague Lisa Melia wondered out loud whether Axon thought he could break into a car or not. She didn't tell him others – including Subaru itself – had failed. Sure, said Axon, always up for a challenge. He'd had to stand at an awkward angle to do so, and jiggle the door handle at the same time as trying to flip the switch with the wire, but he did it.

"Did you find that you could open the door with a piece of basically No. 8 fencing wire through a gap of one inch in the window?" Colin Nicholson asked with a barely concealed triumphal smirk. This was, after all, a Crown witness.

"Yes, in the way I described," confirmed Axon.

"And after that did you hear from the police and they came along and wanted you to repeat the opening exercise?"

"That is correct, yes."

Nicholson looked across to the jury, put his finger to his lips thoughtfully, rocked on his toes briefly, and decided to enjoy the moment some more.

"With your own ingenuity and intelligence you were able to get a piece of No. 8 wire, shape it and put it in, and open the door?"

"Correct."

Given the Crown's stated claim that opening the door with a wire was impossible, Axon's evidence was a kind of inconvenient truth.

The coup de grace on breaking into Subaru cars, however, was delivered by forensic scientist Rory Shanahan, a former senior DSIR expert and another graduate of the Crewe murders investigation 20 years earlier. Shanahan had been hired by Tamihere's defence team to see if he could break into the car using fencing wire.

Initially, Shanahan said he couldn't do it, but he went back to David Tamihere and asked him precisely to illustrate how he'd done it.

"The discussion lasted about five minutes," the scientist later testified. "I suppose he gave me a verbal description of how he constructed the wire, he also sketched it on a piece of paper."

The police had never bothered to ask Tamihere exactly what he'd done, so when the Crown's experts tried to replicate it they were flying blind. For Shanahan, Tamihere explained how he had bent and twisted the wired around its shaft to provide extra strength, and created a loop in the twire at the bottom which he used to rock the toggle switch on the door.

Even armed with that information, however, Shanahan couldn't open the car. As a last resort, the defence gained permission for a handcuffed Tamihere to come and demonstrate on the car itself. The prisoner started with a long length of wire, and proceeded to shape and mould it for the exercise. "At all stages he had some difficulty because he was handcuffed to one of the prison officials," remembered Shanahan.

Just as Tamihere was about to flick the lock and open the car, court officials stepped in and ordered him to step away from the vehicle. Nonetheless, Shanahan had seen enough to know what he had done wrong. A slight tweaking of the shape and a few extra twists around the shaft, and his own wire finally worked the next day. The forensics guru told the court he'd become quite adept at car conversion as a result of the lesson:

"I timed myself on three tests…and the average of three attempts was 25 seconds."

While none of this had a bearing on how David Tamihere had fortuitously ended up with a set of the Swedish couple's car keys, it did prove that the Crown had been wrong to claim it was impossible to break into the car using a wire.

Something else to consider. If the Crown's contention is correct, then Tamihere never broke into the Subaru using a wire at all; he would have used the key stolen from the bodies of Heidi or Urban. However, without having seen the car in over a year, Tamihere was able to describe to Shanahan in detail how to shape a length of No. 8 wire for the precise circumstance of opening the 1976 Subaru with the rocker switch. Not only that, when finally taken to the car in handcuffs, Tamihere was able to show the experts exactly how he'd done it, without fumbling around and trying different things.

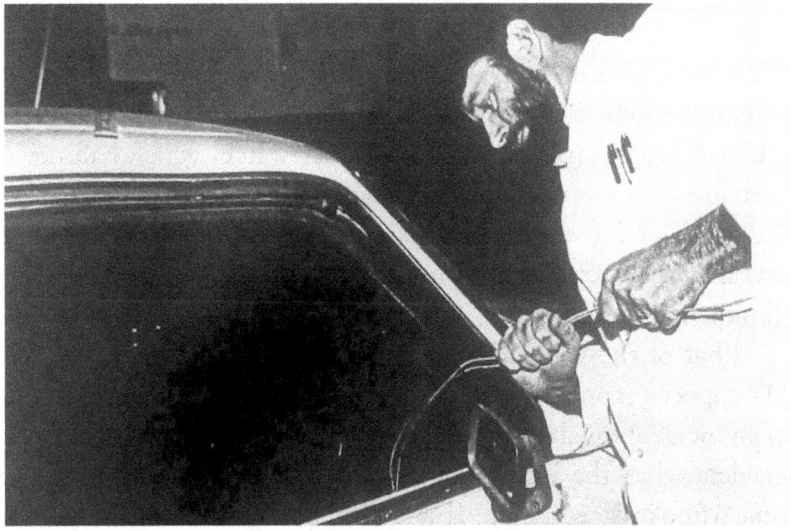

The fact that Tamihere was able to do this from memory suggests he'd done it before, and if he'd had to do it before then he clearly had not had access to a key.

The other major piece of evidence the Police had against Tamihere was a piece of evidence they actually did not have: a men's watch.

When Tamihere had returned from the Coromandel, shortly before his arrest, his wife Kristine had taken a boarder – Duane Davenport – to help pay the rent. Davenport remembered David Tamihere being seated at the kitchen table at the Blockhouse Bay flat when Tamihere's ten year old son Jon came running up to him.

"He seemed excited, like a kid with a new toy or something like that, and he came up to me and said 'Duane, look at this watch Dad gave me!'"

Davenport says he examined the watch for 10 or 15 seconds, then returned to making a cup of tea. He says Jon Tamihere moved a couple of feet away, "and apparently the watch had an alarm or beeper on it and he was playing around with that, and Dave told him to stop playing with it or he will run the battery down."

"Had you seen Jon with that watch before?" asked assistant Crown Prosecutor Paul Davison.

"No."

"Did you see him with that watch after that occasion?"

"No, that was the only time I saw it, that Saturday morning."

Urban Hoglin had a 1981 men's Pulsar watch, which had never been found. It was the Crown's contention that Tamihere had stolen the watch and given it to his son. The biggest problem for police was that they couldn't find it. This was proof, they argued, that Tamihere disposed of it.

"What of the watch?" prosecutor Morris asked the jury. "Mr Davenport got on well with the accused. He has a clear recollection of an incident involving a watch. Obviously his reference was to an incident when the accused came home…Do these things and the time it took place line up? If it is not Urban's watch Davenport is talking about, whose is it?

"Tamihere is not saying. He didn't say it didn't take place… the watch was remembered clearly by the lodger. He had no axe to grind…Don't look at this on its own. The watch – where is it? Which is the watch that was given to that boy?"

CHAPTER 10

Tamihere Cross-Examined

"A couple of days ago we passed Queenstown. Some 5,000 people live there, but there are probably more than 100 shops. Tourists from all over are coming there. River rafting in a rubber boat is very popular, and there's also a new thing that you can do. You tie a rubber band around your feet and then you throw yourself out from a 30 metre high bridge!

"Time flies too fast here and it's coming close now for us to be leaving for home. We are looking forward to all amenities though. We've been living in the tent since Christmas. I can't even remember how it feels to sleep in a bed."

– letter from Urban Hoglin, March 2 1989, Fox Glacier

Scotsman David Morris was a skilled courtroom orator. His rhetoric skills and confidence were like sniper's bullets when addressing a jury. To get a feel for it, take this exchange when he got to cross examine David Tamihere at the October 1990 murder trial. Tamihere, you'll recall, was the gamechanger in the search. The instant police knew a convicted killer and rapist had been in the area, they dropped their theory about accidental death like it was radioactive. The actions of John Hughes, as we've already established, were to pin this crime on Tamihere come hell or high water.

So listen to Morris demanding to know why Tamihere had not

been a good citizen and helped out with the search – on the basis that the couple had accidentally become lost – after being arrested for the car theft:

MORRIS: "Tell me this. In any of the interviews with any of the police officers, did you suggest to the police any place in the Coromandel where they might have gone off the track?"

TAMIHERE: "No, well I would have been able to suggest, but that's not what we were talking about."

Tamihere is correct. What the police had actually asked in the interviews was "Tell us where they are buried, then". Knowing that, but knowing the jury didn't, Morris continued to cast his spell:

MORRIS: "That's what I was asking about."

TAMIHERE: "No, because there was no question as far as the police were concerned of walking off the track or accidents."

MORRIS: "What I'm saying is this, you knew you were the number one suspect, you told me that you knew this area like the back of your hand, did you ever say to the police, 'Look, go and have a look up there, they could have gone off there'?"

TAMIHERE: "No."

Imagine the number of "wasting police time" charges Tamihere could have faced by simply making guesses about where the Swedes might have had an accident. Imagine the field day Morris would have had as Crown Prosecutor: "Ladies and gentlemen of the jury, the accused repeatedly sent police on a wild goose chase, enabling the trail to go cold and wasting valuable taxpayer resources and time.."

What Morris in fact said next was fairly similar:

MORRIS: "Can you tell the ladies and gentlemen of the jury why you didn't make a decent suggestion to find these bodies?"

TAMIHERE: "One, they didn't ask, they never ever asked me whether alternatives could have happened, and two, I wouldn't have helped those guys [the police] across the street."

MORRIS: "Even if it meant getting you off a murder charge?"

TAMIHERE: "Yeah, I'd gone quite a long way towards helping them and it still wasn't changing anything was it."

MORRIS: "Weren't you prepared to even make a suggestion to where this couple might be, to help you get off a murder charge? Weren't you prepared to volunteer that?"

TAMIHERE: "I wouldn't have known where they were. Any alternative apart from me killing them was never brought up by police."

MORRIS: "But that's what you are asking this jury to believe, that they might have just wandered off the track!"

TAMIHERE: "No, I'm not saying anything, even in my statements I never said they would have wandered off and got lost until today."

MORRIS: "You never have even raised the possibility until today?"

TAMIHERE: "No, the only reason it was raised today is because you raised it."

In that exchange for the jury's benefit, Morris instantly put Tamihere on the back foot, defending himself from what was in effect a straw-man proposition, almost akin to the old question, "Have you stopped beating your wife yet?" If Tamihere hadn't killed the Swedes, then he wouldn't know where their bodies were. At best he would be making a guess, and there were already plenty of seasoned Thames Search and Rescue trampers who knew the area better than Tamihere. More to the point, right from the first interview police were telling Tamihere he was the killer, and challenging him to reveal where the bodies were in that context. Yet, in this exchange, that context was lost.

At one point, Tamihere testified in a closed session that the jury were not permitted to hear, how John Hughes had come into the interrogation room, "going on about they had been getting information and it was time to tell them or to admit that I killed the Swedes, where the bodies were…[Hughes] told me like they weren't just going to get up and walk away from it or shelve it, they had unlimited resources they could use on it – the support of MPs, the Swedish government wanted a result, the tourist board were willing to contribute money as well to it.

As Tamihere explained, this was on the afternoon of July 26 1989, the day he appeared in the Thames court on the car theft charge.

John Hughes warned him, he said, that opposition police spokesman John Banks "was going to stand up in parliament and read my track record out". Tamihere alleged Hughes also threatened to charge "the missus with harbouring me" and that police would start "putting the heat" on his family publicly.

Hughes, he said, also made a "bet…that I will hang myself or kill myself", and he told Tamihere that his iwi, Ngati Porou were "pissed off" with him and that they'd had "a big meeting and they were going to put a tapu on the Coromandel until I came up with the bodies". Hughes, he said talked of "the sort of effect more charges would have on my sons".

One of the surest strategies in a courtroom is to make your opponent look like a liar. Morris' next major play on Tamihere did just that. Tamihere had told police, and insisted right the way through the entire process, that when he came upon the Swedes' car he had felt the exhaust pipe to get an idea of how long it had been there.

In the great scheme of things, the comment didn't mean much. If he hadn't mentioned the exhaust pipe at all the case against him would not have been any stronger or weaker. We know April 10 was a hot sunny day, somewhere around 20 degrees. We know the sun was on the bonnet of the car, making the warmth test there useless, so Tamihere tried the tailpipe. He knew the car had been there at least an hour and a half, because nothing had passed him on his journey up the Tararu Creek Road. He told the jury the exhaust pipe "still felt warm" when he stuck his finger on the inside of the pipe. Instantly, Morris was on the attack:

MORRIS: "Did you say anything to the police about putting your finger into the exhaust pipe?"

TAMIHERE: "Yes I did."

MORRIS: "Not in the statement, is it?"

TAMIHERE: "Yeah, but I'm not responsible for what they're writing down, though."

MORRIS: "It's not in the statement is it?"

TAMIHERE: "No, it's not."

MORRIS: "It's a statement you initialled, isn't it?"

TAMIHERE: "Yeah, that's right."

MORRIS: "The officer was asking you questions and noting down your answers, is that right?"

TAMIHERE: "Well, not every answer or question that was asked."

If Morris' theatrics had any actual legitimacy, the credibility of his entire Crosbie's Clearing sighting by Cassidy and Knauf would be out the window on the same basis, given that much of what they eventually claimed was never in their first statements. We have already examined how police statements were written up by police based on answers they had noted down by hand. At that time in New Zealand, witness statements were not recorded on tape. It gave police huge freedom to draft statements. Morris, however, was taking the high ground of moral outrage.

MORRIS: "Are you now saying that this is not a complete record of those questions?"

TAMIHERE: "Well, actually no, it's not. It's not a complete record of everything that was said or asked, it's a fairly good summary of it but there was an awful lot that was said and asked that wasn't written down."

MORRIS: "Are you saying that the officer has missed these things out, even though he was obviously after a detailed account from you?"

TAMIHERE: "Yeah, he has."

MORRIS: "Which officer was that?"

TAMIHERE: "The whole three of them. I told them twice about feeling the exhaust, once here and once again in Thames – twice in Thames."

MORRIS: "Are you saying that all these three police officers, that's Detectives Beard, Kiely and Matthews, put their heads together to not put this in?"

TAMIHERE: "No, I'm saying they were told and it's not here and they weren't writing down everything anyway."

Again, Morris has made it Tamihere the suspect's word against that of three upstanding police officers. The exhaust pipe issue was essentially meaningless, but it was a perfect credibility hit on Tamihere. Morris pulled a similar stunt on Arthur Allan Thomas who was challenging what was later established as fabricated testimony from John Hughes and other police officers in that case. Have a read of this passage from the book on the Crewe murders:

> *In and of itself this wasn't significant, but it grew from a bone of contention to a baseball bat of contention over credibility. When Thomas protested in court that Hughes was mistaken over his testimony or lying, Crown prosecutor David Morris sneeringly invited the jury to 'behold a man' who claims everyone else is lying but him. As a farmer, Thomas should have appreciated what was happening. The wolf was separating the vulnerable one from the rest of the herd, destroying any sympathy the jury might still have for him. Its impact was devastating.*
>
> *As history in fact records, the police officers were lying. It was a very effective wind-up to make Thomas look even more guilty in the eyes of the jury.*[92]

Crown Prosecutor Morris and Detective Inspector Hughes had been a tag-team for decades. There are actually huge similarities between their behaviour on the 1970 Crewe murders investigation, and their behaviour on the 1990 Swedish tourists trial. In the Crewe murders, Hughes and his detectives lied on oath, planted evidence and fabricated notes and statements. At one point, Arthur Allan Thomas, like David Wayne Tamihere, was accused by Hughes of stealing the dead man's watch. In both cases this was later proved wrong, but only after the trials had convicted both men.

Morris was in fine but predictable fettle against Tamihere:

"So [SWA] is lying is that what you are saying?"

---

[92] See *Arthur Allan Thomas: The Inside Story* by Ian Wishart, Howling At The Moon Publishing, 2010, p135

"Yes."

"And this lady has got it all wrong?"

"Yes."

In the "voir dire" – a cross examination of Tamihere the jury were not allowed to see or hear – assistant Crown Prosecutor Paul Davison challenged the accused:

"It's important to you to try if you can to prevent this evidence [the disputed police interview] from being heard by the jury."

"Well, only in so much as that you guys are saying to this court that 'this is a true and accurate account of what happened'. Now I am saying it is not, but I can't prove it though, which makes it pretty dodgy."

"Are you saying you didn't say these things to the police?"

"Exactly…I'm saying what the police are saying is that I told him the bodies were up there and I refused to tell him where, and I'm saying I didn't say anything like that at all."

Reprising his Crewe murders sneer when proceedings went back on the record, Morris invited the jury to behold a man who claimed everyone else was lying except him:

"Everyone else is out of step, who does not agree with him."

Tamihere had already admitted lying about not stealing the car, so painting him as an even bigger liar for the jury came easy for Morris. It didn't matter whether he was telling the truth in everything else, his credibility was damaged.

Morris moved through the key evidential points with Tamihere. Take the panties exchange:

MORRIS: "If what you tell us is correct, these cut panties had been carefully put away in a bag of clothes…you said you got them out, threw the stuff out of a bag."

TAMIHERE: "No I didn't. The only evidence was they were in a bag with other clothing. Now, I said I didn't see them so I may have thrown them – well, obviously I did throw them – I was saying I didn't put them in the bag."

MORRIS: "But you got them out of the bag, if your evidence is correct, to throw them."

TAMIHERE: "No, I just threw the bag away."

MORRIS: "Whatever you did with them, if what you are saying is correct this girl Heidi Paakkonen has gone to all the trouble of packing away a useless pair of panties, right?"

TAMIHERE: "Yeah, but taking your step of it further, I've done even sillier because I've gone and killed them up in the bush, carried the panties down, packed them away in a bag, and then thrown them out at the end of the track."

MORRIS: "You are saying that's what happened?"

TAMIHERE: "No, I'm saying that's what you're saying."

MORRIS: "If Mr Knauf and Mr Cassidy are correct you could have cut those off this girl before you raped her!"

TAMIHERE: "Yeah, but that's what I just said earlier – if they were correct, what you're saying is I took the time out to carry them [the panties] 12km out of the bush to throw them away at the end of the road, or pack them away first with the other clothes and then throw them."

In the heat of a courtroom battle, with prosecutor and suspect going head to head – a rare thing because guilty suspects almost never take the witness stand – the power of rhetoric, flourish and the right sneering tone can overwhelm the jury with the crackling emotion, such that the substance and nuance of the debate gets lost.

Cassidy and Knauf had given absolutely no testimony about the blonde woman's underwear, cut or otherwise, but Morris had suddenly made it seem as if they had.

If Prosecutor Morris is correct, David Wayne Tamihere went to all the trouble to commit the perfect crime, ensuring Heidi Paakkonen's body could never be found, yet took items away from the crime scene deep in the bush, back to a popular public walking track entrance, and dumped them there in plain sight, including Heidi Paakkonen and Urban Hoglin's name labels and clothes he had allegedly cut off the victims.

"If you had killed them up there on the Saturday would you agree you'd have plenty of time between then and Sunday afternoon,

Monday afternoon, to make a couple of trips to get their valuables and dispose of their bodies?"

"I'd either have to do one or the other, I'd say. Either get rid of the bodies or take the car. You can't do both."

But did he have enough time? Remember the testimony the jury never heard, from trampers Tony Goonan and Andrew McLean, who hiked into Crosbie's with their dogs on Saturday 8 April and camped there all night. They saw nothing, their dogs saw nothing.

Covering all bases, prosecutor David Morris dog-whistled the jury into wondering whether Heidi had met her fate at the Tararu Creek carpark, rather than Crosbie's Clearing:

"We know the panties were cut and at the top of the road were discarded by the accused. Do you believe she would retain a useless pair of panties? Isn't it extraordinary the number of things found cut in the same area as the labels. Were they cut when the panties were on her, and was she forced to put them in the back of the car?

"What do these cut panties indicate to you? Someone else? Unless he wished to remove the panties to have intercourse with her."

Would Tamihere have brought Heidi back to the car, raped her there, got her to pack her underwear away neatly in a plastic bag, then thrown the underwear out in the same place? All of this raises some really important points that, again, force readers to ask themselves the question: "What would I have done?"

If the Crown case is to be believed, David Tamihere made absolutely no attempt to distance himself from the heinous double murder he had just committed. Instead of destroying evidence in an incinerator somewhere, or dissolving it with acid, he leaves the victims' name tags around where they can be found, he steals their car and drives around in it, he keeps some of their belongings and takes them home, he sells the rest. He leaves behind some of Heidi Paakkonen's prescription medication, with her name on, at the Sunkist Lodge where he had stayed. When he was first arrested in Auckland on May 24 on the outstanding warrant, he openly told police where he had been.

"He said that he had been down in the bush in Coromandel for quite awhile," arresting officer Ross Johnson testified at the murder trial. "I asked him how long he'd been there, he replied about 8 or 9 months."

He could have said he'd been down in the King Country and police would have been none the wiser. But he didn't, he said Coromandel. If you had just committed a double murder, would you voluntarily cough to police that you'd been active in the area the bodies were?

In summing up, Crown Prosecutor David Morris continually honed in on Cassidy and Knauf's delayed identification of Tamihere, telling the jury that regardless of police hijinks surrounding the process, the men were now certain it was Tamihere they'd seen on Saturday 8 April. "He didn't recognise the accused in the montage, so what?" barked Morris.

"There was no formal identification parade, that is true. As Mr Hughes said, 'I was damned if I did and damned if I didn't'. Also that any identification parade would have been worthless because of media publicity."

What Morris carefully avoided was the inconvenient fact that Hughes had tipped off the *New Zealand Herald* within literally an hour of telling Tamihere they were going to charge him. Hughes did not have to leak that information to the newspaper, and if he hadn't the media would have received a huge surprise at 10am the next morning when Tamihere appeared in court. By telling the *Herald* in advance, Hughes knew a media pack would assemble and get photos. Hughes deliberately made an identification parade worthless by creating the media publicity.

Morris wasn't telling the jury any of this, preferring to pretend the police had been independent of the fiasco.

"There has been criticism that the police have allowed the press to get photographs of Tamihere. Where does that take you? The police don't control the press," he snorted.

Instead, said Morris, ignore all those studies on how witness memories can be contaminated, and concentrate on Cassidy and Knauf's certainty.

"The question is whether you are satisfied that this is the man, that you can accept the identification is reliable and positive and one upon which you are prepared to act."

In the style of an old door-to-door carpet salesman, Morris urged the jury to never mind the quality, feel the width! Look at how the secret witnesses back up Cassidy and Knauf!

"The ultimate question is the worth of the identification amongst the other circumstantial evidence. When you are looking at all this don't forget [Secret Witness C] who was told by Tamihere 'that he had Heidi at some stage in the bush and that a couple came across them and that he almost got sprung'."

It could be true. Morris could be right. Maybe the secret witnesses are all telling the truth and David Tamihere opened his mouth and yapped, not thinking for a moment that anyone would quote him. For all we know there could be some family trait amongst the Tamiheres where none of them ever realise there's a tape recorder on the table. Somehow, it seems unlikely. David Tamihere had served plenty of prison time, he knew the dangers of prison 'narks'. The essence of the Crown case is that Tamihere was cunning enough to pull off the crime, but stupid enough to immediately tell everyone who asked him, what he'd done and how he did it.

Back in the 1980s, New Zealanders were more prepared to give police the benefit of the doubt, but today it's hard to see how a case with so many holes created by the Crown could succeed. This case was brought to you by the team that fitted up Arthur Allan Thomas for a double murder he didn't commit. Always keep that in mind.

Tamihere's own evidence is that he knew very well there was 'a recorder on the table', and treated every fellow prisoner as someone with an agenda.

"I felt the only way I'd get charged was for the police to come up with one or more of these secret witnesses – an inmate jumping up and saying 'he told me this and he told me that'. Now, there were five or six guys in this part of [the prison] so I told each of them nothing very important…I told each of them something different, with the idea being that if it came up while I was getting questioned then I would know which ones were shouting to the police."

Indeed, Secret Witness C even claims Tamihere complained to him about the testimony of the other secret witnesses: "He regretted certain conversations he had with [Secret Witness A] in regards to the Swedish case."

And yet the jury were expected to believe that Tamihere – already gun-shy of jailhouse informants – still had a policy of once-bitten, twice-bitten, even three times bitten by allegedly repeating the same things he'd told SWA, to SWC.

Tamihere admitted discussing the Swedish case with Secret Witness A because SWA's son – also a criminal – had been in the area and was being questioned by police. The official police file confirms this, and Hughes – who was already using SWA as a jailhouse informant, undoubtedly played a part in getting Tamihere placed in an adjacent cell.

Tamihere drew sketches of Tararu Creek Road and the Crosbie's Clearing area – he says in response to SWA's questions about the areas his son was being "hassled" over. SWA, of course, testifies that Tamihere drew the sketches to boast about where he had attacked and raped the Swedes.

Under cross examination, SWA admitted the sketches lacked the features he claimed they were drawn to show:

"I asked him to draw it…so I could visualise what he was telling me that he did with the Swedish couple, and everything that he was telling me that took place up at Crosbie's or The Pines area that weekend."

"Let's look at those please, the first one…shows the Tararu Creek Road….has the top of the Tararu Creek Road a cross, and written in Mr Tamihere's writing the word 'car', is that correct?"

"Yes."

"And that confirms what he told you about finding the car at the top of Tararu Creek Road and where he found it, is that not so?"

"That's where the car was parked, yes."

"Look at the next one please, the one which shows a track with 'Tararu 12kms' at the bottom, and Tapu-Coroglen highway to the top."

"Yes".

"Now, is there any X marked there as to where this alleged rape took place?"

"No sir, he just pointed it out, see where the arrow's going? It says 'remains of forestry hut' into that area sir."

"Well, he put an X and wrote where he saw the car, didn't you ask him –"

"Oh, yes -"

"- 'could you put a cross and mark down where this raping took place?'"

"Again sir, I can only apologise for my incompetence."

"Well, the next one on the other side that shows The Pines area in more detail – there is no X there marking where anything took place, is there?"

"No sir, he never put any X there sir."

"Any mark indicating where he met the Swedes?"

"No, all he said was 2kms from the turn off to the Table Mountain, sir."

Secret Witness C's testimony, said the Crown, was key, yet the jury did not hear who Secret Witness C was, in order to test his credibility.

Crown Prosecutor David Morris told the jury the secret witnesses had testified because they were "disgusted" at Tamihere: "This was a lonely man talking to his mates. He said things that disgusted them sufficiently to break the prison code of silence."

Emotive stuff, especially for jurors who were easily led by Morris' oratory. Was he right?

SWC was actually a double-murderer. In the early 80s he had randomly shot a man in the back of the head, then called a 28

Missing Pieces

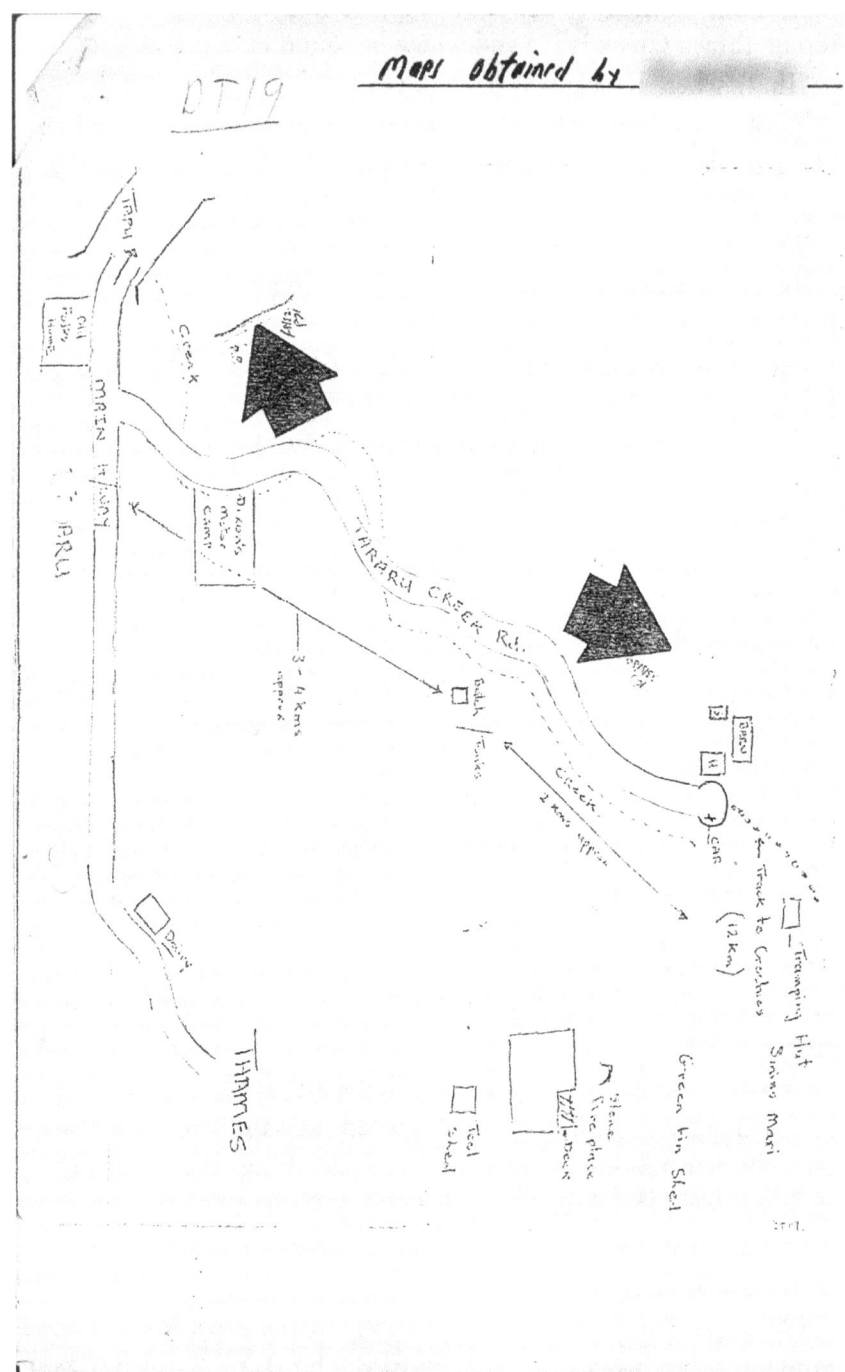

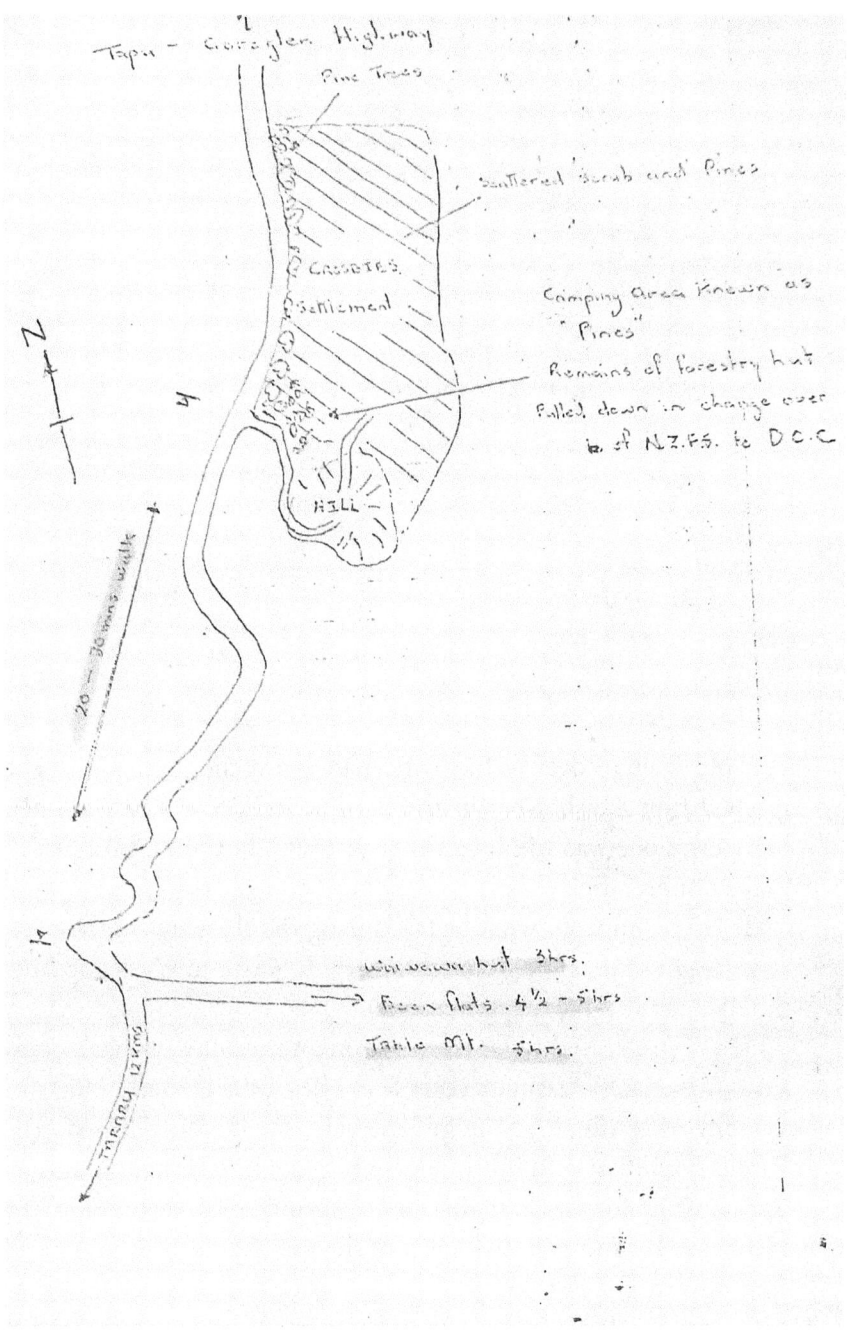

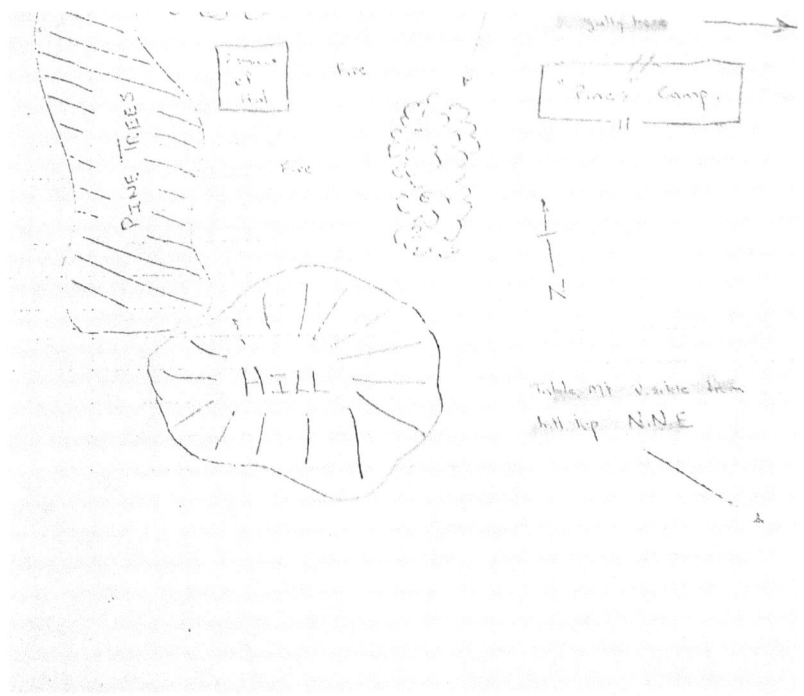

year old woman over to him who had heard the shot. When she reached him, he shot her in the head as well. She died instantly, but victim one was still breathing, so SWC shot him again just to make doubly sure.

He later compared what he felt during the slaughter to the pleasure he got from eating confectionery. It was a motiveless crime, purely a thrill-kill.

He's been released twice from prison and recalled on both occasions – the latest just four years ago when he was found guilty of sexually molesting a young girl the very day he was released. The Parole Board has refused to release him again so far, although he will come up for parole again in 2013, saying he has a record of bad behaviour behind bars and a gift of the gab that he uses to try and spin his way out of trouble.

This man, a double murderer and convicted child sexual offender, said in his statement to police about Tamihere: "I decided to tell the Police about what Tamihere has told me because I don't like what he did. He's nothing but a f***ing animal…in the old days he would of got the shit beaten out of him in prison for the things he has done".

Irony, thy name is Secret Witness C.

SWC added more fuel to the case in later years. In the mid 1990s he recanted his testimony to the murder trial, saying in an affidavit that the police had fed him all the information to say:

"[Det. Sgt. Sanderson told me things that would be beneficial to the Police. Sanderson told me about the blood stains on the tent which David Wayne Tamihere had supposedly concealed in a hut or shed. I as (sic) told about sexual activities involving the female Swede after the male Swede's body was supposedly disposed of. I was told that a watch belonging to the male Swede was given by David Wayne Tamihere to his son. I was told about trampers coming upon David Wayne Tamihere and the two Swede's and that at such time the female Swede was visibly distressed. I may have been told also about a body being dumped at sea. Sanderson wanted me to say that all of this had been told to me by David Wayne Tamihere. Sanderson said he would return with a typed statement for me to sign he also said that the officer in charge was the former Detective John Hughes on whose behalf, he acted."

SWC claimed he'd been offered money by police if he cooperated, and assistance with early parole:

"After David Wayne Tamihere was convicted as the supposed murderer of the Swedes John Hughes flew to Christchurch where I had been transferred, to support me at my parole hearing."

When the Police Complaints Authority commenced an investigation, SWC quickly changed his tune. Through his lawyer Lorraine Smith, he told the PCA that gang elements within the jails had threatened to harm him or his elderly relatives if he did not swear an affidavit accusing the police of corrupt behaviour, as above.

In a new statement to the PCA, he withdrew his affidavit, and instead wrote:

"I wish to apologise for bringing into question the integrity and the credibility of the Police pertaining to this matter. At the same time I would like it noted it all came about due to a life threatening sequences of events. That still concerns me and smoulders on my memory with unspeakable anguish.

"I know beyond question there was no improper conduct by Police investigators regarding myself and the evidence I gave …. Further, the Police did not produce me as a secret witness, I produced myself …."

Whatever the doubts that later sprang up around Secret Witness C, in December 1990 it was his testimony that the jury was told was reliable.

In summing up, David Morris laid into the Tamihere defence teams claims that the Novis and Waters sightings of a young couple in northern Coromandel were the missing Swedes. Apart from the timing conflicts, he told the jury, there was also the inconvenient issue of "boots".

"Mrs Novis wasn't sure whether it was Friday or Saturday that she saw them, but she describes boots. You will not see boots in any photos – merely shoes. Shoes which were bought [after a South Island tramp] after that trip.

"Remember the evidence – the police were required to make an inventory of assets. The resources to hand were a visa card and travellers cheques. All purchases were made under their visa card and accounted for. There were no boots purchased.

"There is nothing to show that Heidi had distinctive boots of any kind. There is no evidence to justify the conclusion that she purchased a pair of boots because it would have been on the visa card…there is no evidence to raise a reasonable possibility that she purchased boots before reaching Thames.

"If she didn't have boots, Mrs Novis didn't see Heidi."

Remember that line. Let it burn into your memory. We have covered part of this earlier in the book, but now, as the main Crown case draws to a close, it is time to revisit the boots issue.

Here's what Anne Novis testified for the Defence: "She had boots, and I thought they were commando-soled boots…they weren't sand-shoes or sneakers or anything, they were boots with proper soles."

Here's what Peter Novis said: "…blouse type top with light tramping boots".

Here's what BMW employee Steve Waters said: "They were wearing a tramping boot of some description, European-style of boot."

Got that so far? Remember what Morris told the jury: if they saw a woman with tramping boots, it wasn't Heidi, because Heidi did not have any tramping boots.

Morris made a huge play of that in summing up. When it came time to sum up on Cassidy and Knauf's identification of the woman at Crosbie's as being Heidi, Morris told the jury the two trampers were "solid types. Their actions show they were taking care. They were observing, and used to, the bush. Not put off by the rain from noting important matters."

Morris reminded the jury that some of Tamihere's witnesses only saw "the car and the girl [at Wilson's Bay] for about 5 to 10 seconds. Can we put a lot of weight on that when compared to a sighting which took place over 13 minutes?

"This is not a sighting from 50 yards away. It was man to man and face to face. Thirteen minutes by responsible and senior people… there is no question of bad light. Nothing to detract from the ability of the man to know who he is talking to.

"The girl? Well, the description fits apart from one or two items. No other man or girl was located despite the wide publicity."

It's in the bag, then. Or is it? What were those "one or two items" about the woman in Crosbie's Clearing that Morris quickly skipped past and which did not fit with what police knew of Heidi:

Cassidy testified: "I purposely looked at her feet and she had on a pair of light tanned boots or beige – what I might call beige coloured boots. They were rubber soled and would be quite appropriate boots for a girl to wear to the bush. They looked, I thought, like Paraflex brand boots, I've got a pair myself and they looked to be very similar to the ones I have."

Knauf testified: "She was wearing boots, that much I could see."

What should the jury have made of this "solid" eyewitness testimony, in light of Morris' warning that Heidi didn't have any such boots, and "if she didn't have boots, Mrs Novis didn't see Heidi".

It should have been that black and white. On the basis of the Crown's case, any blonde woman wearing tramping boots could not have been Heidi. No wonder Morris skipped over it in summing up.

Why didn't David Tamihere's defence lawyers have a field day with this evidence? Because they couldn't. Colin Nicholson QC had anchored his sightings of Heidi and Urban in the testimony of the Novis' and Steve Waters, all of whom had seen a woman in boots. It was impossible for Nicholson to attack the Crown's own contradictions without undermining his own case. He had no option but to leave it. The biggest clue of all that Heidi Paakkonen was not the woman at Crosbie's Clearing that April Saturday sank without trace.

Crown Prosecutor David Morris naturally urged the jury to find Tamihere guilty of double murder. Justice Tompkins was, equally naturally, more cautious in his summing up.

"The issue is clearly one of identification," he warned the jury, "and on that I am required to give you a very clear direction. It is this. I must warn you of the special need for caution before you find that the accused was the man at Crosbie's on that Saturday afternoon, in reliance on the correctness of the visual identification of him by Messrs Cassidy and Knauf.

"The reason why a judge always gives a jury that warning where there is an issue of visual identification is because experience has taught us that there is a possibility that where there are, as here, two identification witnesses, that both of them may be mistaken, and you must be alert to the possibility that a mistaken witness may yet still be a convincing witness.

"Let me refer first to the identification of the woman, and I just emphasise to you again that from the defence point of view, Mr Nicholson's submission, this is a crucially important issue.

"He emphasised that the opportunity to observe the woman was limited because she had the poncho around her face, remember Mr Archibald [Nicholson's co-counsel] put it on, you can see how it limits what you can see of a person generally. Of course, they didn't speak to her so there is no evidence about her accent.

"They did notice that she was wearing make-up and, of course, Mr Nicholson quite properly urges on you that that is a very significant observation, because Heidi did not normally wear make-up. She worked in the store in the make-up department and her sister-in-law said…she never wore bright colours. And when you look through all the photographs as far as one can judge from those, one does not get the impression of somebody wearing make-up so noticeable that two persons turning up at Crosbie's think 'my goodness, she's wearing make-up'."

No evidence had been found that Heidi wore make-up at all on her New Zealand trip, or that she bought or carried any with her. None was ever found.

"Even if there was this rather strange business of the man forcing her to put it on," noted Justice Tompkins, "where did it come from? How did the nail polish and lipstick and powder get there?"

The defence suggests, said Tompkins, "and you may think this may well be right, but it is bordering on the farcical to suggest that the man would have had it with him. Well, it is possible that somebody might have gone back to the car, it is possible she may have had it with her, although one would think that was not to be expected."

Of course, this Crosbie's sighting had been timed at 3pm on Saturday 8 April, yet a police intelligence analyst, Robert Mills, had testified he did not believe Urban and Heidi's car had arrived at Tararu Creek Road until late Saturday afternoon. On this point, the judge gave the jury an explicit instruction:

"We are not interested in Detective Mills' interpretation of the evidence. It is your interpretation of the evidence that counts…I suggest you disregard it completely.

On the breaking into the car issue, Justice Tompkins noted both Crown and Defence positions and invited the jury to make their own minds up:

"The case for the Crown is simply this – that the accused opened the Subaru door with the key he took from the Swedes. He didn't open it with a piece of wire, there was no piece of wire.

"The case for the accused is that the accused opened the door with a piece of wire the way it has now been shown it can be done, and found what may well have been a second key in the glovebox, and they may well have had a second key cut for a precaution, or because the one they received from Andersson was cracked."

Of the disputed police interviews, involving alleged comments that "I'd rather tell one of you" where the bodies were than Hughes, or similar, the judge warned the jury to be especially cautious of the police claims.

"There was a lengthy series of interviews he gave at Mt Eden Prison when he is alleged to have come out with that expression that I am sure you will remember, 'You'll find the bodies up there', and you will remember he immediately said, "That's not what I said! It was, 'if they're up there, you will find them'. And then it was later on the same day when he is recorded of making another statement, 'If you find their bodies buried on the bluff with broken necks, I'm in the shit'.

"Now, I haven't gone into great detail about the circumstances of each of those because the Crown doesn't really place any heavy reliance on them. There are always difficulties about short expressions that are not recorded in their full context."

The statements, said the judge, "were not [tape] recorded at the time and there was an argument about the precise words used, and when they are not accurately recorded at the time it is unsafe to place too much reliance on the precise words used."

It's interesting what else the jury didn't hear about that dispute.

In his Privy Council submissions, Tamihere took issue with the way the Crown had been allowed to downplay what he alleged was fabricated note-taking:

"Both Defence and Crown echoed [the judge's] remarks, during their respective summing ups," wrote Tamihere. "But this was far from what the jury should have been told, and forms the basis of my charge that Detective Kiely had lied, and did so with the full knowledge of his superiors and Crown Solicitors.[93]

"Unbeknown to Det. Kiely, he wasn't the only police officer present during our conversation in the Thames Police cells on 26 July 1989. His superior, Det. Insp. Hughes, had initiated an action codenamed 'Operation Outback'. This involved the placing of an undercover policeman alongside me in the police cells. He would also accompany me back to Auckland in a police van. His job was to record anything I said, and to endeavour to have me implicate myself in the disappearance of the Swedes.

"A situation then developed whereby at approx 8.30pm Det. Kiely tells his superiors that I admitted to the bodies being 'up there' (Crosbie's) and at approx 11.30pm Hughes' own man was telling him I hadn't.

"The Operation Outback file, at least the portion made available to the Defence, came about only after an oft-heated Voir Dire hearing in the final hours (literally) of the trial.

"Regardless of how the judge dealt with this, or the way in which the Crown backed away from this evidence, one fact remains: At the time Det Kiely was giving his evidence, the Crown were sitting on a file showing he was lying. And that, I submit, is perjury on the part of both Crown and Det. Kiely," Tamihere wrote in his Privy Council petition.

Again, it was something the jury never knew about.

On the subject of Urban Hoglin's watch, the judge was careful to point out how the police witness had given evidence that the watch

---

93 Submissions for leave to appeal to Privy Council, p51-52

Tamihere's son was playing with had an alarm chime that he heard go off. Tompkins then reminded the jury that Seiko, who distributed Pulsar watches in NZ, were unaware of any Pulsar analogue models with chimes on sale prior to 1984, while Urban bought his in 1981. But, said the judge, "he accepted in cross examination that an analogue Pulsar watch with an alarm may have been available in Sweden in 1984.

"The case for the Crown is that that was Urban's watch."

It had been a harrowing five weeks for the 12 men and women selected to try David Tamihere against the evidence. They had to endure some of the most gruelling testimony ever inflicted on a jury in regard to the alleged degradations performed on Heidi and Urban. One juror did in fact become physically ill as a result.

Could they overcome the power of such loathsome "evidence" (in the sense it was jailhouse hearsay) and look at the critical evidence more closely: if trampers Cassidy and Knauf had seen Tamihere, why did they say the man they saw had no moustache or a "small" one? If the woman was wearing tramping boots, as both witnesses were adamant, how could it have been Heidi when the Crown had earlier insisted she did not have such boots? What about the haircut discrepancy, or the fact that the woman at Crosbie's showed no evidence of crying or having red eyes, when she would have had only seconds to compose herself as Cassidy and Knauf walked up unexpectedly?

No evidence was presented about the couple's car being seen driving up Tararu Creek Road at sunset on Saturday 8 April, which may have been an oversight on the part of the Defence. But it meant the jury were in the dark on a sighting that would have cast doubt on the 3pm Saturday Crosbie's Clearing sighting. How could it have been Heidi deep in the bush at 3pm if she was still in the car at that time?

The jury retired to consider their verdict at 3.10pm on Monday 3 December 1990. As a matter of historical trivia, the 1990 calendar matches the 2012 calendar day for day. At 5.20pm on Wednesday 5 December, after a marathon three days, they finally had a verdict. Guilty on both counts of murder.

Imagine everybody's surprise, then, when Urban Hoglin's body turned up less than a year later, nowhere near Crosbie's Clearing, and in fact 73 kilometres away from it, with a major highway intersecting the bush in between. To make matters even more controversial, Urban Hoglin was still wearing his watch. He had not been cut into small pieces. He had not been killed by a lump of wood whacking him in the head. He had not been dumped at sea, and he had not been buried at the top of a cliff.

Every main plank of the Crown case was falling apart, and David Tamihere's lawyers wanted answers.

CHAPTER 11

Urban's Body Is Found

"We've been to Punakaiki where you can see some cliff rocks formatted as pancakes on top of each other. It was beautiful and unbelievable nature. It's changing vastly from snow-covered mountains to dry grass hills and even to rainforests.

"We decided to go and visit a guy that Urban met on a fishing tour in Australia, he invited us to stay the night at his house. Simon, the guy that Urban met in Cairns, was going to work so we got a key of our own and a house of our own. Urban made some pancakes and I listened to your tape.

"It's incredible that he trusted us and gave us a key and let us spend the time here all by ourselves. When they invite you to stay overnight and you say no, they can't understand that and they seem to believe that you are rude. To them it's obvious that you should say OK and you should feel at home.

"If it weren't for all these sandflies and the wasps, New Zealand would be the perfect country, almost anyway.

"How is it otherwise on the love front, have you seen Pinnen? I gather you were going to think about Pinnen when you listen to the songs with Chicago and Chris de Burgh. I've heard a really nice song here, but I don't know who's singing it or what the name is. It may be lucky that

Urban's Body Is Found

you can't hear it, because I have a feeling you would think it is a Pinnen song.

"Now I have to quit because Urban is trying to read it, it's better to fold the envelope fast!"

– letter from Heidi Paakkonen, March 11 1989, Nelson

The call to police came at 9.16pm on October 10, 1991. A Whangamata man reported his son had found a body while pig hunting up Parakiwai Valley, just across from the Wentworth Valley, several kilometres west of Whangamata township at the base of the Coromandel peninsula. The call centre passed on the information to Whangamata's local copper on duty that evening, Constable Jury.

By 9.30pm, Jury was in a car with Darren, the informant's son who'd found the remains, travelling out to the crime scene.

"On examining the scene from a distance of no less than two metres, I could see what was obviously a human skeleton and clothing consisting of some form of red pants and a black shirt. Skeleton was not touched in any way," Jury recorded in his notes.

As Darren told it, he and his mate James had been out pig hunting that night when they came across the skeleton.

The Thames-Coromandel area commander, Detective Inspector Lex Denby, was alerted to the find at 11.15pm that evening.

By 8.50am on October 11, pathologists and police were assembling from across the Waikato. As they surveyed the skeleton from various angles in daylight, certain things became obvious. Firstly, what was presumed to have been "a shallow grave" was not: the body had simply been left on the surface of the ground with no attempt to bury it. The shallow indentation was merely where the body had sunk into the ground as it decomposed.

The scene itself was a forestry plantation area comprising a sheltered pastoral glade with a mix of pines and eucalypts providing canopy cover. To the northeast, maybe 40 metres away, a large embankment rose to a steep bluff. The body was lying 36 metres into the glade off the forestry track.

The exposed bones, including the skull and femurs, showed "considerable weathering", leading the pathologist to speculate the body could have been there up to five years. Denby's file notes show there was no obvious "major injury to the skull", and no obvious damage to the rest of the bones save for the fact the skeleton had been trampled by cattle at some point, leaving hoofprints in the vertebrae above the pelvis. Underneath the jaw bone, detectives found a Maori bone carving on a leather thong.

On what remained of the left wrist, police located a men's Pulsar analogue watch. It had stopped at 7.30 on "SAM 15". "SAM", pointed out one of the detectives, could be the French word "Samedi", for Saturday. If so, it was a European watch.

There was evidence that rats had begun squirreling away some of the smaller wrist and hand bones in two burrows up to 34cm deep underground. These, too, needed to be located and cleared. Underneath the torso, as police gently extracted the bones from the remains of a black sweatshirt, detectives made a breakthrough:

"As the area immediately beneath the torso was examined, a gold wedding band was located by Sgt. Pritchard and handed to Det. Macky. The band was in a clump of roots and did not appear to be still around finger bones.

"Prior to the movement of the pelvis and leg bones, Det. Macky cleaned the wedding band and advised me that there was an engraving within the band, of 'Heidi 2.9.86'," reported Det. Insp. Denby. "The finding of this ring immediately raised the speculation that the remains were those of Urban Hoglin."

The moment he realised what he was dealing with, Denby tossed up whether to immediately stop the body recovery operation, or whether to keep going. With a police videographer and photographer already on site, and the pathologist, Denby figured there was no point stopping now. Plus, the skies were threatening imminent rain and he wanted the body excavated before the scene turned to mud.

At 5.45pm on October 11, after returning to Whangamata base, Denby rang Det. Snr. Sgt. Bruce Raffan over in Hamilton, who'd

Urban's Body Is Found

been second in command of Operation Stockholm. "The clothing, the watch and the ring, all sound as though you have found Urban Hoglin," Raffan replied. Within minutes, John Hughes had been called. By 8pm, Crown Prosecutor Paul Davison, Hughes, Raffan and Thames search coordinator John Cassidy had confirmed they were driving down in readiness for an 8am briefing at Whangamata the next morning, October 12.

Ever suspicious, John Hughes wanted to know whether the two men who'd found the body had any connection to David Tamihere. He instructed Whangamata police to reinterview the men and find out why they were really in the area that night and, in particular, "whether or not the finding of the remains was in any way a result of instructions/direction/information supplied either directly/indirectly from Tamihere or his associates."

Both men, Hughes knew, had drug convictions, including possession of cannabis for supply. One of them, James, "has grown cannabis for a number of seasons but never in that area". James was also a bone carver, and Hughes wanted to know whether the carving found around Urban's neck was his work, and whether he'd given such a carving to Tamihere.

Detective Ian Varley re-interviewed the men and came away confident that while they were dope growers, the Parakiwai Valley was not their patch and they were genuinely pig hunting that night. Neither man knew Tamihere, although James confirmed he knew a man named David Reid, who'd seen Tamihere in the neighbouring Wentworth Valley at one point. Reid had given evidence at the murder trial.

As he examined the scene, Hughes was painfully aware the body had not been buried on a cliff top. The nearest steep bluff was 39 metres away, which was too far for Hoglin to have been wandering along the top of the cliff and fallen down as well.

In a crime scene analysis, Det. Sgt. Win Van Der Velde made a number of findings. Firstly, that Urban Hoglin was unconscious or dead when placed where he was found.

"The body was dragged to where it was found, and was dragged by the feet, backwards...the legs were straight and fully outstretched... Both of the arms were outstretched in a forward direction, above the head, consistent with being pulled backwards, whilst arms were released, and the face was down."[94]

"The sweatshirt had concertinaed in an upward direction, consistent with being pulled backwards on his stomach. Through time, undergrowth and roots had grown through the sweat top, causing it to hold its shape."

So Hoglin had not been lifted into position, he'd been dragged there. Police inquiries were turning up other leads as well. They established the bone carving had been purchased only a week before the couple disappeared, which is why there had been no photos or awareness of it at the murder trial.

Checks of the Pulsar watch were also being carried out. When the battery was replaced, the watch began working as normal. Significantly, it had no chime or alarm function, proving once and for all it could not have been the watch that the Crown made so much of at Tamihere's murder trial. The watch had given up the ghost not from damage but simply because its battery had gone flat.

It had stopped at 7.28 on a Saturday 15th. "From the time of the disappearance of the owner of the watch in April 1989 until its discovery in October 1991," noted the forensics report, "the 15th of the month fell on a Saturday in five months. These were April 1989, July 1989, September 1990, December 1990 and June 1991."[95]

Had police thought about this dating on the watch for a moment, they would have realised the calculations were out regardless. Analogue watches with the physical date mechanism run the full 31 calendar days each month unless they are manually adjusted to compensate for differences in the lengths of each month. April of course has 30 days, as do June, September and November, and

---

[94] Job sheet of Det. Sgt W J Van Der Velde, 22 October 1991, "Body Scene Examination"
[95] Forensics report of Robert Winchester, 20 February 1992

Urban's Body Is Found

Hoglin was not alive to adjust it. If the device was still ticking in February 1990 it would have been thrown out a further three days right there. The watch may have thought it was stopping on Saturday 15, but it is certain to have been a different day altogether.

A post mortem on Urban's skeleton was conducted on 22 October 1991 at the Auckland City Mortuary. A trio of pathologists pored over the bones and wrote that they'd been able to reconstruct the entire skeleton, bar a missing bone, the hyoid from the throat, and several minor finger and toe bones, presumed taken by animals.

"No evidence of skeletal injury of any sort whatsoever was found during this examination…We conclude that the skeletal remains of Urban Hoglin, as examined by us, were entirely free of skeletal injury."[96]

Detective Inspector John Hughes just about fell off his perch. Were these esteemed forensic pathologists who'd worked on many cases with him suggesting Urban Hoglin had died of natural causes while wandering in the Parakiwai Valley, yet miraculously then dragged his own dead body backwards by the feet for several metres?

There wasn't even a broken neck to hang a murder on in these results. Fortunately for Hughes, he didn't have to wait too long for hard evidence of foul play.

---

[96] First post-mortem report on remains of Urban Hoglin, 22 October 1991

CHAPTER 12

A Frenzied Attack

"It's funny to see photos of Elin, Johann and Anna. We recognise Elin but Johann has grown so big that we hardly know him. Anna we think of as if she's still newborn, in spite of the fact that she's three months now.

"We have really a lot to do here, there's a lot we want to see but time is rushing by. We don't have any time to work. We tried to see a couple of days ago whether we could help someone with fruit picking but they already had all the people they needed and the season is over. It would have been good for the money, but we have enough to last until we get back. Instead of going to work we tried to find some gold, with meagre results as usual.

"The candle has burnt out now, so I have to end this letter."
– letter from Heidi Paakkonen, March 13 1989, Nelson

The first forensic results on Urban Hoglin's clothing came back on November 5, 1991, and they confirmed Urban may have died a violent death. DSIR forensic scientist Robert Winchester had been tasked with examining the clothes. He began with the black sweatshirt carrying the words "Unbelievable JC", inside of which was a pink t-shirt with the words Marco Polo. Both garments had been a polyester/cotton blend. In both, the natural fibre cotton had decomposed, leaving only the thin polyester layer as the trace remains of the garment.

A Frenzied Attack

"Mr Winchester indicated cuts to the left neck area of the clothing which he considered were consistent with having been caused by a knife. There appeared to be several cuts, with one in particular passing through both articles of clothing," John Hughes later noted.[97]

An expert in this particular field – violent, hacking stab wounds – was Stephen King, police were told, not the author but a forensic scientist based with the Metropolitan Police in London.

Urban had also been wearing underpants, red shorts and a pair of dark blue Lee jeans. Of the underpants, all that remained were the elastic bands, and of the jeans only the Lee label, a couple of front pockets, the zipped up fly and some studs were left. The best forensic clues, then, came from the red pair of shorts.

Robert Winchester told police he'd also found stab wounds in the waist-band of the shorts which, aside from the cuts, "were in remarkably good condition with little or no deterioration."[98]

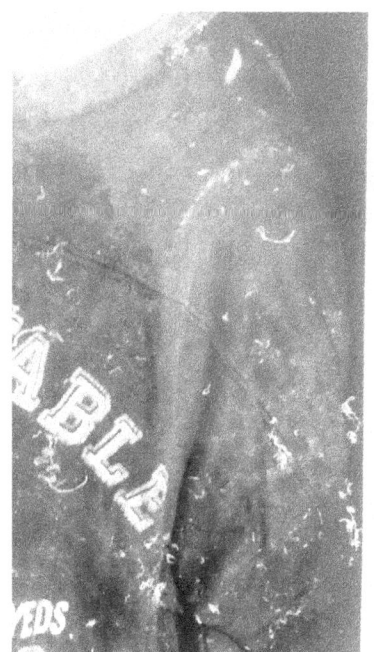

Stephen King, it turned out, was too far away to be of use in this particular horror story, but the DSIR had soon lined up another expert, Harry Harding at the State Forensic Laboratory in Adelaide. Harding was an expert in analysis of damage to fibres under electron microscopes with techniques so accurate that they could sometimes pick out marks on fibres left by tiny defects or nicks in a particular blade.

It was decided Winchester and Det. Sgt. Win Van Der Velde

---

97   Job sheet of Det. Insp. John Hughes, 7 November 1991
98   Job Sheet of Det. Insp. John Hughes, 12 November 1991

would take the slashed clothing to Adelaide for examination, with "exhibits to be sealed and labelled 'Homicide Exhibits' and carried in transit as hand luggage."[99]

They were taking a risk carrying dirt and flesh-encrusted clothing remains as carry-on luggage through Australian Customs undeclared, but Van Der Velde later boasted "Bag never challenged by Australian Customs".[100]

At the South Australian lab, Harding briefed the kiwis on what to expect. The scanning electron microscope would, he said, illustrate pulled fibres or blade-cut fibres, and clues could be gleaned from the type of cut patterns detected.

Arriving back in New Zealand, Winchester and the police officer again opted not to declare their macabre hand luggage and Van Der Velde recorded that "again, he was unchallenged by Customs on either departure from Australia or arrival in New Zealand".

Harding's comprehensive report and electron microscope photos were decisive, however.

"It was determined that the damage to the left shoulder and neck was likely the result of three stabs with a knife to that area… the simplest scenario which comes to mind would be a standing, frontal attack by a right-handed person, though other explanations are possible." Harding added that because he only had the clothes to work with, his report could only cover stab wounds delivered through the clothing. It was of course possible other stab wounds connected directly with skin on the neck.[101]

"The presence of multiple stabs suggests that they were deliberate."

One of those stab wounds appeared to have severed the leather thong holding Urban's Maori bone carving.

On the black sweatshirt, Harding studied a 20mm cut in the left shoulder of the garment in "a fore/aft direction", this hole being

---

99   Job sheet of Det. Insp. John Hughes, 19 November 1991
100 Job sheet of Det. Sgt. W J Van Der Velde, 12 December 1991
101 "Report on the examination of items of clothing etc", Harry Harding, 28 November 1991

about 20mm to the left of the neck band. The back edge of the cut was itself 18mm in front of the shoulder seam. If you put your fingers up to your own left shoulder you will quickly find the spot.

Under the microscope, Harding found the severed ends of the fibres were not frayed, meaning the fibres had not been washed or subjected to any friction from movement, since the cut had occurred. The body, he indicated, lay within metres of where Hoglin had died.

There was a further stab wound to the left neck band of the sweatshirt, and a stab to the forearm of the left sleeve.

Underneath the big cut in the shoulder/neck area, a corresponding stab wound was found in the pink Marco Polo t-shirt that lined up perfectly with the sweatshirt. More stab wounds were found in the neck of the t-shirt.

On Urban's red shorts, Harding confirmed he appeared to have been stabbed twice, about halfway between the centre of the waist band and the right-hand seam. The larger cut had "severed at least

two thicknesses of cloth plus the elastic material of the waistband. A further stab wound was found around the back of the shorts, in the waist band area. Urban appeared to have been stabbed in the upper right leg, close to his groin, the blade penetrating "at least three thicknesses of cloth" before entering the body.

What remained of the underpants nonetheless gave up its secrets under the microscope – the left leg elastic band had been stabbed in two places.

Summarising all this, Harding told New Zealand Police "the damage to the left neck and shoulder region of the sweatshirt and t-shirt is the result of three stab cuts, two of which cut through both garments at the same time (the third only cut the t-shirt neck band), and all of which were 'recent'. In this context 'recent' means that the clothing was not subject to much normal wearing (less than a few hours), nor to any washing, between the time the cutting occurred and when the clothing was found.

"The weapon may have been a single-edged blade (knife). The presence of multiple stabs suggests that this was a deliberate attack."

The cuts to the forearm of the sweatshirt, Hoglin's shorts and underpants also indicate a vicious attack directed to vital organs.

Armed with cutting edge evidence of murder, John Hughes went back to the Auckland City Mortuary and demanded they take a harder look for evidence of stab wounds to the neck, shoulder, arm and pelvic areas.

What the scientists found on their second examination of the body could have come straight from the imagination of Stephen King – the author, not the London cop. On closer analysis, the neck vertebrae showed clear evidence of cuts. The pathologists isolated four vertebrae and sent them across to the DSIR for detailed forensic photography.

The bones were "the middle four of the seven bones in the neck," reported the DSIR's John Buckleton later. What the pathologists found, and what Buckleton confirmed and photographed, were multiple cuts and nicks, some shallow, some deep.[102]

One such cut, on the fourth cervical vertebra, was a centimetre long and 3mm deep. These cuts were unrelated to the stab wounds in the clothing.

"I believe that these marks, which represent two separate cuts, were produced by a knife with a very sharp edge in a probable cutting motion," reported top pathologist Dr Tim Koelmeyer. "I believe that either one or both of these cuts would have divided the major arteries in the neck on the left side (carotid arteries, internal jugular veins) and have caused death."[103]

But that wasn't the worst of it. Whoever killed Urban Hoglin attempted to cut off his head.

"A deep cut…has been inflicted to the right side of the neck and passing backwards to the midline …has shaved off a piece of bone…with the line continuing on to the marks on the left side described previously. I think this kind of cut would have almost certainly divided the spinal cord and could be interpreted as being an attempt at decapitation."

In summary, he told police these wounds were not related to the stabbing cuts to the clothing.

"I believe it is quite likely that the cuts in the bones that have been described could have been produced without having to pass through the clothing worn. In particular, I think there is evidence in the marks in the bone of a more cutting, rather than a stabbing action.

"Therefore, the marks in the clothing reflect stabbing type wounds which could well have produced fatal injuries to the neck structures, but not leave any marks on the bones," concluded Koelmeyer.

For reasons currently unknown, the assailant or assailants of Urban Hoglin gave up on the idea of decapitation, and didn't even bother really hiding the body.

Pathologist Tim Koelmeyer had testified on the different speeds

---

102 Statement of John Simon Buckleton, 20 February 1992
103 "Opinions regarding skeletal remains of Urban Hoglin", Tim Koelmeyer, 25 February 1992

of decomposition at David Tamihere's 1990 murder trial. He told the jury that if Urban and Heidi had been buried in their sleeping bags, the smell of decomposition would likely have still been strong by the time searching commenced at the end of May 1989. On the other hand, bodies left in the open decompose much more quickly, within six to eight weeks.

He told the court that at the end of eight weeks in the open, probably only a skeleton and possibly some skin would remain and that such a body "could not be found unless one physically stumbled over it".

Knowing how Urban Hoglin had died was one thing. The who of it was something different again. The obvious line of inquiry was finding out who had access to the forestry road, 'access' being the operative word. Lyall Bowen worked as a foreman for Carter Holt, and one of his jobs was maintaining the gates leading into forestry areas. The track leading to the body is officially known as Parakiwai Road No. 101.

Bowen and some of his colleagues discovered during a routine inspection in mid May 1989 that the locked first forestry gate to the track had been smashed.

"Before that we had a bit of a problem with cannabis growers in the area," Bowen told police. "I suspect it was them who had damaged the forestry gate. Obviously a 4WD vehicle had pulled the gate out. We found the post in the river. It would have taken a powerful car or most likely a truck to break that gate."[104]

"Trampers don't need to pull out the gates, neither do hunters, and that is why I suspect cannabis growers.

"When I first checked the gate, which was between 22nd – 26th May 1989, I had a look up the track and found a tree lying across it just above the 3rd gate. The tree made the track impassable. There was no room for a vehicle to get past.

"On either 22nd, 23rd, 24th or 25th May 1989, I cut that tree up and

---

[104] Statement of Lyall William Bowen, 16 March 1992

removed it. I know that because it was out by the time I repaired the gate.

"I would say the tree had been lying there for about three months. I say that because of the grass growing around it, the fact that the pine needles had fallen off, the bark had delaminated and sap stains had set in.

"I have had a bit of experience with trees having worked in the forest since 1983, and am confident that tree was there for at least three months."

In other words, at all relevant times, vehicle access to the glade where Urban Hoglin's body was found was impossible, by virtue of a large fallen tree blocking the track at the third gate, halfway up the track.

Farmer John Shearer leased the land to graze stock on up until 1991. He told police there are actually five gates on the track that leads to the glade. "This is the only vehicular access to the block," Shearer explained to detectives. "You can walk in by several other routes but this track is the only way in by vehicle from Quarry Road."[105]

The first forestry gate, he told police, "was constructed of heavy steel" and "it was only damaged for about 2-3 weeks prior to it being repaired in May 1989. It was never damaged after that time."

This too is important, because it indicates that around the time period the Swedes went missing, criminal activity was taking place on the very track where Urban's body was eventually found.

"I remember a tree lying across the track just above the 3rd gate," Shearer said. "I don't know how long it was there or when exactly it fell there. It was sometime between January 1989 and May 1989.

"I am sure that a vehicle could not get past the tree where it was lying across the track. On the left side was a bank, and trees were close to the track on the right. You could walk past but you certainly could not drive past it."

This information conflicted with a vague sighting by Whangamata

---

105 Statement of John Percival Shearer, 13 March 1992

resident Heather Lindsay. She told police that in the first week of April 1989 she was at the top end of the Parakiwai Quarry Road – (the road, not the forestry track) and saw a car similar to the white Subaru parked there.

"There were three vehicles there, the [Subaru] station wagon, a blue early-model square-shaped Falcon station wagon, about late 60s, rust spots etc all over it. There was also a little red Honda Civic". She thought she'd seen it there on Thursday 6 April and Friday 7 April.

The problem with that sighting is that it conflicts with sightings of Urban and Heidi in Thames on those days. Although the couple did not introduce themselves to Thames shopkeeper Graham Manning on the 6th, or hairdresser Merilyn Round on the 7th, both are certain they spoke to Heidi and Urban, and the final letter from the Swedes to their family back home was postmarked "Thames, 7 April".

Nonetheless, to complicate matters, Heather Lindsay's 22-year old son Darren told police he'd gone up a track and found a white Subaru station wagon parked there as well. When police asked him to show them where he saw the car, it was about 100m north of where Urban's body was found on the forestry track.

Darren Lindsay was also shonky on dates, but felt that it was "a Monday".

"It was parked on the right hand side of the track and was slightly off the track on the verge. The car was facing uphill…I walked over and had a look inside through the window. There was a backpack on the back seat. It was dark blue in colour but that's about all I can remember."[106]

Lindsay also says he saw a camera on

---

106   Statement of Darren Mark Lindsay, 15 October 1991

A Frenzied Attack

the back seat, pointing upwards, "black in colour. It looked to have a big lens on the front of it but I'm not too sure about cameras."

The witness recalled seeing the word "Subaru" painted on the rear doors, but made no mention of seeing bullbars.

In a further statement to police, two days later, Darren Lindsay added, "The pack was dark blue or black and had red piping around the edges. I remember my eye being drawn to the red on the pack and the camera…The camera was not a big flash one but an older box-shaped one with red trim, either around the lens or on the body of the camera."[107]

If police had not shown Lindsay photos of the Swedes' missing gear, or indulged in leading questioning that put words in Lindsay's mouth, then it's almost certain he saw the Swedes' car on Monday 10 April. The reasons for this follow:

Firstly, he positively identifies a white Subaru station wagon parked on the forestry track about 100 metres north of the crime scene.

Secondly, he sees a dark blue day pack with red piping. There are photos of Urban Hoglin wearing such a bag, and it remains missing.

Thirdly, he describes a boxy camera with red trim around the lens

---

107 Second Statement of Darren Mark Lindsay, 17 October 1991

and possibly on the body. The Swedes had with them a Panasonic Zoom C-900ZM camera, featuring red trim on the front of the lens and on the body of the camera. A camera like this was seen in the car when it was parked at Tararu Creek Road on Sunday 9 April.[108] Tamihere also told police he'd found one in the car when he broke into it.

One of these items might be a coincidence, but to have three specific identifications within 100 metres of the body scene on what may have been the morning of Monday 10 April is too much to ignore.

The only problem with Lindsay's sighting was his dates. He was extremely vague. You cannot, however, ignore the specificity of his description. It must have been Monday the 10th, because no other Monday would fit. There are clues that firm this up.

Darren Lindsay told police he'd been living in Thames until 13 April 1989, when he moved to Whangamata. "I remember the date I moved out because it was Black Friday," he said. "Then on Monday two weeks later I decided to have a break and go for a walk."

The police were critical of Lindsay's credibility, pointing out that there was no "Black Friday" in April, and that the 13th of April was in fact a Thursday.

In his second statement to police, Lindsay admits he must have "got some of the dates mixed up…It may have been April Fool's Day that stands out in my mind but I'm not sure. I just know that around the time that I move to Whangamata there was an important day on the calendar."

Indeed there was, and everyone seemed to have forgotten it, even the police. *Good* Friday had fallen on March 24. Two weeks after "Good Friday" was the crucial weekend the Swedes disappeared: Friday 7 April, Saturday 8, Sunday 9 and Monday 10 April. It was a Monday two weeks after an important Friday, when he took his "walk" – Monday 10 April.

Darren's mother, Heather, also told police her son "would have

---

108 See evidence of Harry Goodwin.

arrived back in Whangamata the last week of March, first week of April", ie, Easter weekend.

What Lindsay's testimony also meant, however, is there must have been a way for that car to have made it up that track, or driven into the area.

The travel time between Whangamata and Thames was one hour at tourist pace – a distance of 59km. It could be done faster in a hurry.

The question is, was it?

CHAPTER 13

A New Scenario

"We have been travelling the West Coast up. First, we visited Milford Sound where amongst other things we took a boat trip with a lot of Japanese people. It was just impossible to hear the captain's voice in all that chatter. When we finally managed to climb up the steep road towards Homer tunnel we met a whole gang of keas (probably the ones you heard Johni) and some tourists were feeding them.

"After [the west coast] we went towards Marlborough Sounds...we are leaving the South Island soon, probably Thursday or Friday (if there's any vacancy on the ferry because we haven't got any tickets). After that it's only five weeks left here in New Zealand unfortunately."

– letter from Heidi Paakkonen, 15 March 1989, Marlborough Sounds

Sometimes, it is said, we fail to see the wood for the trees. We are so busy looking at something one way, that we lose the ability to see it from other angles.

There are huge – massive – problems with the theory that Heidi Paakkonen and Urban Hoglin died *at* Crosbie's Clearing at the hands of David Tamihere. If that's the case, how did he get the body from 12km deep in the bush to a location 73km away? For a fit tramper travelling lightly, Crosbie's to Tararu was a three hour walk. If that same person was lugging a body for those 12km on their own, you can call it 16 hours – if they didn't collapse first. The risk of being discovered on this journey over such a timeframe is so obvious it should not need further consideration.

If the Coromandel bush around Crosbie's was rugged enough to bury Heidi in so that she'd never be found, why go 73km to dispose of Urban? It just doesn't make sense. The Crosbie's Clearing issue has more than a hint of sideshow about it, as if the killer distributed items of the couple's belongings up around Crosbie's to throw searchers off the real trail, and only after the interest in Crosbie's became public.

None of the key items at Crosbie's and on surrounding tracks had been found by either the public or search teams initially, despite the Kauaeranga/Crosbie's/Tararu track being described as a busy and popular hiking route.

The post-mortem evidence – that Urban's body was literally found at the spot where he had been killed – ruins the theory that Hoglin had been manhandled out of the bush on Tamihere's back, dumped in a car and driven to the Parakiwai Valley. According to pathologists, the bone injuries when examined microscopically showed no evidence of movement after death. No friction from the rubbing of flesh on the knife cuts. Nor of course did luminol tests reveal any blood in the car.

Ergo, Hoglin was alive in that clearing in the Parakiwai Valley; he arrived there alive. This too makes the Cassidy/Knauf sighting at Crosbie's on Saturday 8 April irrelevant. It was already dodgy on the identification evidence – no moustache, woman wearing tramping boots, tent fly blue instead of silver – now it is doubtful on timing. If it was Tamihere acting alone, as the Crown claim, he cannot have been in two places at once – he cannot have been with Urban Hoglin alive in the Parakiwai, and simultaneously been with Heidi Paakkonen at Crosbie's Clearing pitching a tent. Controlling Urban Hoglin would have been a full time job.

Let's re-trace what we know.

- Witness John Kennedy saw a white Subaru station wagon with

a couple in, drive up Tararu Creek Road on the Saturday just before sunset at 6pm. He never saw the car come down that night.
- We know someone lit a campfire at the top of Tararu Creek Road, close to where the couple's car was seen parked. Knowing their propensity for roadside camping, this could explain where Heidi & Urban spent the Saturday night, ready for the hike the next day.
- We know the couple's car was parked there from at least 12:30pm on Sunday 9 April through to about 5pm when witnesses left the area.
- We know the couple's Subaru was seen on Monday 10 April at Parakiwai, parked 100 metres from where Urban's body was later found.
- We know travelling time between Tararu Creek Road and Parakiwai is about an hour.
- We know David Tamihere checked into the Sunkist Lodge at Thames on the afternoon of 10 April and had possession of the couple's car by this point.

Sharp-eyed readers will have noticed no mention in that list of the possible Sunday morning church appearance, or Tamihere's discovery of the car at Tararu Creek Road on the afternoon of the 10th. No one independent can verify seeing Tamihere on Tararu Creek Road. It may well be the truth, but it comes down to being his word for it. With the church, the descriptions and Heidi's name match, and it fits the appearance of the car at Tararu on Sunday afternoon, but it is a tangent rather than a crucial ingredient.

So here's a scenario.

Heidi and Urban entered the bush at Tararu on late Sunday morning at the latest. They made Crosbie's Clearing and set up an overnight camp there.

Is it possible that someone after sunset came across the couple camping at Crosbie's Clearing, slashed open their tent, surprised them in their sleeping bags and quickly overpowered Urban? It's possible. A threat to kill Hoglin would certainly have kept Heidi under control, and it is feasible that the couple were marched out of Crosbie's back down to their car in the dead of night and driven to the Parakiwai Valley.

Such a march, in the middle of the night, was almost guaranteed to go unseen by anyone else. The departure of the car, particularly if it left Tararu Creek Road after midnight, would also have gone unnoticed by residents safely tucked in their beds.

A midnight drive to Parakiwai, likewise, meant little chance of anyone seeing them. The area was remote, people were asleep, it was dark. Obviously it had to be a person or persons familiar with the Parakiwai Valley area – it is not a road you would randomly choose and it is literally about as far as you can get from Tararu Creek Road and Crosbie's Clearing. It is sufficiently remote that any screams would have been heard only by the owls.

The area where Urban died was frequented by cannabis growers, and he was in a glade close to the track. His body was not buried, it was left on the surface of the ground. It could easily have been found much sooner than it was. It was not buried at the top of a cliff where pig hunters don't go. It was lying in a highly accessible spot, and it was found, ironically, by pig hunters.

The seclusion of Urban's final resting place is another clue that Heidi was alive, and probably with him or nearby when he died. As long as the killer had one of the couple hostage and under threat of imminent danger, the other person would have remained compliant. The killer had to have walked Urban into the clearing away from the car, and Urban would likely only have walked if Heidi was still with him. Otherwise why comply? His instinct to protect Heidi would have raged. The only other alternative is that Hoglin by this stage was so overpowered and under threat that Heidi obeyed orders and walked with him in the hope they could stay together and alive.

One thing is clear, the killer would not have left Heidi alone in the vehicle while he took Hoglin away, unless she was well tied up or others were guarding her.

Darren Lindsay says no one was with the car when he saw it on Monday 10 April at Parakiwai, nor did he call out to try and find the owners. He left well enough alone and walked away.

The car, however, had to be back in Thames later that day, because we know Tamihere had it when he checked into Sunkist. Tamihere, however, says he stole the car from Tararu Creek Road and this brings us back to the evidence he gave at trial for which he was scorned. All the way through, from the very first day he was questioned, Tamihere has insisted he felt the exhaust and it still felt warm. The evidence has been that the exhaust should have been cold, therefore Tamihere is lying.

It seems a strange lie to die in a ditch for, however. It was meaningless in the great scheme of things – even his defence lawyers in summing up for the jury suggested their client had probably made a mistake. Yet he has always denied that. "It felt warm", he repeated under cross-examination.

If the car was seen at Parakiwai on Monday 10th, then later – an hour away – at Tararu Creek Road, then possibly the exhaust could indeed have been warm. If the killer/s had dropped the car back to Tararu, and Tamihere the car thief stumbled across it, that would explain the apparent inconsistency.

Is there evidence that the Subaru was seen driving up Tararu Creek Road on that Monday? Funnily enough, there may be, but the witnesses were never called to testify.

John McCullough and Simon Whitta were working on the deck of McCullough's Tararu Creek Road house around 10am, when "something drew my attention to the Subaru," McCullough told police, "so we looked at the car going up the road."[109]

"The car I saw was a white Subaru station wagon, early model, black roo bars on the front, and it was going fast. He was going fast and looked like he knew the road. I say that by the way he came around the corner, I would say he was a good, competent driver,

---
109   Statement of Terrence John McCullough, 28 June 1989

A New Scenario

he came around the corner which is quite sharp and had the car under perfect control.

"I have a mental picture of the car, but I can't zero in on the occupants.

"The car gave me the impression that it was full. I was looking down on an angle inside it, I think the speed of the vehicle was such that I couldn't see in it properly. The car just seemed full, I can't say whether it was people or what. I said to Simon, 'they're in a bloody hurry'."

Under further questioning from police, McCullough said "I'm sure I saw it go up and come down."[110]

The second comment is interesting, because the description fits the scenario of the killer/s returning from Parakiwai, and the car later being taken by Tamihere.

"On this day...it would have been half past two, three o'clock in the afternoon – I think we were on an afternoon coffee break – we were sitting in the guts of the house when we heard a car coming out from the end of the road [the Subaru had a distinctive exhaust].[111]

"I looked down on the road and it was definitely the same Subaru station wagon. It was going fast, I only just saw it, right in front of my house is a sharp bend and I just saw inside the car as it went past.

"The car seemed full."

McCullough thought he caught a glimpse of what he described as "the arm of the passenger", a man wearing a black jersey. Given his angle of view, this was probably the left arm of the driver, as he should have been able to see most of the body of any front seat passenger if one had been in the car.

The 2.30pm timing fits Tamihere's admission to police that he arrived at the car around "quarter past two", and spent 15 minutes breaking in and ransacking it before stealing it.

So, two clear points arise. Firstly, the car comes up the street mid

---

110 Job sheet of Det. P J Devoy, 28 June 1989
111 Statement of Terrence John McCullough, 28 June 1989

morning in "a bloody hurry", and he had the impression several people were in it, although he could not be sure. Mid afternoon, the car comes back down Tararu, around the same time Tamihere admits stealing it and driving to the Sunkist Lodge.

Again, the timing is such that Tamihere could not have driven in at 10am, tramped three hours into Crosbie's Clearing, tramped three hours back, and be stealing the car at 2.15pm.

Why was McCullough never called as a witness? Because his dates were vague. He told police this had been Monday 3 April, but the Swedes and their distinctive Subaru with the bull bars were still down in the Bay of Plenty that day. Monday 10 April fits like a glove.

You may be asking yourself why the killer would return the car to Tararu Creek Road. Well, the killer had to have come from somewhere. As far as we know the killer/s either met the Swedes randomly in the bush, in which case he/they probably had a campsite of their own they needed to return to and clear, or alternatively the killer/s came from the Tararu Creek Road area themselves.

Police knew there was a cannabis growing operation in that area. Coincidentally, or perhaps not, the Parakiwai Quarry area was also a big cannabis haunt.

If it was a local Tararu criminal, the attack would probably have begun on the Saturday night while the couple were camping at Tararu Creek Road. In which case it wasn't a very long march to the car after all if they were surprised there. If the couple were attacked in the bush, however, then such could only have happened after they entered the bush, and the culprit/s is more likely to be someone used to the bush environment like a fellow tramper – police testified drug dealers did not bother venturing too far into the rugged hinterland as they needed their crops to be close to road transport.

Ironic as it may seem, there's one person for whom taking the car back to Tararu – if he was the killer – does not make sense. At least, not within the parameters of the big picture. That person is David Tamihere.

Granted, if Tamihere was the killer he may have needed to clear a campsite. His fingerprints, so to speak, were all over the Crosbie's Clearing area – many people had seen his tent with the signed note from "Pat Kelly" begging people not to steal it. The evidence shows, however, that Tamihere did not clear his campsite that April weekend, because at least one police witness testified to seeing the Pat Kelly tent in the bush the following weekend.

Moreover, if Tamihere had indeed killed the Swedes, why would he knowingly dump named clothing of theirs at Tararu Creek Road, on a bush track leading to an area he was known to frequent? Would you do that? If Tamihere had killed the couple after spiriting them 73km away from the area, why on earth would he dump evidence in plain sight at the scene of the abduction, when he could have dumped it anywhere else? There did not have to be anything linking the Swedes to Tararu Creek Road, but by his actions Tamihere made certain there was, and it was evidence that nailed him to the crime.

If Tamihere was the killer, then he already had the car and had no need to return to Tararu Creek Road from Parakiwai, he could have driven straight to Sunkist. And yet, the couple's dirty washing and other clothing were dumped out of the car at Tararu Creek Road, and Tamihere admitted doing it. Are we to believe that upon first abducting the couple, that he decided to go through their washing before kidnapping them? For what purpose? How did he maintain control over Hoglin – who'd recently finished a year's military training – and Paakkonen whilst deciding what clothes to toss? If it seems hard to believe that he ferreted through their stuff for 15 minutes while they were alive and in the car, it's easier to accept he did it when he says he did it – in the process of stealing the car.

Much as Tamihere has prior form as a killer and a rapist, it just doesn't make sense for him to have gone to all the trouble of removing the couple from the area, yet leaving all their clothing there as clues. The killer must have had all of the Swedes' gear in the car at Parakiwai – if it was Tamihere why didn't he find an old mineshaft and drop the clothing into that? Why transport it all the way back to where he had taken them from?

It actually makes more sense that it's just a bizarre coincidence – that Tamihere genuinely stole the car, not from Heidi and Urban directly but from their killer. What are the chances of the killer returning to Tararu Creek Road late on Monday morning, and then in turn having his car nicked just because Tamihere by chance has turned up in the area? Expressed like that, the probability seems hugely low, but the law of chance doesn't actually care about back-stories.[112] Someone's car gets stolen or broken into every 15 minutes in New Zealand, regardless of whether they had "just dropped it off" or "my back was only turned for thirty seconds". Opportunists take their chances when they arise. Tamihere was an opportunist.

For all we know, the killer might actually have hoped the car would be stolen, and that's why a set of keys was left in it. That would put someone else's fingerprints in the vehicle, and connect that someone to the crime when it was eventually discovered.

In which case Tamihere was a schmuck, and tossing the Swedes' clothing out and name tags out was consistent with the behaviour of a schmuck who thinks he's scored a car, not a possible rap for double-homicide.

A schmuck might happily drive around in a stolen car and even take his mates on joyrides in the vehicle, but the killer of two young tourists who knows for a fact the couple will be reported missing soon would be much more careful about so blatantly linking themselves to the victims, you would think.

Leaving Heidi Paakkonen's named prescription medication behind in the room he'd rented at the Sunkist Lodge, where staff later found it, is the behaviour of a schmuck who'd stolen a car, not a master killer who'd gone to all the trouble of removing Heidi and Urban from the area.

Having said all this, the discovery of Hoglin's body in the Parakiwai Valley still leaves Tamihere in the gun, as far as the police files are concerned, as you are about to see.

---

112 In fact, that portion of Tararu Creek Road housed a number of criminals at different addresses along the road, so within one square kilometre there was actually quite a high proportion of criminally-minded active individuals.

CHAPTER 14

Back In The Gun

"The nights are starting to get a bit chilly and it's getting dark earlier. It's going towards autumn in other words. If you want to send anymore letters, the last address here in NZ is Auckland and you have to send it by 1st April at the latest. Then on 20 April we are going to the Cook Islands where we will stay for two weeks. After that it will be Tahiti for four days and Los Angeles for one day.

"We reckon we will be home on the 7th of May so we won't miss the big party. Send our love to Illi and Ia from us, and we hope that everything is well with you all."

– **letter from Urban Hoglin, March 16 1989, Picton**

To get access to the Parakiwai forest track where he saw the Subaru, Darren Lindsay had walked up the back of Pat Taikato's farm, which adjoins the forestry block. Lindsay's mother Heather told police in 1991 that the forestry track was not the only way vehicles could reach the quarry up there.

"There are a number of roads and tracks that can be driven by 4WD that will give access to the top of the forestry road where the body was located. You can get up there by crossing the river on Pat Taikato's farm, where Darren is living, and drive the fence line to within a few metres of the track. You can also get there very easily by turning off the Parakiwai Road just past the orchard. You can drive across the Berry farm and right to the top.

"There are about five different ways also to get in from Knight's place on the Wentworth Valley by the airstrip."

Within one week of finding Urban Hoglin's body, police had also found this man, Don Turner:

"I bulldozed the tracks from the river where the tin bach is on Parakiwai Road, all the way up to the fence on Lindsay's property and the boundary of the forest block. During the summer you could drive up there in a car.[113]

"I opened the area up so me, Dick Hauraki and Lance Tamihere could take the ti-tree out for firewood."

Yes, you read that correctly. Lance is David Tamihere's brother.

"In 1987 we were hauling out ti tree. Lance was staying in a tent with his girlfriend over the river. The bach wasn't there then. David Tamihere used to visit him. He came two or three times that I know of. Lance will deny that, though.

"I actually dropped David off one time at the tent, he had been walking, this was in 1987...He was wearing army-type gear, khaki green longs, camouflage windbreaker and an army-type framed pack. Sometimes he used a blue and black swanni. He had a shovel, a black billy and a tomahawk hanging off the pack.

"He was always walking. I would see him on the road all the time. He spent all his time bumming around, walking from place to place. Everybody was talking about him being up for interfering with a young girl, but we found out he had raped an old lady. People wouldn't let him stay, [they'd] just give him a feed and off, that sort of thing.

"I have never seen him driving a car on the road. One time I saw him down at Mataora driving an old Falcon. It was an old '66 station wagon. I think it was Lance's car. It was two-toned blue-grey, a rusted-up dunger."

Again, sharp-eyed readers will recall Heather Lindsay had claimed to have seen a Subaru together with a rusted, blue, 1960s Falcon station wagon parked up at the end of Parakiwai Quarry Road (not

---

113 Job sheet of Sgt. W J Pritchard, 18 October 1991, interviewing Don Turner

the forestry track) on the 6th or 7th of April. If Heather Lindsay's dates are right, it cannot have been the Swedes' Subaru. The police file notes Lindsay is hazy on the dates.

There had already been plenty of evidence linking David Tamihere to the neighbouring Wentworth Valley area, and he had freely admitted as much at his trial. David Thorp, a Rotorua bookshop owner, had been tramping the Wentworth at Easter of 1989 with his wife and a friend when they came across Tamihere.

Now that Urban's body had been found, plenty more locals were prepared to tell police they'd seen a man they thought was Tamihere.

A year earlier just before Cyclone Bola hit the area in February 1988, Whangamata resident Barbara Thorburn took her brother and sister-in-law up to the Wentworth Valley waterfall. When they arrived back at the carpark they found a person "bent over, leaning into the boot" of their car. "He was hunched up, I only saw the back of his head and shoulders."

When challenged the man legged it: "Straight away this bloke ran off, crouched over. I never saw his face. He was very quick with long loping strides".

Despite never seeing his face, Thorburn told police that after Tamihere had been convicted of the Swedes' murders, "I saw a documentary on the whole case. I saw pictures of him. Straight away I knew it was David Tamihere."

Amazing what the power of suggestion can do in the absence of actually seeing a face. The sasquatch-like creature that Thorburn saw thieving from the boot of her car was wearing a black and blue swanndri, and he escaped with "ninety-eight dollars out of my bag and my sister-in-law lost $380."

Much closer to the relevant time, and on this occasion a full facial view, were sightings by Wentworth Valley resident Russell Nelley, beginning in December 1988.

"I picked up a hitchhiker at the quarry on the Wentworth Valley Road. He was a male person [you can tell these statements are written by cops] dressed in camouflage army-type clothing with a huge pack on his back. I was in my car and when he threw the pack in the car it really rocked the car. The pack must have been really heavy, 80 to 90 pounds at a guess."[114]

Tamihere's huge pack was his trademark. It was so heavy he'd felt confident leaving it on Karangahape Road while he sold the Swedes' packs, knowing nobody was going to be able to pick it up and run with it.

"He wore a Rambo-type sweat band around his head. He was big, strong built, black staring eyes....He wasn't hitchhiking he was trudging. He looked surprised when I stopped for him to give him a lift. He had big eyes."

Nelley recalls real problems with vehicle break-ins at the Wentworth Valley that summer of 88/89, but never made the connection with his hitchhiker whom, he assumed would have been "long gone". He positively id'd Tamihere from one of the same coloured photos that Cassidy had picked him from.

In the second incident, sometime after Easter 1989, Nelley says he found a "bright red tent" pitched in his avocado block just on dusk. The tent really glowed a "yellowy orange colour". He'd called out to see if anyone was in it, and jumped when a voice behind him growled, "who wants to know?"

He didn't recognise the owner of the voice, although later told detectives he was "a dead ringer" for David Tamihere's brother, John Tamihere.

Police appeared very excited about Nelley's sightings. Det. Sgt. Knight called him "an excellent witness who is absolutely positive on what he has seen. A confirmed sighting of David Tamihere in the area, December 1988, and again after Easter 1989…a brilliant, straight person, very credible.[115]

"This second sighting of Tamihere places him in the Wentworth Valley, a short distance from the scene where the body of Urban Hoglin was located."

---

114   Statement of Russell Nelley, 17 October 1991
115   Job sheet of Det. Sgt. R A Knight, 21 October 1991

Det. Sgt. Knight may not have realised at this point, but the fact that Tamihere was in the Wentworth Valley after Easter 1989 was not news, it had been well canvassed at the murder trial, and Tamihere had never denied it.

Knight found two more witnesses to corroborate Nelley. Teachers college lecturer Robin Patchett and his partner Colleen McClenaghan went tramping in the Wentworth Valley over Easter. While at the waterfall on Easter Sunday morning, March 26, they met a man wearing "a green and khaki camouflage patterned jacket…he had a moustache and may have had a stubble beard.

"The general gist of the conversation was that he indicated that he had come from over the ridge on the south side of the Wentworth Valley and I remember him being quite surprised at the short length of time he said it had taken him."

The man "told us he was going over the top to the Coromandel side…he said he was going to _____ Flat ((something) Flat)."

The man was undoubtedly David Tamihere and we know this because he testified at his trial to coming across from the Wires camp south of Wentworth that day:

"I crossed over into the Wentworth and then made my way up, there is a ridge track that will take you up through the Tairua forest." Tamihere told the court he had come out on the Kopu-Hikuai Highway, and hitched a lift into Thames, where he checked into the Sunkist Lodge on the evening of the 27th.

After checking out four days later, Tamihere hitched back down to the Wires camp and started the same journey again.

"…picked up my gear and on the Sunday I crossed over into the Wentworth Valley."

"Is this about Sunday 2 April?"

"Yes".

"We heard from Mr Thorp and Jones about bike riding or something like that, can you remember them? Yes, I ran into them about 4kms or 5kms up the bush."

"Where was that?"

"Wentworth Falls."

Thorp had arrived at the falls just on lunchtime and says Tamihere arrived after him. They talked for awhile, and Tamihere then walked off down the hill.

On this particular journey, Tamihere told the court, he'd spent the night of Monday 3 April at "Boom's Flat", or, as Robin Patchett recalled it "something Flat".

To give you an idea of the problems with witness memories, however, the Thorp/Reid sightings provide an excellent example. David Thorp described Tamihere as wearing "tramping boots, rugby socks (maybe blue and white), light nylon shorts (possibly blue), top may have been a t-shirt, head band."

Lynn Jones (Thorp's wife) couldn't recall the clothes, and David Reid said Tamihere was wearing "a bush shirt of some description, some sort of trousers…his trousers were stuffed into his socks and he was wearing a heavy pair of boots".

Clearly, David Tamihere knew the Wentworth Valley well, and according to Don Turner he'd been to Parakiwai to see his brother Lance Tamihere two years earlier. This is on the record, and much of it since 1989. It is certainly all contained in the police files.

By the same token, there are many people who frequent the bush tracks of Coromandel, all the way from Waihi in the south up past Parakiwai and the Wentworth, through the Kauaeranga and Crosbie's. We know this because of the large number of sightings. When someone is in the dock, they become the focus of our collective attention. All the evidence is measured against that person. In a murder trial however, sometimes the culprits are the ones who are not in the dock, the ones we don't know about.

Circumstantially, there is strong evidence that puts Tamihere close to where Urban Hoglin was killed, although not on the day in question. Equally circumstantially, objective readers need to weigh up whether Tamihere's subsequent actions in throwing out the couple's gear at Tararu Creek Road are consistent with a killer/s who had gone to extreme trouble to remove Heidi and Urban from the Tararu area.

Schmuck or double murderer? That remains the essential question. One thing we do know is that David Tamihere was not the only criminal wandering the Coromandel that April.

CHAPTER 15

New Suspects

"We are in the Tongariro National Park in the North Island in an area with some volcanic activity. As recently as 1974 Mt Ngauruhoe had an eruption. We've been walking some tramps in the area around here and seen where the lava has been pouring.

"We went to Mt Egmont National Park, that's on the western side of the North Island. We found a very nice camping spot that was also cheap, and the guys who ran the site invited us for dinner. They served lamb chops, beef, salad and potatoes. For dessert we got Mum's fruit salad and ice cream. It was a really nice meal for us.

"We are going to Coromandel and Rotorua. It feels strange that it is Good Friday today because at home it is going towards Spring when Easter comes, and here it is the other way around. They've got a special Easter bread here, Urban likes it, it's spiced (so it tastes almost like soft ginger cake) and there's some raisins and fruit in it.

"Sorry this letter is so messy but it's a bit hard to write in the light of the candle."

– letter from Heidi Paakkonen, March 24 1989, Tongariro

At some point in early 1989, a Rotorua man named Huia George Foley left, or escaped, from a mental health institution and made his way to the Coromandel gateway township of Waihi. Twenty-eight year old Foley stayed there long enough to become an occasional visitor to St Joseph's Catholic Church, but one afternoon his demons got the better of him.

"He went into the Waihi Catholic Church. He said he went to have a rest, but he was after the donations in the church and he asked the priest then if he could have some," recalls 88 year old Tuhourangi kuia Ngawai Davis, who knew Foley personally as the son of her sister's good friend. The children had all attended Auckland's Wesley College together.

"The priest said 'No, I can't give you this', and he stood up and the priest knew he was going to chase him. He chased the priest outside, through the back door, once, twice around the church. The priest ran into his own place and rang police, and they rang Foley's mother about it, what happened," says Davis.

Huia, however, had fled into the Coromandel bush. Weeks later he turned up at Whitianga, on foot, carrying a green army surplus sleeping bag.

"When he turned up at our place I was talking to my dad on the deck," recalls Bill Davis, Ngawai's son, "and we were looking right down the Esplanade at Whitianga, and my dad said to me, 'here comes trouble'. And all we could see was a black dot. My dad was dying of leukaemia but he was able to pick that up."

It was 6.30 in the morning, and Ngawai says her ailing husband didn't want Foley around.

"My husband was up and spotted him, and he said, 'what the hell are you doing here? I don't want you mixing with my sons'. He said, 'It's alright Martin, I'm only here to see your boys and I'll be on my way'. I followed him out of the house and that's when he told me how he'd walked there," explains Ngawai.

"When he left Waihi he walked around the edges of the road to Whangamata, then from Whangamata over to Thames and Coromandel, then over the range to Whitianga. He told me. So I asked him where he slept. 'Oh, I slept in the bushes'. But look, he was the height and he had the build of that fellow David Tamihere. And he was strong, very strong. A young fellow."

The unstable Foley's zig-zag path through the Coromandel could easily have put him in contact with the Swedes, either while they were tramping or alternatively by hitching a ride with them as he walked the roadsides.

Bill Davis, interviewed separately, says Foley seemed nervous when he showed up in Whitianga.

"He was quite a bit agitated, quite agitated. He had mood swings. He looked like David Tamihere. He fits the ID, he was the same size as David Tamihere. He had a beard and moustache. Looked very similar to David Tamihere. If you stood them 15 metres away you'd think they were related. If you got a photo of Huia and put them side by side, they'd look familiar."

Bill, Ngawai and her husband Martin were due in Rotorua that day and couldn't delay their departure. Foley remained at Bill's place with Bill's younger brother. When Bill returned from Rotorua, he was stunned to hear what happened while he was away.

"When we came back my brother's car was missing. My young brother said Huia threatened him with a softball bat and said 'I'll smash your head in if you don't give me the keys to your car'.

"He was capable of using that softball bat, he wouldn't think twice. I know Huia. I know this chap. I went to college with him at Wesley College and I've seen the potential of how angry and violent he can get. And he did get violent.

"So he bolted. Took the car, took some of our gear, left behind this sleeping bag he'd brought with him.

"He then proceeded to go up to Auckland. Apparently he had an accident. There was a truck parked up on the side of the road, and the police officer told my brother and I that it was strange, because they'd spoken to the truck driver who said, 'This guy was coming straight for me. He knew exactly what he was doing, he was coming right towards me, waving his arm out the window, as if he was trying to commit suicide. He had issues'.

"He lost his arm in that accident."

New Suspects

It was just then, late May 1989, that news broke of the two missing Swedish tourists. Six weeks later, "Wanted" posters seeking information on an itinerant named "Pat Kelly" – an alias of Tamihere's – were placed around the district.

Bill Davis was one of those who took part in the official police search for Hoglin and Paakkonen, and he became convinced Huia Foley had something to do with it. More to the point, so did Huia's own mother, says Tuhourangi tribal matriarch Ngawai Davis.

"A few days later we heard about the missing Swedish young people, and I had a funny feeling. I rang my sister to talk to her, and she said that Huia's mother, as soon as she heard about these two young Swedes, she said 'My son did that'. She knew he was walking in that area, and the police had already rung her to tell her what happened in the church, and she went to see my sister and said, 'he did it', and this was before he told her what he did."

As the Davis family remember it, Huia's mother told them her son had confessed to her when she finally confronted him. "I was surprised," says Ngawai. "I thought the mother might get in touch with police in Rotorua and tell them about what her son did. I guess they didn't want to see their son in trouble."

The Davis family tried to ring police but Operation Stockholm detectives refused to show any interest in the tip off, or the German army surplus sleeping bag that Foley had turned up with and left at the Davis house.

Colin Nicholson QC says police developed a one-track mind on the case.

"I do know, from my inspection of the police discovery documents, that they definitely had another suspect who they were pursuing, until such stage as Tamihere was identified as having taken their car and selling some of their tramping gear, at which stage police just turned their focus completely on Tamihere."

It may have been simply a case of the bird in the hand being worth two in the bush. It was easier to fit the crime to David Tamihere than it was to pursue a fresh lead.

"We tried to explain to the Police that Huia Foley was the man, but they just said 'you haven't got enough evidence, blah blah," recalls Bill Davis.

The evidence, however, was this. A 28 year old man, of similar muscular build and appearance to 36 year old David Tamihere, decamped from a mental institution and tried to attack a Catholic priest inside his Waihi church. He then fled into the Coromandel bush heading for Whangamata at the same time as the missing Swedes were in the general area. Hoglin's body was found in the Parakiwai Valley, due north of Waihi on the route to Whangamata. Although off the main road, it was accessible from an access road.

Foley's trek, by his own admission, takes him from Whangamata back over to Thames and Coromandel, then across to Whitianga over a long period of time, during which he has suddenly come into possession of a European sleeping bag, which he dumps at Whitianga, then steals a car after threatening the owner with a softball bat. Foley then manages to take his right arm off by driving directly up against a parked truck on the other side of the road at speed while waving his arm out the window.

Clearly, a mentally unstable and violent man was on the loose in the Coromandel at the time the Swedes disappeared. Foley knew the area well. His old schoolfriend Bill Davis recalls Foley was a frequent hitchhiker and transient in the Coromandel.

These facts are indisputable, attested to by multiple witnesses. The alleged confession to his mother, and his mother's subsequent confession to her friend, are more problematic because both Foley and his mother are now dead and their secrets have gone to the grave with them.

Ngawai Davis' sister June once confronted Huia Foley in the main street of Rotorua.

"I know what you did to that Swedish couple", she challenged. Foley just laughed.

"You'll never find her, they'll never prove it".

Could it have been Foley, on the run from police for the robbery

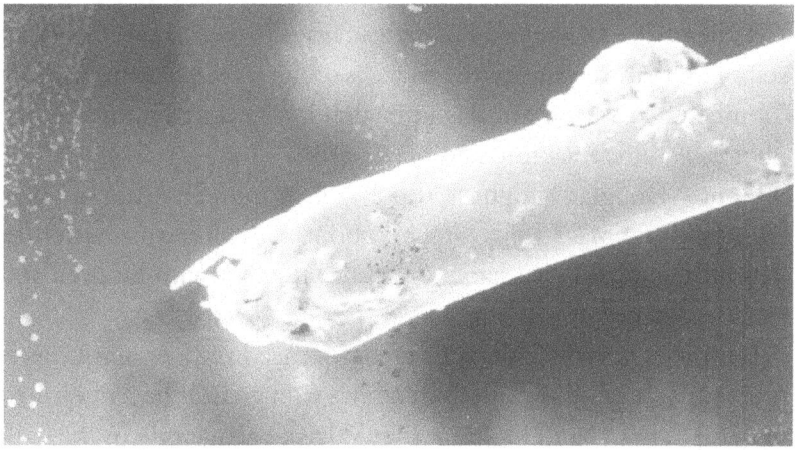

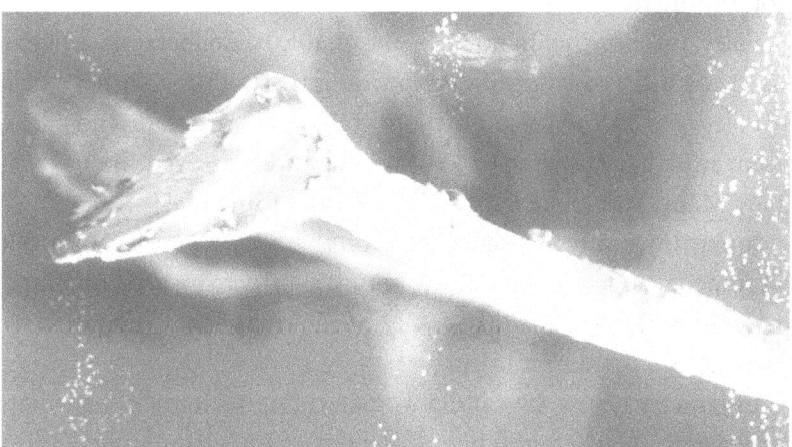

Electron microscope photos of cut sweatshirt. The top image was damaged caused by the killer's knife. The lower image is damage from a test stab using Tamihere's blade

of a Waihi church, a mentally unstable and extremely violent man bearing close resemblance to David Tamihere, who stumbled across the Swedes in the bush and marched them to their car?

The post mortem on Urban Hoglin showed he'd been subjected to a frenzied knife attack, and a subsequent decapitation attempt, before being dragged into some scrub and left there. It has the hallmarks of an attack by someone mentally insane, rather than a calm cold-blooded killer.

Remember too, that when forensic experts compared the actual stabs in Urban's clothes with test stabs of the same garment made by Tamihere's knives, there was no match in the electron microscope photos. A different knife had been used.

Hunter Douglas Knight told police he'd found a knife in bush, "not far from your body scene", about eight months earlier, in February 1991.[116] Presumably the police tested it with luminol and found nothing.

Tamihere, you'll recall, was an experienced trapper and hunter, quite capable of killing and butchering wild boar. If he had wanted to decapitate Urban Hoglin, it should have been a walk in the park for Tamihere.

Foley, on the other hand, was so unstable he deliberately drove so as to ensure his own arm was ripped off in a collision with a truck.

Foley was in the area, on those tracks, when Urban and Heidi went missing. He wasn't blond-haired and blue eyed, he too was part Maori and looked at lot like David Tamihere.

It may by now have occurred to you that this is a perfect example of someone 'not in the dock'. While all eyes were focused on Tamihere, it appeared he was the only possible suspect. Now, we have two. Could there be a third?

In January 1987, a 32 year old woman tramping in the Waitawheta Valley near Waihi found herself the victim of an attempted abduction:

"I was attacked by a Maori man posing as a Forestry Ranger in the Waitawheta Valley. He told me he had just come out of jail and he was lonely. He tried to drag me from the hut clearing into the bush and I fought him. He then ran off.[117]

"I was very shaken and reported it to police. I felt they should have tried to find him, as he had stolen the uniform, pack and supplies from a forestry depot and was still in the bush. Other people would

---

116 Job sheet of Det. Sgt. W J Van Der Velde, 22 October 1991, "interview with Douglas Jackson Knight"
117 Email correspondence with author, 27 February 2012

be at risk. However, as apart from a few bruises I wasn't injured, they didn't seem interested.

"It wasn't David Tamihere," the woman added.

For the sake of completeness, it's worth covering off some other leads floated in these pages. Readers may recall the testimony of Air Cadets Flying Officer and Volvo service manager Robert Owens who'd seen the Subaru at a remote campsite in the upper reaches of the Kauaeranga Valley at 2.30pm on Saturday 8 April. He remembered the little yellow AA sticker.

You may also recall shopkeeper Graham Manning advising Heidi and Urban they should go up the Kauaeranga track, rather than Tararu.

Police discounted the Kauaeranga sightings early on, because they couldn't find anyone else apart from the Air Cadets who'd seen the car, and because the park management had found no evidence that Heidi and Urban had used their "honesty box" payment system for camping in the valley. That's a bad reason to discount sightings, because if Heidi and Urban had been abducted before they had a chance to pay, obviously there would be no record. Absence of evidence is not, as you will recall, necessarily evidence of absence.

What if, however, someone had come along and said, "I can guide you into the bush, it's quicker through Tararu Creek." The Swedes were very trusting. This would explain the disappearance of the Subaru from Kauaeranga, and it later being seen arriving at Tararu Creek Road sunset Saturday.

If the Kauaeranga sighting at 2.30pm is correct, then the McDonald/Gray sightings of a woman south of Coromandel taking photos by a white Subaru with bullbars become difficult, but not impossible. Wilson's Bay was about 40 minutes north of Thames, so within reach, but it would then mean the Swedes were perhaps driving around with their newfound friend/s and that they had backtracked on ground already covered in the trip down from Port Jackson that morning, as seen by farmer Albert Bowers.

If Kauaeranga is where Heidi and Urban's attacker/s first met them, then presumably that was the round trip through the bush they took after dumping the car at Tararu Creek Road on the Monday after Urban's murder, the place they ultimately returned to. That might explain the scattering of some of Heidi's and Urban's gear along the way, and why it stretched all the way from the Jam Tins down towards Kauaeranga.

All of this is purely speculative, however, and that trail is coming up 24 years cold. The car may also have been one of the three other white Subarus with bullbars known to have been on the Coromandel at the time.

Perhaps the biggest mystery of all, however, is the whereabouts of Heidi Birgitta Paakkonen.

CHAPTER 16

Where Is Heidi?

"Last night we went out in the middle of the night and looked for some kiwis. As you may know, they are nocturnal and sometimes you can hear how they scream when they are looking for food. The kiwi has diminished a lot and is now seen just in some areas. It's almost impossible to see them because of the very tight vegetation. So far we have not seen any, but we haven't given up.

"The weather hasn't been that good since we came to the North Island on 17 March, and right now it's raining. It's starting to get really cold during the nights. we may get away with it as we have just four weeks left here. Otherwise, everything has gone really well with sleeping arrangements. We haven't paid for one single night since the 29th of December 1988 in Auckland. Most of the time you can find a nice little grass spot close to a small river... the tent feels like a home now."

– letter from Urban Hoglin, March 24 1989, Tongariro

For Urban Hoglin's family, a quiet gravesite back in Sweden has been a focal point for the past 21 years since his body was recovered. For Heidi's family, their daughter/sister/aunt is still out here, somewhere. They have no closure.

A police search of the Parakiwai Valley in 1991 failed to find any sign of Heidi Paakkonen's body, and Google Earth photos show the pine forest in the area has since been harvested and replanted in that time. Both of those events, labour intensive as they are, should have turned up Heidi's body if it had been there.

Instead, nothing. No one, none of the tens of thousands of trampers and hunters who have used the Coromandel Forest Park over the decades, have found any further trace of Heidi anywhere. Like Marlborough teenagers Ben Smart and Olivia Hope a decade later who were last seen disappearing on a ketch,[118] Swedish tourist Heidi Paakkonen dropped off the map on April 8th or 9th 1989, and was never seen again.

Or was she?

In 2010, longtime *Investigate* magazine subscriber Neville Logan died. Included in his personal papers was an envelope forwarded to the magazine, which contained a report marked "Confidential" and for the eyes of former Police Commissioner John Jamieson.

Logan was a Christian, and friends with John and Mary Heaven, also Christians, who had operated the campground on Kawau Island in Auckland's Hauraki Gulf. Commissioner Jamieson, likewise, was a Christian.

Kawau Island, whose first notable European inhabitants included Governor Sir George Grey, can only – as the name suggests – be accessed by boat. Apart from a couple of small tracks, there are no roads to speak of on Kawau. Virtually every home has its own secluded private jetty.

Neville Logan had been asked to act as a go between after the Heavens came across what they suspected was a major drug smuggling operation in a large home on Kawau they'd been to. The property was owned by a "local underworld character" and "massive excavations were undertaken to allow for a large development underground."

As a staging point for narcotics shipment, Kawau had certain

---

[118] See *Ben & Olivia: What Really Happened?* By Ian Wishart & Jayson Rhodes, Howling At The Moon Publishing

advantages. International yachts could arrive at any one of the private jetties never having cleared Customs, and with no record of their visit to Kawau being taken.

The Heavens, who had visited the house in question on several occasions, became suspicious of certain activities which, combined with basement facilities capable of allowing people to be "held there against their will", moved them to visit Auckland Police in 1986 in the company of Logan.

The police politely agreed to maintain a watching brief – the information was given to the CIS – criminal intelligence section. The incident was duly forgotten.

Then, at some stage over the summer of 1988/89, the Heavens had two Swedish tourists come across on the ferry from Sandspit wharf on the mainland, having left their white Subaru station wagon parked there. The tourists, they recall, introduced themselves as Heidi and Urban, and explained they were on their dream holiday tour of Australia and New Zealand.

With foul weather closing in, the Swedes were invited to stay at the Heavens' home, rather than get washed out in the tent.

"We owned the camping ground on Kawau. The weather was pretty bad and so instead of them being out in tents, we invited them to come over and camp in the lounge. We found them to be very presentable people – both of them," remembers Mary Heaven during an interview.

"They introduced themselves as Heidi and Urban?"

"Yes, they even came and had a meal with us," says John Heaven. "They slept inside, it was so wet."

Mary Heaven remembered Heidi wearing a gold neckchain with a cross on it.[119] The couple told the Heavens how they hoped to see the Coromandel as part of their visit. The next day, still raining, they left to continue their tour of New Zealand.

---

119 Still listed as missing along with Heidi is a "gold neck chain with heart, cross and anchor in three separate pieces on chain".

"There wasn't any problem whatsoever," continues Mary, "and when the weather cleared they went on over to Sandspit to pick up their vehicle. We went over to Sandspit too."[120]

Heaven insists the car she saw them get into at Sandspit was the white Subaru.

For the purposes of their reconstruction of Heidi Paakkonen and Urban Hoglin's movements throughout New Zealand, police intelligence analysts checked bank transactions, credit card payments, photographs and letters home to try and work out where the couple had been.

A "Flow Chart of Couple's Movements" was introduced as a court exhibit, but noticeably missing from that reconstruction is any explanation of where Heidi and Urban stayed between Christmas of 1988 and the first week of January 1989.

From Christmas Eve they had stayed with Canadians Ron Lewis and Sharon Stray at a bach in Paihia. They left that town on December 27, and arranged to meet Lewis and Stray in the South Island later in January. The Swedes' whereabouts from that moment remained a mystery to investigators, because Heidi and Urban next popped up in Turangi on January 3 1989, on their journey south.

The only time window in Heidi and Urban's itinerary that could have accommodated a Kawau visit was during that week, and the most likely date was 28 December. It fits the timing, and it fits the weather.

Urban Hoglin wrote home at one point that the last time they'd paid for a night's stay was 29 December 1988, at Auckland after leaving Paihia. Sandspit was only an hour and a half's drive north of Auckland, putting them comfortably in the city on the night of 29 December.

Of that period, Heidi Paakkonen wrote in a letter:

"After boxing day it rained almost all the time until the 3rd of January. It got a bit boring travelling south in that weather. When

---

120   Interview with author, March 2012

we left Auckland it rained so much that the roads got closed in some places."

It was still pouring on New Year's Eve, south of Auckland.

"I will now tell you how we celebrated New Year's Eve. We took the car to a small lake, then went for a short hike up the beach and put the tent up when we found a good spot. Even then it was raining but it was really cosy.

"We thought we were going to have chicken that we just had to heat up for tea, but all the wood we found was wet so we couldn't light the fire. Instead we had to sit in the cold black tent (because we had left our torch in the car) and celebrate the New Year.

"The Kiwis are really open people and very nice, you can talk to them for an hour or so and then they invite you home for dinner or to stay with them for the night."

The Kawau matter might have ended there, a bedraggled footnote so small in their trip that it did not rate a mention, except for a second sighting of the woman they identified as Heidi Paakkonen, without Urban.

"They saw Heidi Paakkonen near their home just as the police were starting to search for them in the Coromandel (they live nearly two hundred kilometres from the Coromandel). Heidi was with a dark-haired man, definitely not David Tamihere, and was struggling to hoist a very heavy pack on to her back. The straps were down near her elbows and she was clearly distressed," Neville Logan wrote to former Police Commissioner John Jamieson in 2002.

"My friend's wife stepped forward to help lift the pack, whereupon the man snarled, 'Don't touch her!'. He then walked on and impatiently beckoned her to follow. She seemed terrified and kept scanning the surrounding bush as if anticipating something.

"My friends were convinced it was Heidi and so phoned Detective Hughes who was heading the investigation... Detective Hughes thanked them for the information but assured them that it couldn't have been Heidi as they were sure she was in the Coromandel. The police did not contact my friends any further regarding their sighting."

Logan wrote that Heidi looked very frightened:

"Yes, she was, she was," Mary Heaven murmurs 23 years later as her mind drifts back to that day. "That's quite so, that is exactly right, what Neville is saying. Yes, she did come back with somebody and she was frightened."

It was Heidi's body language that spoke to Mary – the young Swede was too terrified to actually speak – and her eyes told the story for her.

"She didn't really say a lot but she was trying to get a message across to me that something wasn't right.

"It was just the way that she was, she was trying to let me know that the person who had brought her wasn't doing it correctly, that he had no authority to be putting her in this position. That was very definite, very evident."

The man with Heidi was a thin Pakeha. "He certainly wasn't a podgy person, quite slim in fact. He wasn't Maori," Mary Heaven, now 75, says.

What innocent explanation could there be for a man to snarl "don't touch her" at someone trying to help with a heavy pack? That encounter has haunted Mary Heaven for nearly two and a half decades.

If you're thinking the couple could be mistaken and there's no hard evidence it was Heidi they saw, well, perhaps you are right. But a man was convicted and given a life sentence for murder on the basis of a sighting of "Heidi" by two men who'd *never* seen her before, and to whom she never said a word, and of whom they were trying to recollect a fleeting meeting that had taken place eight weeks earlier, and they hadn't really seen her face, hidden behind a hood. Heidi had not been in Cassidy or Knauf's homes, sharing a meal.

What scenario would bring Heidi back to Kawau? The timing is vague after 23 years, but the Heavens say the sighting came shortly before news broke in late May 1989 of the couple's disappearance. It was the news coverage that prompted Mary Heaven to call police. The man Heidi was with was not Urban Hoglin, and it was not

David Tamihere. By a simple process of logic, if the Heavens are more accurate in their sighting than Cassidy and Knauf were in theirs, then regardless of whoever killed Hoglin, Tamihere could not have killed Heidi Paakkonen.

What happened between that eerie forest glade in the Parakiwai Valley where Urban Hoglin was murdered, and Heidi's appearance on Kawau Island weeks later as the terrified captive of a man who wasn't Hoglin or Tamihere? It's a void we cannot currently explain.

There are a series of tantalising sightings on the eastern Coromandel seaboard of a woman who looked like Heidi, in the company of a man or men, a week after she disappeared.

On the weekend of Saturday April 15, witness Michael Burns told police he'd seen a woman who looked like Heidi "with a number of men" by the Wentworth Track.

Waihi woman Linda Millen told police, and later the *Woman's Weekly*, she believed she'd seen Heidi with a man who looked like Tamihere on remote Ohui beach, 20km north of Whangamata, on April 17:

"We drove down the beach and as we got closer we could see the man was kneeling in the sand dunes and the woman was standing about three feet away from him, staring in our direction," she told journalist Megan McChesney.[121]

"She was about five foot eight and her blonde hair was tied back in a ponytail. The man was a short, stocky, half-caste Maori with a moustache and a five o'clock shadow.

"As we came closer to them, the man stopped what he was doing and went and stood next to the woman. He put his hand out and held her by the arm, by the wrist.

"We kept on going along the beach and the woman just kept watching us. Her body stood rigid and only her head moved. I felt the woman was pleading to me to stop and I desperately wanted to go over to her, but we both really panicked and we kept on driving.

---

121 "Haunted by Pleading Eyes", by Megan McChesney, NZWW, 15 March 1993

"Even now, all I can see are her eyes just pleading, saying please, please....," Millen told the magazine four years later.

Intriguingly, McChesney sought comment from John Hughes, who'd by then retired, and says "he told the *NZ Woman's Weekly* it was likely that David Tamihere had, in fact, met the Swedes in the eastern side of the peninsula, possibly in the Wentworth Valley where people can camp without charge.

"Police believe, however, that by April 10, 1989, seven days before Linda's sighting, the pair were already dead. That is when they say David Tamihere left the bush and travelled around the Coromandel with other tourists before driving to Auckland."

The alleged admission by police that Tamihere might have met the Swedes at Wentworth, not Crosbie's, is a massive abandonment of the entire case that Tamihere was actually convicted on.

But look at the wider implications of the sighting. There's no question that Tamihere was no longer in the Coromandel by April 17 - he had returned to Auckland on the 12th. Clearly he could not, even on the police scenario, have been in control of Heidi after April 10. Millen's suspected sighting therefore lends weight to the theory that Tamihere didn't do it, and that another or others did. Where did Heidi go from there? Was she ultimately abducted by a drug smuggler exporting the famed 'Coromandel Green' out through Kawau? We just don't know.

Perhaps the answer lies buried somewhere in the evidence originally collected by police, but tossed aside when they assumed Tamihere was guilty. Retired judge Colin Nicholson evidently suspects so.

"There were something like 80 volumes of Eastlight folders of documents associated with the inquiry which, as they were required to do, Police made available for inspection by the defence."

Although Nicholson isn't holding his breath, he says he'd like to think Police will try and follow up the latest leads.

"Well one would think so, but the police were zealous in pursuing Tamihere once they had him in their sights, and they are perhaps not as enthusiastic to make further inquiries that show that they were wrong."

As for the Court of Appeal's willingness to allow police to break the rules, the former judge also feels the judiciary sometimes lose sight of the important things.

"I don't like to criticise my former colleagues, but there's no doubt that an appeal is heard in a court of appeal in a completely different way than an actual trial is heard and determined in the first instance. Things can tend to get a bit academic without appropriate weight being given to the importance and impact of evidence [on a jury]."

David Tamihere did go to the Court of Appeal, and you might be surprised at what they said.

CHAPTER 17

Your Verdict

"Next time you hear from us may be from the Cook Islands. It's exciting to see think we will be on a real South Pacific island. I hope it's as nice as we've imagined. If I can find any, I'll but some grass skirts to bring back home. So then we can sing and dance hula-hula on your deck in the summer, whole gang of us, with Putti and Juho in the front. Till next time, all the best and send our love to all."
– **letter from Urban Hoglin, April 2 1989, Rotorua**

The Court of Appeal, despite the discovery of Urban Hoglin's body in 1991, threw out Tamihere's appeal in May 1992. Among other things, the court ruled that the jury would not have taken the evidence of the three secret witnesses seriously.

"The Crown called three fellow prisoners whose names were, and continue to be, suppressed from media publicity, although they were of course disclosed to the Defence, the Jury and all in Court at the time, so it would be misleading to describe them as 'secret' witnesses.

"The accounts are plainly inconsistent with each other. He denied them, but with the curious qualification that he fed false stories of different kinds to five or six fellow prisoners, so that he could identify those whom he believed might try to wrongly inform on him to the police.

"The Crown did not contend that these accounts given to fellow prisoners…were necessarily correct. They were significant as demonstrating that he had been talking about his involvement in murdering the couple; that he was closely following the police investigations; stating repeatedly that they 'would never be found'...a comment borne out by the discovery of Urban Hoglin's body so far away from the searches.

"We would be surprised if the Jury had given much credence to any of the detail in the stories Tamihere was said to have told these witnesses. In the case of two of them, there are doubts over whether he said anything at all, apart from his own admission that he spread disinformation to suspected inmates."

It would be surprising if the prime suspect in one of the country's biggest murder mysteries had not taken an interest in everything the police were saying about him and the case, and it would be surprising if other inmates were not asking questions about it. However, it's one thing to feed unimportant false information to other prisoners to figure out which one is an informant, it's a totally different thing to suggest that such false information includes boasts about how one disposed of the bodies.

After all, this was a case without bodies, so if your idea of feeding false information was to boast about how you'd chopped them up so they'd never be found, that would make you the dumbest inmate in the prison system.

Have a look at the Court's reasoning in there and you will note it is circular in places. While suggesting no one gave the secret witness statements credence, the Court itself gives them credence when it suits them – "talking about his involvement in murdering", "stating repeatedly that they 'would never be found'". You might also remember it was the Court of Appeal that allowed Cassidy and Knauf's shonky identification evidence back into the trial, on the basis that the secret witness testimony provided "quality" corroboration.

The Court now appeared to be admitting the secret witness evidence was doubtful, but it didn't matter anymore because Cassidy and Knauf were credible.

The Jury, of course, had been told that if they wished they could take the Secret Witness testimony as honest from men who felt sufficiently repulsed by Tamihere's crimes they had broken the criminal code of silence, as Crown Prosecutor David Morris put it.

The Court took a similar view of the watch evidence, saying:

"...this evidence of a direct association between the accused and Urban Hoglin can only be regarded as very tenuous...if the jury had accepted that the watch belonged to Urban Hoglin...One may wonder why it still took them a full two days to reach their verdict... coupled with the inconclusive nature of Davenport's evidence, suggests that the jury may well have put it to one side."

In fact, it took the jury that long to reach a verdict because one or two jurors remained unconvinced and for a while it appeared there was going to be a hung jury. There is no evidence that the jury placed no weight on the watch.

By ruling that the jury would not have placed weight on these issues, the Court of Appeal was able to then rule that new evidence regarding them was not sufficiently weighty to force a new trial. Again, it is circular reasoning.

Tamihere's legal team had mounted the Appeal on the following grounds:
- That the discovery of Urban Hoglin's body so far from the alleged crime scene was hugely relevant to the Crown's case the way it was constructed
- That the jury might have reached a different verdict if they had known Tamihere had not stolen Urban's watch
- That Hoglin had not died the way the secret witnesses had testified
- The secret witnesses had lied
- The Crown and Police had knowingly presented false evidence by leading fictitious and emotive testimony from the secret witnesses, and by telling the jury that the beeping watch could have been Hoglins, even in the face of denials from Seiko/Pulsar that such a timepiece was available. Hoglin's brother had also provided a statement that the watch had no chime.

As per their above reasoning, the Court of Appeal were brutal:

"Is the new material so material that a verdict returned without it might amount to a miscarriage of justice?

"We are quite satisfied that the answer must be no…as was clearly recognised at the Trial, crucial to the whole case was the sighting of the man and woman at Crosbie's, by two trampers. They said the man looked like Tamihere; he wore a belt with a pouch, and was using an axe similar to those items found at Tamihere's house; he was putting up a tent of an unusual design, and of interest to them, which both regarded as similar to the tent found at his house.

"The girl was remembered as similar to a photograph of Heidi with blonde hair and fine features; and she was wearing an unusual poncho similar again to one found at Tamihere's house. The discovery of such a garment and tent at his house would be a most extraordinary coincidence. In conjunction with other matters just described, it makes the odds against the couple being other than Tamihere and Heidi so high as to put that possibility beyond rational consideration.

"Once that identification is accepted, the rest of the Crown's evidence falls into place as convincing circumstantial proof that the couple were murdered by Tamihere."

That is the hub of the Court of Appeal's decision not to order a retrial of this case. Where does it go wrong? A number of places.

Firstly, the new forensic evidence was that Hoglin died on the spot where he was found, 73km away from Crosbie's Clearing. The Crown's new evidence is that this may have happened on the morning of Monday 10 April, when witness Darren Lindsay saw the Subaru parked up the forest track, 100m away from the murder scene. No Crown narrative given to the original jury allowed for this possibility. The charge was murder at Crosbie's Clearing. If Tamihere was actually marching Heidi and Urban out of the bush to drive to Crosbie's, what on earth would he be doing pitching a tent at Crosbie's?

Secondly, as you have seen earlier in this book, Cassidy and Knauf did not give detailed descriptions of the alleged Tamihere camping gear initially. Those descriptions only turned up in revised witness statements after police had shown Tamihere's gear to the two trampers at the Thames Police Station – another identification blunder.

Thirdly, and this is not the Court of Appeal's fault – the young trampers Goonan and McLean were not called at trial to give evidence that they camped at Crosbie's on Saturday 8 April with their dogs and saw and heard nothing, right beside the area where the alleged attacks that went on "for ages" were supposed to be taking place.

Fourthly, the Court of Appeal had ignored the Crown's own glaring inconsistencies, such as Morris' insistence that Heidi "didn't have boots". How could the Crown then get away with saying the woman in Crosbie's, wearing boots, was Heidi?

According to the Court of Appeal, the entire case could be hung on the credibility of the Cassidy/Knauf evidence, yet their sighting went directly against what police knew about Heidi Paakkonen. How could it possibly underpin the conviction?

At this point, some readers will undoubtedly be saying, "Yeah, but on the balance of probabilities we think Tamihere could be good for this." Great, and he has served 20 years for it, but the balance of probabilities is a 50/50 coin toss. The criminal standard – the standard for which we used to hang people – we need to be more than 50/50 sure, the actual test is beyond reasonable doubt. In other words, that there is no other possible explanation, no one else known or unknown who could have done this, and the evidence points not just probably but definitely to the accused.

Look back through the book and identify what makes Tamihere good for this. Prior form, yes. Being in the wrong place? Yes. But was he the only dangerous man roaming the Coromandel bush that weekend? No. We've looked at an example or two.

Additionally, before they seized on Tamihere, police had another suspect in mind, a figure in the drug industry who fled the scene. The sheds where the tent was found had reportedly been used by cannabis growers on the sly.

Then there's the "schmuck factor" we touched on earlier. If you really were the killer, would you drive around in their distinctive car so blatantly, and – as Tamihere said in his failed bid to the Privy Council – "would I have used Hoglin's name when selling the property?"

You have now been presented with the relevant evidence in the case, including material the jury either were not allowed to hear or which simply was not known at the time they deliberated on their verdict.

Like it or not, our justice system requires a high standard of proof when allegations are made of a criminal nature, because everyone's liberty is at risk if standards slip.

At the start of the book, three options were posed:

One, the jury convicted the right man for the right reasons.

Two, the jury convicted the right man for the wrong reasons.

Three, the jury convicted the wrong man for the wrong reasons.

If you support option one, then after reading this book you will have found the Crown's evidence as presented in court compelling beyond reasonable doubt. If you support option two or option three, only a retrial can test whether the Crown case was flawed.

Why should we care? After all, Tamihere has served two decades for this crime, does it even matter? Put yourself in the same position. If you or one of your children became prime suspect for a crime you/they did not commit, would you want the state-funded justice system to be permitted to take short-cuts to get a conviction, simply on the basis of a "hunch" or "gut instinct"? Or would you like to know that justice is done without fear or favour, according to accepted community standards?

And if you are the victim of crime, wouldn't you sleep easier at night knowing police had made a genuine effort to find your attacker, rather than just grabbing a quick and easy lookalike off the street?

No one is denying Tamihere was bad in the eighties or that he was capable of committing this crime, but if in fact he did not, as he has insisted all the way along, then locking up the wrong bad guy for a double murder doesn't really do anything for community safety or closure for the family of victims.

This, then, is the evidence. I have tried to cast a critical eye over the Crown case whilst including all the major relevant information. The hearings and evidence run to thousands of pages, but much of it was dotting i's and crossing t's. There may never be a retrial, so the verdict ultimately now falls on you, the readers, to determine.

> *"We are right now on a peninsula called Coromandel, situated a bit south of Auckland. We have only 14 days left here in New Zealand.*
>
> *"Here in Coromandel are a lot of beautiful beaches and the weather is really nice. There's a lot of lying around on the beach. Often we are on our own so there is no crowd.*
>
> *"Last night we slept in a camp for a change. Most of the time we are just staying out in the open, in the countryside. The camp ground had its own thermal pools and it was rather nice to sink into the pool at 9:00 in the evening with all the stars in heaven above us.*
>
> *"I wonder if the same songs have been popular at home as here. Every big city here has its own radio station and they play mostly pop and a lot of songs from the 50s.*
>
> *"A couple of songs have been John Farnham (different songs), Chicago – Look Away, Poison – Every Rose Has Its Thorn, Wet Wet Wet – Angel Eyes, Chris de Burgh – Missing You, Eric Carmen – Make Me Lose Control, Moody Blues – I Know You're Out There Somewhere...*
>
> *"Until we meet again... Urban & Heidi"*
>
> *– final letter from Urban Hoglin & Heidi Paakkonen,*
> *April 7 1989, Thames*

Your Verdict

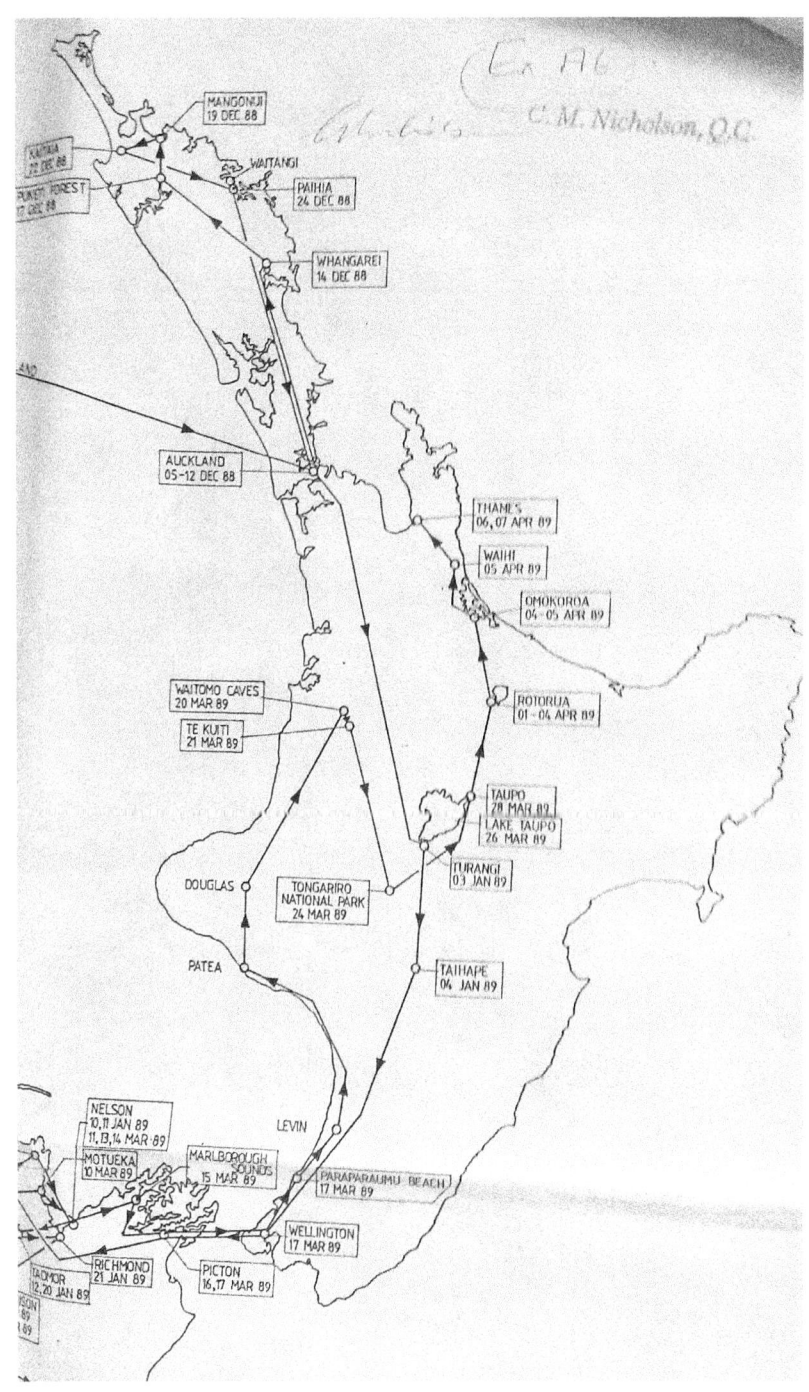

Missing Pieces

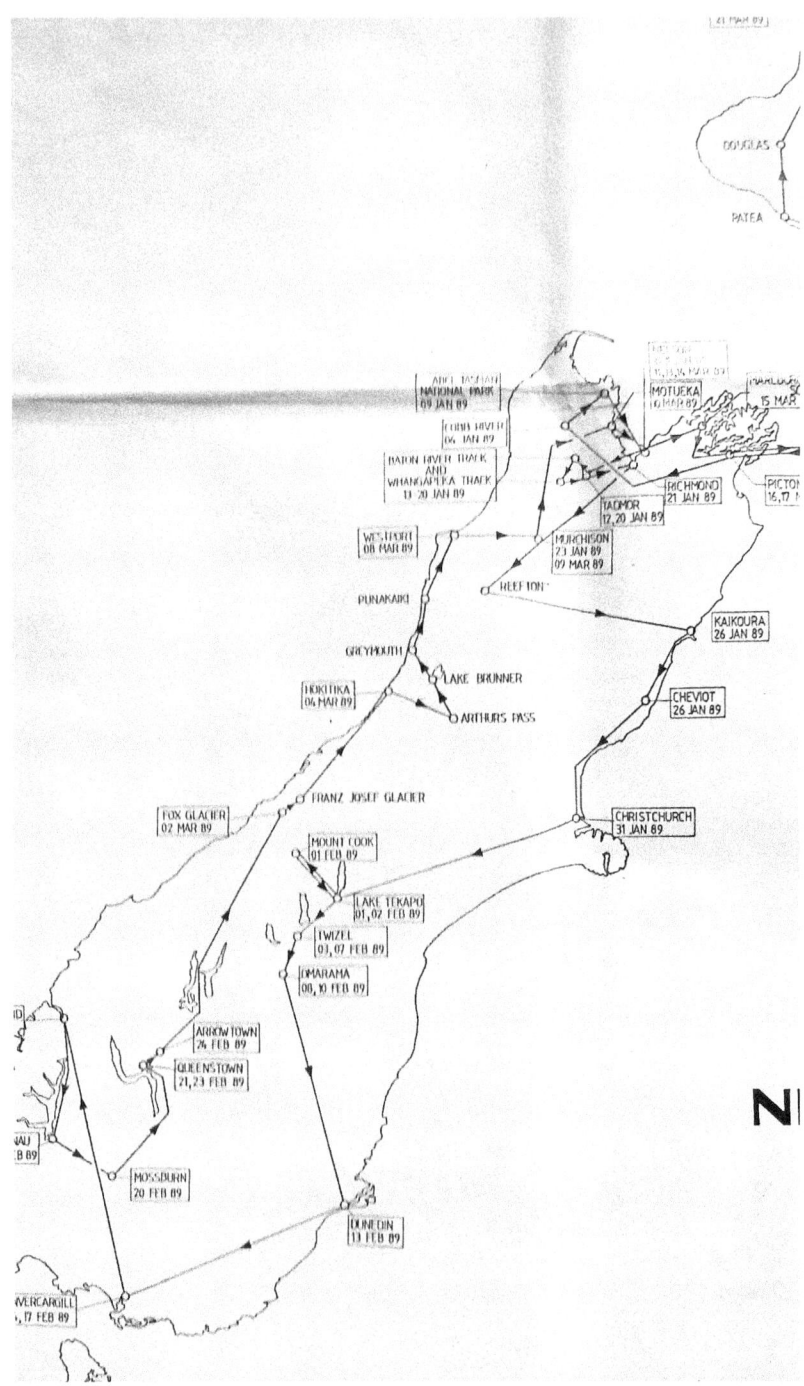

**See Amazon.com or www.howlingatthemoon.com
for more Ian Wishart books**

FROM THE AMAZON REVIEWS

5.0 out of 5 stars
By Dr William B. Grant, San Francisco
This book is the latest popular book on vitamin D. It covers topics of current interest including autism, cancer, erectile dysfunction, hospital-acquired infections, pregnancy, heart disease, infectious diseases, and autoimmune diseases. The research journal literature on vitamin D is growing at the rate of about 4000 papers per year yet the health system in the U.S. accepts the evidence only for falls and fractures. This book makes the case well that there are many, many beneficial effects of vitamin D. I strongly recommend this book.

5.0 out of 5 stars
By Barbara Locke
I felt this book was a great summary of the research around Vitamin D and its health effects, and the excellent referencing made it easy to read more technical research if i needed to. A very thought provoking book.

5.0 out of 5 stars
By Ivan Lowe
My first degree was in Human Biology, and now as an Associate Professor I teach courses on evidence and research methodology. Therefore, I was at first both attracted and sceptical about this book. The title put me off. I would have preferred: Vitamin D: reassessing the evidence.

I came to the book familiar with Wishart's science books. I knew he would be readable, courteous, firm, and well referenced. Wishart is well acquainted both with the science and the politics of medicine. He presents the science so that non-technical people can see the point, and technical people can have precision and detail. Wishart is NOT jumping on a bandwagon: he has been researching and writing about the importance of Vitamin D for over seven years. His basic approach, as always, is to follow the evidence wherever it leads, even if the conclusions are contentious and uncomfortable.

The first chapter introduces his argument. Chapters 2-12 cover the role of Vitamin D in (2) Alzheimer's, (3) Autism, (4) Asthma and Allergies, (5) Breast Cancer, (6)Colon and Prostate Cancer, (7) Heart disease, (8) Flu and colds, (9)Pregnancy and childhood, (10)Mental Illness,

(11) Multiple Sclerosis (12) Chrohn's Disease and Type 1 Diabetes. His basic thesis is that Vitamin D is needed, in large quantities. It is vitally important in a wide range of biological systems and diseases. For instance, Wishart presents loads of evidence in chapter 2 that high blood levels of Vit D are strongly associated with a lower risk of Alzheimer's. The natural level of Vitamin D in people who work outside is 50ng/ml (125nmol/L). This should be the pre-winter target.

So, what is the problem? Surely a balanced diet provides all we need?

Wishart shows that diet is not sufficient. The main source of Vitamin D is through the influence of sunlight on skin. Everyone is agreed that sunburn is to be avoided, so the exposure needs to be limited and frequent. Dietary supplements are possible, but they work best for those who already have reasonably high body reserves. Wishart is careful to warn that large supplements can be dangerous.

So the problem is that we have a generation educated to believe that skin cancer must be avoided by regular use of sunscreen, which blocks the sun and as a consequence prevents the production of Vitamin D. Chapters 13&14 cover this. He explains that sunscreens do help to protect against the less dangerous "squamous cell carcinoma" but provide no protection at all for the dangerous kind: "melanoma". In addition, those with the most exposure to sun are more likely to survive the dangerous cancer, and are less likely to get it!

I wish Wishart had gone into more detail on what to do. I immediately stopped using suncream, but will continue to wear a hat and sunglasses. Sunlight is after all associated with glaucoma and cataracts is it not? I live in Tunisia and walk to work. Before I started using sunscreen two years ago I had become skilled in avoiding prolonged exposure to sun, while tolerating a little reddening.

Both sides of the debate agree that burning is bad. Suitable clothing is the best way to avoid that, in unavoidable circumstances such as driving. But how can I avoid burning and blistering on my face? Is there a case for limited sunscreen use? I would also have liked a systematic evaluation of ALL the major components of sunscreens – not just Vitamin E, Titanium derivatives, Nanotechnology, and Oxybenzone. I hope that in the second edition he will answer these questions.

Buy this book. Send your doctor a Kindle copy, and catch as much Autumn sunlight as you can. If Wishart is wrong, then he will have only saved you some money. If he is right, then high levels of naturally produced Vitamin D will reduce cancers and boost the immune system.

THE CRITICS ON *THE GREAT DIVIDE*:

"*The Great Divide* is the book that somebody had to write."
– Phil Hayward

"I can recommend it, I think it is a fascinating read and I think everybody should be reading it. We've all read Claudia Orange and the other books – this is an updated version." – Doris Mousdale on Newstalk ZB.

"A page-turner that tells the story of pre-Maori history, of explorers who met a sudden death, of brave missionaries, musket wars, of the beginnings of British rule, the ins and outs of the treaty, land clashes, sovereignty wars, of the role of Christianity, and implications for today. His chatty, colloquial style could and should keep a wide range of readers on the edge of a chair…

"The chapter "Waitangi's fairytale godfathers" shreds Waitangi Tribunal arguments… Those chiefs who opposed the unity of the races under one sovereign became the Maori king movement, and the focus of the so-called Maori renaissance in the 20th century, Wishart wrote. "Their followers, however, are the ones now in charge of the Waitangi debate, the cultural gatekeepers. They are the ones who can make the majority voices from the past fall silent – their words left out of the popular history books and not quoted in universities."

So here we are in the 21st century still fighting the 19th century sovereignty war, this time using words instead of bullets. The book is a must-read." – Mike Butler

"It had been my impression that Ian was a polemicist, an extremist, even a writer of scurrilous pamphlets. (This may demonstrate the efficiency of the Establishment's knocking machine).

"However, when I opened *The Great Divide* I found it moderate in style, clear in expression and thorough in discussion.

"I noted with interest his references to Michael King's hitherto lauded *Penguin History of New Zealand*. Wishart confronts King. Clearly we agree that King was a member of the 'politically correct brigade' (though Wishart does not say so in as many words.)

"Wishart…most importantly in my view, gives thorough attention to the Kohimarama Conference of 1860 which has been so notably discounted by Orange and Salmond. In Ian Wishart's words, 'What we see at Kohimarama…is an evolution of consent. After 20 years of partial integration, the chiefs not only ratified Waitangi in full but expressly called for a complete adoption of Pakeha tikanga'.

"…There can be simply no doubt that *The Great Divide* must find a place…on the bookshelves of every educated New Zealander. In short – read it." – Bruce Moon

THE CRITICS ON *BREAKING SILENCE*:

"*Breaking Silence* is not on my recommended read list. I firmly believe it is *compulsory* reading for anyone over 18." – Andrew Stone, *Albany Buzz* business magazine

"The book has real value" – Larry Williams, Newstalk ZB

"I found it an incredibly surprising book, and a very relevant book, and a very important book". – Anna Smart, Newstalk ZB

"I had no particular views on the case before this book came out but I have to say it's a powerful read. An influential read, one might say... All those people who poured out their invective when it became known the book was about to hit the book shops really should just read it for themselves. It may not be quite what they think." – Helen Hill, *The Marlborough Express*

"*Breaking Silence* is a chilling narrative and the most important I have read. Adults may need to read the story to gain any understanding. Younger people should read in it a warning: that it is the way we make decisions early on that may determine the course of our life and the lives of those entrusted to our care." – Pat Veltkamp Smith, *Southland Times*

"The book so many maligned before it came out reveals a mother we haven't met. When I last wrote about Macsyna King, I said I didn't think I'd like her. I've changed my mind. I certainly think she outclasses the Wellington radio announcer who posted on Facebook that after receiving her advance copy of *Breaking Silence*, she had "spat on it, wiped my ass on it, and ripped it up". – Tapu Misa, *NZ Herald*

"Actually, the rumours of Wishart's death as an investigative journalist turn out to be greatly exaggerated. *Breaking Silence* will likely enhance his reputation considerably. As we said at the outset – we are very, very glad to have read the book." – John Tertullian, *Contra Celsum*

THE CRITICS ON *THE INSIDE STORY*:

"Undeniably...when Wishart hits he hits big. *Arthur Allan Thomas: The Inside Story* is a book two generations of New Zealanders have waited for...Wishart...offers an explosive new theory about who pulled the trigger of the gun that killed the Crewes in their Pukekawa farmhouse and theorises about the mystery woman who fed their infant daughter, Rochelle, for days after the murders.

"...With his thorough analysis of the evidence and his generous use of first-person accounts it's a stellar piece of journalism..." – *Southland Times*

"Wishart has a brand new prime suspect and he lays out his case in this fascinating and highly readable book. Wishart is painstaking in his investigation, and his interviews with the man at the centre of the case, Arthur Thomas, offer a remarkable insight into one of New Zealand's most memorable characters. " – Kerre Woodham, Newstalk ZB

"Wishart's report of Detective Sergeant Len Johnston's brazen arrogance collecting items for later use as evidence from Thomas's farm – pieces of wire, .22 shells and axle stubs – exposes a dark and scary side to our guardians.

"Through the book Wishart lays the ground for his claim that Johnston was actually the murderer and by his position on the inquiry team and proximity to Hutton, was able to influence an outcome which saw Thomas convicted twice of a double murder. Wishart's conclusions are disturbingly possible in my view.

"The question of to what extent Hutton had the wool pulled over his eyes by Johnston is moot. Based on Wishart's debunking of transcripts and evidence previously recorded, I think Hutton could well have been fooled by his best mate. Which means so too were the rest of the team deluded." – former Det. Insp. Ross Meurant, *NZ Herald*

THE CRITICS ON *AIR CON*:

"*Air Con* is a thorough summary of the current state of the debate, the science and the politics; it will be an important reference in any AGW skeptic's arsenal." – Vox Day, *WorldNetDaily*

"I started reading this book with an intensely critical eye, expecting that a mere journalist could not possibly cope with the complexities of climate science...[But] The book is brilliant. The best I have seen which deals with the news item side of it as well as the science. He has done a very thorough job and I have no hesitation in unreserved commendation." – Dr Vincent Gray, *UN IPCC expert reviewer*

"Ian Wishart's *Air Con* is another masterpiece of scientific reason, letting the thinking world know that so-called man-made global warming is the greatest scam ever aimed at humanity. Please read this book." – Professor David Bellamy, England

"This book by New Zealand journalist Ian Wishart – a #1 bestselling author four times – surprised me by the completeness with which he reviewed and presents alternatives to the plethora of IPCC inspired spin and publicity which floods our media today.
"His sixteen chapters examining aspects of the debate are meticulously footnoted and thus are a valuable reference resource for those wishing to dig deeper or keep up to speed with the unfolding global warming / carbon reduction political drama in years to come." – Dr Warwick Hughes, climate scientist

"Ian Wishart carefully and painstakingly looks at the topic, examining the evidence and weighing up the pros and cons. He not only finds the science to be unconvincing, but believes that following the proposed remedies will well-nigh bankrupt the West and in fact compound problems. An eye-opening treatment of a controversial issue. – *Quadrant* magazine, Australia

THE CRITICS ON *LAWYERS, GUNS & MONEY*:

"Wishart has grown as an author" – *Otago Daily Times*

"He's onto another winner. Wishart is…exceptionally thorough. He skilfully blends official documents with his own observations and material from his own inquiries, giving a more informative picture than could ever have been possible in the daily media." – *Manawatu Evening Standard*

"If you like to mix business with pleasure, take *Lawyers, Guns & Money* to your beachside accomodation with you" – *North & South*

THE CRITICS ON *THE PARADISE CONSPIRACY*:

"*The Paradise Conspiracy* is required reading...pacey, penetrating scrutiny" – *New Zealand Herald*

"It is the closest thing to a John Grisham novel, but it is the real thing...among the best investigative stories about New Zealand business for many years" – *Waikato Times*

"...a compelling book...a Watergate-type tale" – *NZ Listener*

"Sensational stuff and hard to fault. Wishart is a professional...it is the most controversial New Zealand book that I can remember"
– Bruce Jesson, *The Republican*

"Wishart presents facts he can totally substantiate, and leaves readers to draw some obvious conclusions...compelling, revealing and worrying reading" – *BOP Times*

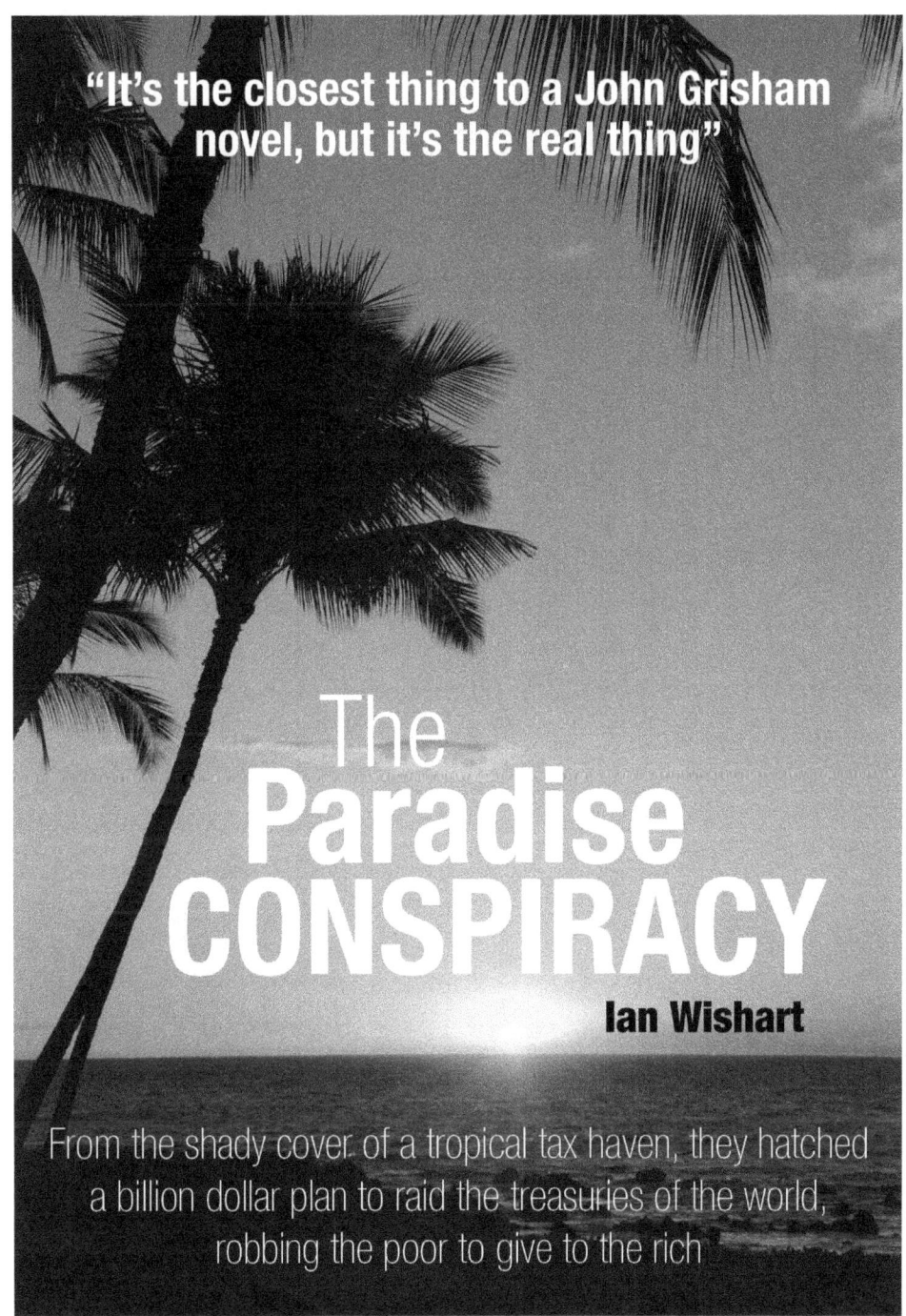

www.ingramcontent.com/pod-product-compliance
Lightning Source LLC
Chambersburg PA
CBHW050555170426
43201CB00011B/1705